SLAVISTIC PRINTINGS
AND REPRINTINGS

edited by

C. H. VAN SCHOONEVELD

Indiana University

104

THE RUSSIAN FOLK THEATRE

by

ELIZABETH A. WARNER
University of Hull

1977

MOUTON

THE HAGUE - PARIS

ISBN 90 279 3325 1

Printed in the Netherlands

To the memory of the late Petr Grigor'evič BOGATYREV,
a constant source of advice and friendly encouragement.

CONTENTS

INTRODUCTION

The student of folklore, wherever his particular interest may lie, will find in Russia a richness and diversity of material which can scarcely be equalled in Western Europe. Compared with most other genres of folk literature, however, the repertoire of the folk theatre is considerably less prolific, less varied, less immediately appealing and partly for this reason it has been largely ignored both by the folklorist and the theatrical historian.

There are many other reasons for this relative neglect of the folk theatre, however. Historical factors produced an artificial break in the development of spontaneous drama in Russia. Indeed, the history of the folk theatre in Russia may be roughly divided into two phases. There is firstly the period ranging from the earliest beginnings to the end of the reign of *Car'* Aleksej Mixailovič, a period characterised on the one hand by ritual drama and mummings of partly pagan origin together with the gradual development of dramatic games and scenes, nonritual in intent but clearly deriving some of their material from earlier sources, and on the other by the activities of the *skomoroxi*[1], Russia's first professional wandering players, who participated in both these and other types of entertainment. The general trend of this phase was a slow movement towards a more secular concept of theatre but with ritual as its foundation and starting point. It was of necessity basically rural in character. The latter half of the period was characterised by increasing conservatism and antagonism in the attitude of the official church towards folk entertainment in all its manifestations, culminating in *Car'* Aleksej Mixailovič's *ukaz* of 1648 prohibiting all forms of public entertainment:-

> ". . . Скоморохов з домрами и с гусли и с волынками
> и со всякими игры . . . в дом к себе не призывали, . . .
> и медведей не водили и с сучками не плясали, и никаких
> бесовских див не творили, . . . богомерзких и скверных
> песней не пели, и сами не плясали и в ладоши не били, и
> всяких бесовских игр не слушали, и кулашных боев меж

себя не делали, и на качелех ни на каких не качались,
. . . и личин на себя никаких не накладывали, и
кобылок бесовских не наряжали . . . А которые
люди от того ото всего богомерзкого дела не отстанут,
и учнут впредь такова богомерзкого дела держатся,
и по нашему указу тем людем велено делать наказанье."2

The folk theatre, closely connected as it was even in the seventeenth century with lingering pagan beliefs and rites, was particularly vulnerable to such attacks throughout its history. It is largely because of this that there is such a lack of information about the development of folk drama in this early period.

The second period of the folk theatre was inaugurated mainly by the reign of Peter the Great. Relaxation of the power of the Church and of the strict ecclesiastical morality which had up to this time suppressed or destroyed much of the spontaneous amusements of the people, dramatic or otherwise, coupled with Peter's own interest in the theatre and his introduction of Russia's first completely secular theatre for all classes of society, were followed during the whole of the eighteenth century by a flourishing of theatrical arts on a variety of levels. Most important among these for the future of the folk theatre was the growth of the largely amateur urban democratic theatres which not only provided both entertainment and education in theatrical methods but also a platform upon which the ordinary people were able to practise and develop their own skills. One such amateur company, that of F.G. Volkov, which began its activities in Jaroslavl' in 1750, eventually laid the foundation of Russia's national theatre. The early eighteenth century too saw the expansion, mainly in the hands of foreign troupes and entrepeneurs to begin with, of the fairground *balagan* theatres popular in both town and country, and this movement in one form or another continued to flourish and increase in popularity throughout the eighteenth and nineteenth centuries. These theatres, many of which, particularly in Petersburg towards the end of the last century, attracted actors and entrepreneurs of considerable talent and renown made a valuable contribution to the growth and development of a secular popular theatrical tradition in Russia. Between these and the folk theatre, the actors and audiences of which were drawn to a considerable extent from similar backgrounds with similar tastes and demands, there was clearly much mutual interchange of experience and ideas.

During this second period of the folk theatre the remnants of ritual drama were still very much alive but the new dramatic games and plays which evolved at this time were completely secular in origin, although even here borrowings and influences from the rituals can still be seen.

The repertoire of this latter stage in the history of the folk theatre was not highly developed; the same small group of popular plays was performed time and time again up and down the country. Fear of the powers of the censor in the eighteenth and nineteenth centuries must have had some effect upon the number of texts in circulation. Many of the themes of the folk plays were satirical in nature and some (e.g. the puppet play *Petruška*) had a number of versions for general consumption and others reserved for small, selected audiences. Puppeteers, actors and those who knew of such versions were suspicious of outsiders making enquiries and naturally unwilling to communicate the full text to strangers. Nikolaj Vinogradov, one of the early collectors of folk plays, found himself at a distinct disadvantage for this very reason, during an interview with two puppeteers he had met on his travels:-

"Путем перекрестных вопросов, подзадориванья и даже лести, мне удалось выспросить почти все, что было нужно. Одного только не удалось дознаться ни коими хитростями — их имен и фамилий, звания и точного местожительства. На зтот счет у них крепко язык был связан: "Потому, хоть ты и душа—человек и нам пóлюбе пришолса, а чево бы не было, — хто тебя знает!"[3]

Many genres of folk literature were already familiar to a wide audience in Russia from the eighteenth century, but, partly as a result of its chequered history, the Russian folk theatre as such was not widely read or known among the scholars and intelligentsia of the nineteenth century and if known it was not generally considered as worthy of serious attention. Broadly speaking it is true that the works of the folk theatre are of a lower artistic and aesthetic standard than most of the other genres of folk literature. The epic *byliny* and the *skazki* for instance, even in the printed form, contain much to grip the attention and imagination. The melodies and wide emotional ranges of the lyrical songs hold an immediate appeal for both reader and listener. The attraction of the folk theatre, however, is more elusive. Plots are almost nonexistent, consisting at most of a series of episodes loosely woven around some central character or conflict. In the *skazki* and *byliny* a high moral tone is sustained; in the eternal struggle of good against evil the forces of evil are invariably defeated and virtue is rewarded. In the folk theatre life is seen as through a distorting mirror and much that is less than noble finds not only expression but approval; satire, parody, open mockery and abuse, anti-semitism, chauvinism, all these elements can be traced in the folk dramas. The language is rough and unpolished and the verse structure where it exists at all of uneven standard. Humour is often produced from crudities of language, gesture and situation. For all these reasons the folk theatre was largely despised during most of the nineteenth century as an entertainment for the ignorant masses.

Much, however, can be said in defence of the folk theatre and unsuspected qualities can be revealed by delving beneath the surface of first appearances.

First of all it should be remembered that the theatre is an essentially non-professional type of folk literature. The variants of the ritual dramas and playlets are not connected with particular artistic 'schools' or with specific performers in the way the best of the *byliny* and *skazki* often are. It is certainly true that gifted, untrained actors did emerge from among the folk, such as the talented comics and *dedy* of the fairgrounds whom A.Ja. Alekseev-Jakovlev remembered with such affection.[4] But in general the success or failure of each performance depended upon the indifferent skills of a group of amateur actors, varying from year to year and from place to place. The impression made by each individual song or tale is not totally lost on the printed page, but the impact of a work created both to be heard and seen is drastically reduced in this form. To appreciate the play fully it is necessary at least to imagine it in its authentic surroundings. Much of the enjoyment of the folk audiences, and there is no doubt that they themselves enjoyed the plays tremendously, stemmed from their own direct or indirect participation in the performances. So much of the humour, for instance, depended upon the mood of the moment, upon a good rapport between actor and audience. So much depended upon being physically present. People enjoyed the costumes and make-up, guessing their own acquaintances among the actors, comparing one year's performance with another. Divorced from the excitement and moods of the festive seasons during which the plays were predominantly performed they naturally lose much of their original attraction. Similarly, the connection, however subconscious, in the mind of the peasants between the agricultural rituals with their embryonic dramatic qualities and the sense of awakening nature, the return of warmth and the emergence of the land from under the snow, the preparation for the spring sowing cannot be gleaned from the written text, yet it was an essential part of the joy of participation.

The folk theatre perhaps more than any of the folk literature genres sprang from the loins of the masses as a spontaneous, collective expression of thoughts and feelings, antipathies, prejudices and joys, fears, demands and protests not always reasonably or aesthetically expressed. In spite of the lack of interest of the scholars, the folk theatre in its various manifestations constituted one of the most popular features of the fairgrounds and the spring and winter village festivities from the earliest times and its vigour and lively high spirits, colourfulness and bucolic fun not only interested but inspired many of Russia's writers, painters and musicians; and after all, as Puškin himself said:- "Драма родилась на площади и составляла увеселение народное".[5]

NOTES

1. *Infra*, pp. 187-189.
2. Quoted by A.S. Famincyn, *Skomoroxi na Rusi* (St. Petersburg, 1889), p. 186.
3. N.N. Vinogradov, "Velikorusskij vertep", *Izvestija otdelenija russkogo jazyka i slovesnosti*, Vol. 10, Book 3 (St. Petersburg, 1905), p. 361.
4. A.Ja. Alekseev-Jakovlev, *Russkie narodnye guljan'ja* (Leningrad-Moscow, 1948), pp. 55, 56 etc.
5. A.S. Puškin, "O narodnoj drame i drame *Marfa posadnica*", *Polnoe sobranie sočinenij v šesti tomax*, Vol. 5 (Moscow, 1950), p. 159.

PART ONE

RITUAL DRAMA

CHAPTER I

RITUAL DRAMA IN THE LIFE OF THE PEASANT COMMUNITY

Ritual drama along with the games and dramatic scenes which emerged from it represents the theatre at an embryonic stage of development and a close examination of the principles upon which ritual drama is based reveals much that is essential to an understanding of the subsequent evolution of the folk theatre in Russia.

In many primitive, economically underdeveloped communities, especially before the advent of professionalism, the development of labour into specific trades, people had little leisure for esoteric pursuits like art and literature, since they were almost wholly occupied with obtaining food. Where art existed in such communities the impulse towards its creation was almost certainly of a predominantly utilitarian nature. "Primitive art," writes Raymond Firth, "is highly socialised. To begin with, in many respects it is the handmaid of technology . . . In a primitive community, art is used by the ordinary people in embellishment of their domestic implements and in their ordinary social gatherings".[1] Looking at it from a slightly different viewpoint primitive art might also be said to be the 'handmaid' of religion. In many respects, religion itself in primitive communities served a utilitarian function when we consider man's total dependence upon nature and his need to control the spirits who apparently manipulated its course.

The utilitarian aspect of early art, closely linked as it was with man's personal and communal struggle for survival, is clearly to be seen in early drama, much of which was of a ritual nature. It is logical to suppose that these dances or dramas were performed originally not so much for purely aesthetic reasons but because they were intended to achieve something, to influence the spirits, help the community to transmit through mimesis certain work processes (as we find in many initiation ceremonies) or even as a sort of group therapy (as in many wedding or funeral rituals) designed to facilitate the transition of individuals from one social sphere or one plane of existence to another. Many of these ritual dramatic forms fall into one or other of two categories. Although there is a considerable amount of overlapping one group may be said primarily to involve man as a member of a community while the other is concerned with the fate of man as an individual.

Ritual, dramatic or otherwise, in the Russian village was inextricably inter-woven into the fabric of day-to-day existence. It reflected the occupations of the peasants and the conditions of life in the village; it answered in some measure the peasant's need to examine, understand and, in some cases, even to influence the complexities of nature, in particular the changing seasons and the vagaries of the weather, upon which his livelihood depended. As far as the contents of these ritual dramatic games are concerned, two major themes emerge: on the one hand the importance of the crops and vegetation in gen-eral and on the other concern for the domestic farm animals.

The relative importance of agriculture, animal-breeding and hunting among the East Slavs in pre-Kievan times has been a constant source of disagreement among both Russian and Soviet scholars. Most Soviet historians play down the role of hunting as a means of obtaining food in favour of the early devel-opment of agriculture and animal husbandry.

B.D. Grekov, for example, basing his views on quantities of seed grains found in archeological excavations, suggests that even during the pre-Scythian Tripoli culture (3rd — 2nd mill. B.C.) Slavonic tribes living in the Dnepr basin were already acquainted with agricultural processes.[1a] The pattern of ritual observances among the East Slavs seems also to indicate an agricultural way of life deeply rooted in the ancient past. Among the Russians, White Russians and Ukrainians there is an almost total absence of hunting rites compared with a superabundance of ritual connected with every aspect of the changing seasons, the crops and the usual occupations of a farming community.

There can be little doubt, in any case, that at least from the foundation of the Kievan State until the Revolution agriculture was the main occupation of the Russian peasant. Each month of the peasant year contained a wealth of ritual activity connected with his work and his environment ranging in com-plexity from simple prognostications of the weather to the elaborate festiv-ities of the Christmas and Shrove periods. The coming of Christianity at the end of the 10th century did little to slacken the almost organic link between the peasant, his land and nature as he understood it. The Christian saints, for example, were quickly absorbed into the more ancient calendar of ritual events. Saints were identified not so much by their deeds or virtues but by their role as agricultural sign-posts; St. Peter's day (16th January) was known as *Petr Polukorm* (January being the time to assess the amount of fodder left for the rest of the winter), St. Simeon and St. Anne's day (3rd February) was known as *Semen s Annoj sbruju počinajut* (this being the time to prepare farm implements for the spring), and St. Avdot'ja's day (4th August) was *Avdot'ja Ogurečnica* (the time when the cucumbers ripened).[2]

Animal husbandry was also an important occupation in some regions settled by the early East Slavs, particularly in the steppe lands towards the South and down to the shores of the Black Sea. Even in the far north where hunting was always relatively more important excavations of sites dating to the 8th century A.D. near Lake Ladoga have produced larger quantities of bones from *domestic* animals (pigs, cattle, sheep and goats) than from wild animals.[3] Cattle, horses and pigs were widely distributed over the territories of the East Slavs, the horse being particularly necessary for work in the fields of the more agriculturally advanced areas. Goats, on the other hand, were relatively unimportant in the husbandry of the Great Russians, although abundant in White Russia and, to a lesser extent, the Ukraine. As one might expect it is in these areas that games involving the ritual goat are mostly to be found.

The peasant agricultural year can be divided into two major work cycles. The first and most important of these began towards the end of winter with preparations (maintenance and repair work mainly) for the renewal of outdoor activity and continued into spring and early summer with ploughing, sowing and tending the new crops. The second covered the late summer-autumn period and was concerned mainly with the rewards of the year's labour, the gathering in of the harvest. Within these periods of particular importance to the peasant agriculturalist we find corresponding climaxes of ritual activity. The earliest of these fell during the week of winter festivities known as *zimnie svjatki.*

1. *Zimnie svjatki* (Christmastide)

The period known as *zimnie svjatki* extended from Christmas Eve to Epiphany (24th December — 6th January) and corresponded to celebrations of the winter solstice to be found among many ancient heathen peoples such as the Scandinavian *Yule* or the Roman *Saturnalia* which culminated on 25th December with the festival *dies natalis solis invicti* dedicated to the birth of the new sun.

Many remnants of the festival's pagan origins survived in Russia well into the 19th century, among them the customary lighting of bonfires at this time and the many practices designed to ward off the synonymous powers of evil, darkness and winter in their final struggle against the regenerating strength of the sun and nature. On the Eve of Epiphany (*Kreščenie*), for example, in many parts of Russia the peasants used to burn crosses on the doors and windows of their houses to prevent evil spirits from entering.[4] Indeed, Christmas celebrations among the Russian peasantry, apart from actual attendance at church, had very little connection with Christianity. Even their Christmas carols (*koljadki*) contained more secular or pagan elements than Christian. It is true, however, that scenes from the Nativity accompanied by suitable hymns were performed during the Christmas period in the *Vertep*, a type of puppet theatre popular throughout Russia but particularly in the southern regions and the Ukraine.[5]

Church and state dignitaries aware of the non-Christian nature of the festival tried in vain to abolish it, providing us in passing with some picturesque accounts of the conduct of their wayward flock. Here, Patriarch Joachim writing in 1684 describes the *zimnie svjatki* in Moscow: —

> "Тогда . . . ненаказаннии мужескаго полу и женскаго собравься многим числом, от старых и молодых, мужи с женами и девки ходят по улицам и переулкам к беснованным и бесовским песням, сложенным ими, многия сквернословия присовокупляют, и плясание творят, на разжение блудных нечистот и прочих грехопадений, и преобразающеся в неподобная от Бога создания, образ человеческий пременяюще, бесовское и кумирское личат, космат ые, и иными бесовскими ухищреньми содеянные образы надевающе, плясаньми и прочими ухищреньми православных Христиан прельщают . . ."6

The Christmastide festivities, providing as they did a welcome period of rest and entertainment before the hard work of preparation for the spring, were highly developed in the Russian village, especially by the younger people. These would often club together and for a small sum hire a house or a room for the night, or even for several days if they could afford it, as a base for their winter parties (*posidelki*). Here they would amuse themselves with eating and drinking, dancing and singing, games, cards and the telling of fortunes. The latter was a favourite occupation of the girls who hoped to find out whom and when they would marry; they would pour melted wax into water, watching the various shapes thus formed or throw a shoe over the house gate to see in what direction it would point when it landed. Less innocent forms of fortune telling were also known. The bolder peasant girls would brave the terrors of the barns, out-houses and bath-houses where evil spirits were believed to lurk and try to conjure up the shade of their future lover.

a) The mummers

Another popular amusement at Christmastide was masking (*rjažen'e*), a custom which, as in other European countries, originated in pagan times. The earliest references to masking in Russia date to the 11th and 12th centuries and are to be found in sermons and religious tracts denouncing the survival of heathen worship among the ordinary Russian people. Even by the 17th century the attitude of the Church to these residual 'pagan' practices had not substantially changed. A work on ecclesiastical law (*Nomokanon*) published in Kiev in 1624 tells us that: —

"Ныне Христианския дети сия творят: в одежду женскую мужие облачатся и жены в мужескую; или наличники, якоже в странах Латинских зле обыкоша, творят, различныя лица себе претворяюще."[7]

The bands of mummers (*rjaženye*) who used to roam the countryside and even the towns during the Christmas season and who often became as much of a social menace to the law-abiding villagers and citizens as their ancestors had been a spiritual menace to the Russian church, were known by a variety of different names in different parts of the country; *xaljavy* in the Jaroslav government, *narjadixi* in Archangel *oblast'*, *kudesniki* and *okrutniki* in and around Novgorod. The Novgorod *okrutniki* led by a sort of master-of-ceremonies, the *rol'nik*, whose particular function was to sing songs and tell stories, looked for the houses displaying a lighted candle in the window as a sign of invitation and welcome. Some of the *okrutniki* were dressed like bizarre brigands in long tunics made from scraps of different coloured materials with scarlet sashes round their waists. They carried weapons; a large kitchen chopper suspended from a towel slung across one shoulder and a hunting knife stuck behind the sash. Others wore outlandish costumes made from bits of sacking and decorated with bells, reminiscent of the grotesque garments of the Shrovetide period. The parade of the *okrutniki* resembled Shrove in other respects. In Tixvin, for example, a ship covered with brightly coloured flags was drawn through the streets of the town by a team of horses and used as a sort of mobile stage on which the mummers danced, sang and performed comic sketches.[8] The ship, as will be seen, also formed an integral part of the Shrovetide celebrations.[9]

The *kudesniki* too wore ragged garments or sheepskin coats turned inside out and carried guns, brooms, spades, oven forks and other such implements frequently found in rituals designed to frighten away evil spirits.[10]

In early 17th century Moscow bands of Christmas revellers known as Chaldeans (*xaldei*) ran riot through the city practising their jokes and tricks. The Dutch ambassador, Adam Olearius, was fortunate enough to see them during his stay in Moscow in 1636: —

"These are a sort of rascally fellows, who get leave of the Patriarch to disguise themselves, by putting on Vizards, and to run up and down the streets from the 18. of December, till Twelve-tide, with Fireworks, wherewith they set fire in their hair and beards whom they meet. Their main spleen is against the Peasants, whom they force, every time they are met, to pay a Copec ere they get out of their hands. They are all disguised, and have on their heads great wooden hats, fantastically painted, daubing their beards with honey, that the sparkles might not fasten in them . . . These men,

as they say, represent those who heated the Oven, into which
Shadrach, Mesak and Abednego were cast, by the command of
Nebuchadnezzar."[11]

It is possible, as Olearius suggests, that the Chaldeans began their outrageous
career as participants in the Church play *The fiery furnace* (*Pеščnoe dejstvo*),
about the martyrdom by fire of the three youths Ananija, Azarija and Misail,
similar in content to the tale of Meshach, Shadrach and Abednego in the Old
Testament *Book of Daniel.* The *Fiery Furnace* was played in Moscow and
several other cities during the sixteenth and seventeenth centuries, to which
period belong the only extant copies of the text.[12] Eventually, the activities
of the Chaldeans were seriously curtailed and in the end banned altogether
because of the dangers incurred by the lives and property of Moscow citizens.[13]

The motives behind different examples of masking may vary widely. The
desire to hide or protect one's person by disguise from the attention of the
evil spirits was a common motive and it is possible that some such idea originally lay behind some of the most popular Russian forms of masking such as
the customary exchange of clothing between men and women and the habit
of wearing clothes inside out, shoes upon the hands, boots upon the head and
like absurdities.

The exchange of clothing was a widespread and ancient custom. Note, for
instance Bourne's reference to the Synod of Trullus,

> ". . . where it was decreed, that the Days called the Calends,
> should be entirely strip'd of their Ceremonies, and the Faithful
> should no longer observe them. . . . They therefore decreed, that
> no man should be cloathed with a Woman's Garment, no Woman
> with a Man's."[14]

In order to enhance their absurd or horrific appearance the mummers would
also daub their faces with soot, flour, beetroot juice, charcoal, etc. It is highly
probable that this primitive form of 'make-up' originally had no aesthetic or
dramatic function at all but served merely as a protection, soot and ashes
being a powerful antidote to the malevolence of evil spirits.

Extremely popular among the Christmas masks were those of the 'old man'
(or 'beggar') and the 'old woman'. The appearance of these characters was
deliberately grotesque and their antics often of an erotic nature. The old man
normally had a hump-back, long, tangled hair and beard, and might be lame
as well. His dress consisted of a sheepskin coat sometimes made from alter-
nate black and white skins, worn inside out and tied with a piece of string. A
stuffing of straw inside the sheepskin formed the hump while hair and beard
could be augmented with tow. He carried a cudgel.[15] The old woman was

depicted in like grotesque fashion, her face daubed with soot and an old rag wound about her head.[16] It is interesting to to note that 'old man' and 'old woman' masks were among those seen by Professor P.G. Bogatyrev during his visit to the Balkans in 1947. These mummings took place during the Bulgarian winter festivities on and around *Vasil'ev den'* (1-14 Jan.).[17] Indeed, the comic old hump-back is a figure known on the popular stage of many lands and many ages and was one of the most constant of the Russian folk theatre. We shall meet him again in the agricultural rituals and the folk plays *Tsar' Maksimilian* and *Lodka*.[18]

The old woman, too, appears to have many sisters among the Russian popular masks such as the witch *Baba-Jaga* or the *kikimora*. The *kikimory* were dwarf-like spirits hostile to man, the souls of children who had died unbaptised or cursed by their parents. They were usually female, preferred to live indoors and enjoyed spinning at night and playing tricks with any spinning equipment left lying about by the women of the house. They sat on the stove, whispering and hopping about and threw things at people when they got the chance.[19] At Christmastime the *kikimora* was a favourite mask among the older women. They would dress themselves in rags and tatters and wore on their heads a pot (*goršok*) covered with a scrap of cloth in mocking imitation of the *kokošnik*, the fan-shaped piece of head-gear worn by Russian peasant women. Thus attired they would make their appearance at the winter evening parties in the villages. Seating themselves on the *polati*,[20] they would begin to spin. The young girls watching them were highly amused and used to tease them, receiving in return for their interference sharp taps from the stick the old women used to carry their yarn.[21]

This mask also bears a strange resemblance to the quasi-pagan, quasi-Christian figure of *Parask'eva Pjatnica*, often equated in folk legends with the Virgin Mary. She was the patron saint of spinners and weavers (a predominantly female occupation) and could mete out dire punishment to those who broke the taboo against spinning on Fridays, the day sacred to herself.

Although the original pagan significance of such masks had disappeared long before, a certain lingering awareness of impropriety was clearly felt by some of the villagers taking part in the Christmas mummings even by the end of the 19th century. Maksimov, writing of this period, suggests that women of respectable peasant families considered masking indecent and even village lads who bought ready-made masks in the town shops were made to bathe in the ice holes at Epiphany (*Bogojavlen'e*),[22] as a penance.

Although the people wearing these semiritual garments were, in a primitive way, acting a part, the real dramatic games at Christmas involved not human but animal masks, in particular those of the horse, the bull, the goat and, in a somewhat different category, the bear.

The importance of animal breeding among the early East Slavs has already been mentioned and the value which the Russians attached to their farm animals can be seen from the many and often complex rites designed to protect them from harm. Thus, the last sheaf from the harvest which was supposed to contain special magic powers was carefully preserved until the beginning of October and then fed to the cattle to help them withstand the rigours of winter. Many animals in Russia had their own patron saints; Sergej of Radonež protected domestic fowl, St. Anisim sheep, the martyrs Flor and Lavr horses.[23] Flor and Lavr's day (18th August) was known as the horses' festival; on that day the horses were given a complete rest from their labours to help preserve their strength and health. They were washed and ribbons were wound in their tails and manes. On the same day special biscuits with a horse-shoe shape stamped on them were baked and offered to the village priest.[24]

b) The ritual horse

The Russian horse mask usually consists of two simple parts, a head and a body, both of which may be made from a variety of materials and fashioned in a variety of different ways. Sometimes the head was crudely carved from a piece of wood or sewn from a piece of rough canvas filled with straw, or again a real horse's skull might be used. To give credibility to the figure ears and a mane were often added, the former consisting of two pointed sticks or bundles of straw, the latter of straw or strands of hemp (pen'ka). The horse's head was then fixed to a pole which was in turn held by the youth (or youths) whose task it was to play the horse. The simplest method of forming the body of the animal was to drape some suitable garment such as a sheepskin coat or a horsecloth over the bent figure of the boy. This basic structure could be strengthened by the addition of a rough framework, two straight poles placed across the shoulders of two peasants and covered over with a blanket or curtain.[25]

A somewhat more imaginative use of the available materials is to be seen in this 'horse' from Mogilev government (Gomel'skij uezd): —

> "Подобие головы шьют из холста и набивают соломой; из пеньки делают гриву и хвост. Весь скелет обшивается белыми скатертями, отчего получается "как есть белая кобыла". На голову кобылы надевается уздечка и привешивается колокольчик.
> В лозовые ребра кобылы влезает человек и покрывается длинными простыгями—попонами, так что ноги закрыты."[26]

The appearance of the horse mask was not restricted to Christmastide. It was also a feature of the spring festivals and often took part alongside the goat and other masked figures in the spring processions of Semik, Rusal'ja and

others. It was during the spring festivities that the following lively description of the horse's antics and its reception among the young people of the village was taken. Here the horse's head, a skull, was fixed to a pole which was covered with a piece of material and bound with string to form the neck. One end of this string was left loose; a youth then took hold of the horse by these makeshift reins and tried to parade it round and control its movements. The horse, however, was extremely frisky, and in spite of all his efforts still leapt about and chased the girls and boys in the crowd.[27]

Around both the ritual horse and the goat there evolved an extraordinary dramatic game, a close parallel to many spring and summer rites, in which the death and subsequent resurrection of the animal was performed with much bucolic humour and boisterous play.

Here, for instance, is a comic scene from Smolensk *uezd*, revolving round the supposed illness of a peasant's horse and its miraculous recovery through the agency of an old wise woman: –

"Кабыла шутки притваряла, абмахнулась—упала, семь дней пралижала.

– Люди добрыя, ти ня иость са старых бабурач кабылу вылечить? Или змяя яе укусила или чемирь пристала? Прашу я вас, штобы вы мне кабылу вылечили.

Падходить баба, лет семидесяти, стала кабылу лячить; вылячила кабылку очень скора; в адно вуха дунула, в другой ветер дугул—кабылка устала.

– Уижжай, мужик, на сваей кабыли: а то нас нехароший народ, сглазить яе — неустанить кабыла. — И он валакеть кабылу, старается увалочь паскарей, кала яво смяютца."[28]

The horse in general was looked upon as a good luck or fertility symbol. It was for this reason that many peasants decorated the roofs of their houses and the shelf where the icons stood with stylised wood carvings of horses. The horse was also supposed to have powers of healing. In the Penza government, for example, superstitious people went to the smithy to collect parings from the horses hooves. These were then burnt and people sick with a fever were given the remains to sniff as an aid to recovery. In other places sick people washed in water left in the bucket after a horse had drunk from it.[29]

c) The goat and the bull mask

Similar to the Christmas horse both in the primitive methods of construction and in ritual significance were the goat and the bull masks. One of the simplest ways of making the goat was as follows: –

"Один парень закутывается с головой в вывернутую шубу, выставив в рукава две палки, изображающие рога."[30]

The head of the goat could, however, be of more sophisticated design with, for example, a mobile tongue which could be made to click up and down by pulling on a string attached to it. This mechanism was put to good use by the actor who would tease the bystanders, pretending to bite and snap at them. A goat of this type is shown in a *lubok* (popular print) from the latter half of the 19th century.[31] Here, a trained bear is performing tricks to a drum accompaniment while a little to one side stands the costumed goat. The actor's body above the knee is completely enveloped in a gaily patterned sacklike garment drawn in tightly at the top of a long, thin neckpiece surmounted by a replica of a goat's head. The animal's jaws can be manipulated by a string which runs down inside the sack. The most essential part of any goat costume was, however, the horns.

Like the horse, the goat was often the central figure in a death and revival scene. In the following example the goat, accompanied by its 'owner', an old man with a hump-back, wearing a sheepskin coat turned inside out, runs about, butting the girls in the crowd until it is eventually taken ill: —

"Кызинка пляшет, падает, валяется по полу. Хозяин говорит, что она заболела.
— Принесите водицы, надо ее збрызнуть, у ей живот заболел, — говорит он.
Ее обрызгивают водой, она поднимается и пляшет."[32]

The erotic elements (butting etc.) in the goat's playfulness were also a common feature of the bull mask. Maksimov, describing a typical bull game at a village winter party points out that the main aim was for the bull to butt the girls in such a way that this was not only painful but also embarrassing; the girls were thus set squealing and shrieking in half serious, half mock indignation. The actor playing the bull wore an earthenware pot on his head with real bull's horns fixed to it. When the game was over the bull was 'killed', that is, the earthware pot was smashed and the fallen animal carried out.[33]

d) The bear mask

Another animal mask which deserves to be considered here, although its origins and historical connections place it somewhat apart from the others, is that of the bear.

The bear, of course, was an animal of the hunt rather than agriculture and although its importance to the economy of such northern peoples as the

Voguls, Jakuts, Surguts etc. is indisputable, among the Slavonic tribes it was territorially limited and sought after mainly by those living in the northerly forest regions. This, coupled with the fact that even among these northerly Slavonic tribes its importance both for food and pelt died out at a comparatively early stage, helps to explain the lack of ritual ceremonies involving this animal. There is nothing among either the Russians or the East Slavs in general to compare with the variety of rites and dramatic games (depicting the hunting and trapping of the beast, the dangers incurred by the huntsmen and so on) to be found among the northern Siberian tribes. Yet in spite of this, the bear, live or masked, played a major role in Russian popular entertainment.

From the earliest times bear-baiting (*medvež'ja travlja, medvežij boj*) in which battles were arranged between bears and dogs, men or even other bears, was highly popular among all sections of the Russian public. There is much documentary evidence as to the existence of bear-baiting at the Russian court from the time of Ivan the Terrible onwards. Among the most interesting accounts are possibly those of foreign travellers such as the Englishman Giles Fletcher, writing in 1589: —

> "On other speciall recreation is the fight with wilde Beares, which are caught in pittes, or nets, and are kepte in barred cages for that purpose, against the Emperour be disposed to see the pastime. The fight with the Beare is on this sort. The man is turned into a circle walled round about, where he is to quite himselfe so well as he can, for there is no way to flie out. When the Beare is turned loose he commeth upon him with open mouth. If at the first pushe hee misse his aime, so that the Beare come within him, hee is in great daunger. But the wilde Beare being very fearse, hath this qualitie, that guiveth advantage to the Hunter. His manner is when he assaileth a man, to rise up right on his two hinder legges, and so to come roaring with open mouth upon him. And if the Hunter then can pushe right into the very brest of him betwixt his forelegges (as commonly hee will not misse) resting the other ende of their boarespeare at the side of his foote, and so keeping the pike still towards the face of Beare, he speedeth him commonly at one blow."[34]

Siegmund von Herberstein, who visited Russia several times on his ambassadorial missions during the first two decades of the 16th century, also witnessed bear-baiting at the royal court and noted that the men who provided the sport were highly regarded by the prince and even well rewarded for the considerable danger they faced: —

> "If in the encounter they happen to be wounded by the irritated

and, maddened bears, they run to the prince, crying, "See my lord, we are wounded." To which the prince replies "Go, I will show you favour," and then he orders them to be taken care of, and clothes and certain measures of corn to be given them."[35]

Such performances could take place at any time of the year although they were more usual in autumn and winter. In Moscow they were usually held in the Kremlin itself on one or other of the main courtyards in a place which had been specially prepared beforehand. In the 17th century a favourite spot for the entertainment was the *Car'*Boris' Courtyard near the Patriarch's palace.[36]

Bear-baiting was not only a sport for royalty. It was followed with keen interest by the ordinary people too. In Moscow itself public spectacles took place behind the *Rogožskaja zastava* up to the sixties of the 19th century, and crowds of people would gather to watch them every Sunday.[37] The sport was abolished in the 1860s when an animal protection society was formed.

A milder form of popular entertainment involving the bear was the custom of training these animals to perform tricks and imitate the actions of human beings.

The extreme popularity of the trained bear among all sections of Russian society can be seen from the many references to them in early documents (particularly ecclesiastical) as far back as the 13th century.[38] The 17th century traveller Adam Olearius remarks several times on bear-baiting and performing bears in Muscovy. At the village of Soliza in 1634, for example, he says: —

"We slept not, but made sport with a young bear, the Pristaf had brought us, which could show a thousand tricks."[39]

In old Russia the performing bear was popular among all levels of society from the *Car'* himself to the poorest peasant. Ivan the Terrible and Mixail Fedorovič both kept bears and even as late as the 18th century the custom was still maintained. The Empress Elizabeth, for instance, enjoyed watching them perform. She herself kept a number of bear cubs which she sent to the Aleksandronov Monastery to be trained. Here the Bishop of St. Petersburg, Feodosij Jankovskij, who himself patronised the keeping and training of tame bears, had a servant, Karpov, who taught the cubs in his care such tricks as walking on their hind legs, dancing and performing other such antics. It was to him that the Empress sent her pets.[40]

As for the peasantry, Rovinskij's graphic account of the arrival of the bear trainer with his performing animal in a Russian village speaks for itself: —

"Приход вожака с медведем еще очень недавно составлял

зпоху в деревенской заглушной жизни; все бежало к нему на встречу, — и старый и малый; даже бабушка Анофревна, которая за немоготою уже пятый год с печки не спускалась, и та бежит.

— Куда ты это, старая хрычевка? — кричит ей вслед барин.
— Ах батюшки — прихлебывает Анофревна: — Так уж медведя—то я и не увижу? — и семенит далее."[41]

The popularity of the performing bear among the ordinary people is also attested by the Russian folk pictures where he was a common subject. In the collection *Russkij lubok XVII-XIX vv.*[42] there are several pictures showing the bear being put through his paces. No. 63, for instance, shows the bear rearing on his hind legs with every appearance of ferociousness. It was usual to have the claws and sharp teeth cut or knocked out, but sometimes these were left in their natural state to provide more excitement. Nearby a youth plays a little drum, stamping time with his foot, and to this accompaniment the bear is forced to dance.

Sometimes, to enhance the overall effect, the bear was dressed up in human garments. No. 18 in the above collection depicts a dancing bear wearing a plumed hat and a tasselled collar while his companion, a castinet playing goat, wears a loose fitting frock.

The main part of the repertoire of these performing animals was made up of a series of imitative actions. Here, for example, are only a few of the tricks performed by two bears shown in St. Petersburg in 1771 by a group of peasants from Nižegorod: —

". . . 5) Натягивают и стреляют, употребляя палку, будто бы из лука . . .

10) Ходят, как парни и престарелые, и как хромые ногу таскают . . .

12) Как сельские девки в зеркало смотрятся и прикрываются от своих женихов . . .

13) Как малые ребята горох крадут и ползают, где сухо на брюхе, а где мокро, на коленях; выкравши же, валяются . . .

22) Кто поднесет пиво или вино, с учтивостью принимают и, выпивши, посуду назад отдавая, кланяются . . .[43]

The antics of the bears were, of course, accompanied by a continual stream of patter from their trainer.

P.N. Berkov tells us that the leading of tame bears was banned at the end of 1866,[44] but it must have continued for some considerable time in spite of this; Vsevolodskij-Gerngross refers to tame bears appearing in Moscow and Leningrad even as late as 1928.[45]

The purely embryonic nature of the performing bear as a form of drama is obvious; although it is true that it represents one of the earliest forms of non-ritual, quasi dramatic entertainment it remains extremely primitive in structure. There is no plot, only a series of mimetic gestures corresponding to the monologue of the bear trainer. Of much greater interest, from our point of view, are the bear masks and games whose evolution was, nevertheless, considerably influenced by the traditions of the performing animals.

The bear mask existed alongside those of the horse, bull and goat during the Christmastide festivities, and in construction bore a strong resemblance to them. As in the other costumes the sheepskin coat was a major item for making the body. In one of the games collected by Vsevolodskij-Gerngross the lad playing the part of the bear was dressed in two black sheepskin coats, with the fur to the outside. The sleeves of one of the coats were pulled on to his arms and the sleeves of the other on to his legs. The loose tail and front parts of the coat were then either sewn or tied together with string. To complete the costume a black astraxan hat was put on the bear's head and his face was smeared with soot.[46] Sometimes the figure of the bear was made with a hump-back.

Instead of the sheepskin the bear could also be made from withered pea-stalks, which are a similar colour to the browny fur of the bear. This looks quite effective as a disguise when bound neatly round the arms, legs and body of the mummer.[47]

This bear mask, which rivalled in popularity the live, performing animal, represents an interesting phase in the development of ritual drama, for the ritual significance of the animal's appearance survived only in a few, minor details, while the construction and content of the 'drama' which evolved round it was borrowed from almost totally nonritualistic sources.

The early Russian church had no doubts about the connections between the bear games and the ritual animal games which have been examined above, condemning them all equally as pagan and unholy. Lack of documentary evidence makes it impossible to say whether or not the bear was, like the other animals, a central figure in East Slavonic agricultural fertility rites, but it is certain that he was regarded in their territories as an animal with considerable powers for good luck and increase both at home and in the fields. Note, for instance, the appearance of the bearskin as a fertility symbol in the Russian and White Russian marriage rituals.[48] Then again, in many parts of Russia it was believed that the bear could cure illness if he stepped over a sick person. Attempts were also made to secure the good health of the cattle through the intervention of the bear. Such methods as censing the peasant home with burning fur taken from the bear's coat or asking a bear trainer visiting the village to lead his animal round the farm and outhouses were thought to be efficacious in warding off the evil eye, and similarly the health and fertility of the cattle and horses was thought to be ensured if a bear's head could be hung up in the stables.[49] Finally, the approach of the Christmas (or Shrovetide) masked bear was accompanied by many popular songs and jingles which again expressed the hope that those who offered the maskers hospitality would receive a little more than mere entertainment for their trouble: —

> "Медведь пыхтун
> По реке плывет,
> Кому пыхнет на двор,
> Тому зять во терем."[50]

An interesting analogy to the Russian beliefs concerning the masked bear, which still further underlines its original purpose, can be seen in descriptions of a Moravian game where the bear was usually played by a farm labourer whose body was covered with pea-stalks. To complete the picture a straw tail was stuck on and a bell hung round his neck. The performance at each cottage consisted of a little dance with the daughter of the house, and it was thought that this would produce good crops of flax and hemp. Bad luck, on the other hand, would follow those who refused to dance with the bear. A piece of fur from the bear was often used as a good luck charm and placed in the nests of the farm geese.[51] A similar dancing straw bear was known in England and other parts of Western Europe; Frazer considered it to be a representative of the vegetation spirit along with the horse, goat and other animal masks. However this may be, it is certainly true that all the animals involved in these games, whether live or merely masked were respected by the Russian peasant as harbingers of good fortune.

e) The secularisation of ritual masking

In spite of the many indications of the masked bear's origins, the external form of the bear games as they are best known was strongly influenced by the repertoire of the live performing animal. Like the real bear its masked counterpart was often accompanied by a 'gypsy' trainer and made to perform similar tricks. Šejn describes the masked bear who frequently appeared at Christmas gatherings in the Vjatsk government (Kotel'ničeskij *uezd*): —

> . . . "Который покажет вам, как старуха шла на барскую работу; при чем медведь и скобянится и со стоном и почти ползком пойдет к дверям; а когда спросят его, как эта старуха просила у барина милостины, то медведь встает на колени и с плачем кланяется в ноги."[52]

Small dramatic scenes grew up around the bear such as in the White Russian games played to celebrate the birth of a child. Here, not only the bear and his gypsy trainer played a part but also a whole suite of gypsy women who went round the village together telling fortunes, offering cures for all ills and collecting small gifts for their performance.[53]

The bear mask was not the only one to attract nonritualistic elements and to become in this way a part of the new secular repertoire of the folk theatre. The horse was often joined by Russian cavalry officers or by costumed gypsies, since gypsies were well known, even notorious horsedealers, particularly in southern Russia and the Ukraine, and a scene depicting the buying and selling of the horse would take place. Of this type was *Igra v kobyly*. For this game played at winter parties the boys divided the girls into pairs and told them to pretend to be mares. They sang: —

> ”Кони мои,
> Кони вороные . . .”,

then one boy, supposedly the owner of the herd, asked the others to buy: —

> ”Кобылы славные, кобылы! Покупай, ребята!”

A buyer would then choose a girl and examine her as if she were a horse. The sale went ahead with many indecent gestures and vulgar songs. Finally the 'mare' was shod. For this one boy would light a bundle of straw while another blew upon it (like bellows). A third (the smith) beat the girl about the heels and ankles while the buyer held her legs to stop her running away.[54]

From such small beginnings something approaching a primitive play might eventually emerge. Such is the case in a playlet from Mogilev government which appears in Vsevolodskij-Gerngross's collection of Russian games. In it the traditionally constructed horse mask is accompanied by an officer, a lady (*barynja*) and a gypsy: —

> ”Один из парней рядится офицером; надевает солдатские мундир и штаны, на голову бумажный кивер с султаном из бумажной кисти, через плечо голубая лента из бумаги. Другой парень одевается в женскую рубаху с расшитыми рукавами и в андарак, на шею надевает монисты, на голову — платок. Это — барыня. Третий парень наряжается в солдатский мундир, но без ленты, с головным убором вроде уланского. Четвертый парень — цыган — надевает синий армяк, рваную шапку, подпоясывается веревкой. С кнутом в руках он ухаживает за кобылой.”[55]

The action of this dramatic game consists quite simply of a series of gay dances between the actors and an attempt on the part of the gypsy, who comically extols the animal's dubious virtues, to sell the horse to the owner of the house in which the performance is taking place. It should be noted that while the external appearance of the ritual mask remains unchanged in such games, some attempt is made, as can be seen in the above description, to portray the nonritual characters more realistically. The liberation of such masks from their original ritual setting by their adoption into situations drawn from the everyday social contacts of the people had a decisive effect upon the development of nonritual drama in Russia. The addition of new characters (officers, gypsies, etc.) inevitably led to the introduction of new scenes, and these to the introduction of dialogue drawn from everydayspeech, as opposed to the mimetic actions and static monologues of earlier works.

Not only were the ritual masks often joined by others of a nonritual nature but they themselves could be used as the basic for quite new creations. Thus, in all probability, the nonritual camel mask was based upon the construction of the ritual horse. The similarity in appearance is obvious. A typical camel was made by two peasants tied back to back in such a way that they could still bend over in opposite directions. Each peasant was then given an arc-shaped yoke which, as he bent forward holding it in his hands, was meant to look like the camel's legs. The whole ensemble was then covered over with a sheepskin rug, fur to the outside.[56]

Many of the Christmas masks were, of course, wholly secular in origin; regional and native costumes or costumes drawn from characters and professions seen in the everyday life of the people or borrowed from popular literature; soldiers and officers, Arabs, Turks, Jews, Cossacks, gypsies and brigands were among the most popular. In the Novgorod *uezd* (Gruzinskaja *volost'*), for example, whole groups of 'gypsy' girls dressed in brightly coloured frocks and shawls would appear in the village streets going from house to house, dancing and singing gypsy songs to a balalajka and accordion accompaniment. This was known as *cygan'ičan'e*. An unusual feature of this custom was that the girls used to ask their hosts to give them any object they had taken a fancy to in the house. In the case of a refusal they tried to 'remove' the object anyway and the householder was obliged to ransom his belongings. The girls bought themselves sweets with the proceeds.[57]

Although the ritual masks retained their popularity and a certain flavour of their original purpose the fun of dressing up to amuse oneself and others became an end in itself and the Christmas mummers were accepted as simply another part of village entertainment over Christmas and the New Year to be enjoyed along with the carols and fortune-telling, boxing and sleighing, feasting, drinking and other pleasures of the festive season.

2. Maslenica

Towards the end of winter when preparation for the resumption of agricultural field work had already begun there took place the second of the two major Russian festival periods, *Maslenica* (Shrove/Carnival). This was a moveable feast dependant upon the date of Easter but generally took place in February[58] during the week immediately preceding the beginning of the six weeks' long Lenten fast.

Shrove week was originally intended by the church to be a period of preparation for the rigours of Lent but in Russia at least it appears to have degenerated into an excuse for excesses of all kinds, particularly eating and drinking. A foreign visitor to Russia at the end of the 17th century commented that the Russians, instead of preparing themselves for the solemnities of Easter, "had abandoned their souls to the Devil." During the whole of the Shrove period they gave themselves up to feasting and drinking, lechery, games of all kinds and even murder "so that any Christian would be horrified to hear of it."[59]

At this time every village had its riotous celebrations, the focal point of which was often the ice hills built up for tobogganing. Around these would would congregate all the attractions of the fairground with performing animals, puppet and theatre shows, acrobats, conjurors and comedians. Youths would amuse themselves with rounds of fisticuffs and by building 'snow towns' (*snežnye gorodki*) which one band would defend against the attacks of the other until either the town was captured and destroyed or the attackers admitted defeat. These amusements were not the prerogative of the village, for the townspeople too took part in the fun. From the middle to the end of the eighteenth century ice hills with their attendant side shows were built in St. Petersburg on the Field of Mars (*Marsovo pole*) and the Admiralty and Palace Squares and later on the Neva and in other places. Even royalty took part in the celebrations. Peter the Great was responsible for a grandiose Shrove procession to celebrate the Peace of Neustadt in 1722. Elizaveta Petrovna enjoyed riding in her sleigh around the royal village of Pokrovskoe and Katherine II after her coronation in Moscow organised a three day mascarade for the entertainment of her people.[60]

Each day of Shrove week had a special name indicating a particular aspect of the merry-making. Monday was *vstreča* (the meeting) on which Shrove was ceremoniously welcomed into the village; Tuesday was *zaigryš* (the beginning of the games) on which the fun really began; on Wednesday, *lakomka* (the *gourmand*), the making and eating of pan-cakes, so much a part of this festival, got under way; by Thursday, *razgul* (revelry), *perelom* (half-way), *širokij četverg* (lit. 'wide' Thursday), the festivities were in full swing; Friday and Saturday, *teščiny večorki* and *zolovkiny posidelki* respectively (evening parties at mother-in-law's and sister-in-law's), were days for the exchange of family visits; and finally, on Sunday, *provody, proščanie, cerkovnik, proščal'nyj den'* (the parting or farewell), it was time to sober up for the beginning of the fast and escort Shrove out of the village. Generally speaking then, there were three main parts to the Shrovetide celebrations: firstly, on the Monday, the reception of the Shrovetide procession with Shrove at the head of it, second- ly, a period of riotous gaiety, of overeating and getting drunk, visiting the fair-ground, playing games and acting comic scenes, and thirdly, on the fol- lowing Sunday, the *provody* or 'leading away' of the departing Shrove.

The formation of the final Shrove procession was always basically the same, consisting of a long train composed of sledges, logs, or sometimes even heavy armchairs, bound together and dragged along by between ten and twenty horses. This train would be decked out with streamers and flags or, for lack of better material, simply with straw. Many of the participants, dressed in fancy costumes, would ride on the sledges, which held various symbolic objects — a sapling (*derevco*), harrow (*borona*), carts (*telegi*), a *kibitka* (sort of covered wagon), and a ship. But there is no doubt that the most popular of these was the ship, often of complicated structure complete with mast and rigging.

Typical of the Shrove procession in general is Morozov's description of *Maslenica* in the Jaroslav government where ten or more horses were har- nessed one behind the other to a specially prepared cart. Each horse had a rider dressed in ragged, soot-soiled garments. They carried a variety of differ- ent objects, one a whip, another a broom. Bells and rattles were hung every- where, even round the mummers' own necks.[61]

The Shrove procession was invariably accompanied by crowds of people, joking, singing and carousing amid the jingle and clatter of bells and other objects beaten or shaken to produce as much noise as possible. At the head of the procession rode Maslenica, symbol of departing winter. This creature, who might have either male or female sex (in spite of the customary title of *Čestnaja Gospoža Maslenica*, was portrayed either by a human being or by a suitably attired doll). The keynote of the whole procession, in contrast, as will be seen, to the mood of solemnity or quieter gaiety which attended some of the later agricultural festivals, was one of exuberant high spirits, a sort of Slavonic *Bacchanalia*, encouraged by liberal libations of vodka.

The Bacchanalian nature of the festivities comes out clearly in the follow- ing description where the part of Maslenica is taken by a peasant dressed in female clothing: —

> . . ."После этого возили Масляницу, почему—то из красавицы
> —богини превратившуюся в наряженного бабою мужика,
> увешанного березовыми вениками и с балалайкой в руке . . .
> Мужик—Масляница, кроме балалайки, держал время от
> времяни штоф с 'государевым вином', помимо него иногда

прикладываясь и к бочонку с пивом, стоявшему подле о—
бок с блинным коробом."[62]

A similar impression of disreputable habits on the part of Shrove is received
from Morozov's description from the Jaroslav government, where Maslenica,
another drunken peasant, was dressed in tattered *beer-stained* garments.[63]

Maslenica as a doll was usually feminine and made out of wood or straw.
The material was given a roughly human shape with a head and arms at least
and dressed in female clothing — an undershift, a *sarafan* and a scarf round its
head. However, male dolls with grossely exaggerated sex organs were also
known.

An interesting substitute for the doll Maslenica was used in some cases.
This was a wheel, symbol for the sun in many ancient mythologies: —

> "На санях, запряженных парою—гуськом, вместо козел, где
> садится кучер, утверждено горизонтально простое тележное
> колесо. В это колесо вделан высокий остроконечный шест,
> середина которого украшена снопом ржи, перевязанным
> лентами, концы которых облегают сноп. Выше снопа, на
> шесте, близ самого шпица, приделана деревянная розетка,
> имеющая в середине черный круг, от которого к краям
> розетки идут белые и черные полосы. Вдоль белых полос
> проходит несколько черных линий в виде лучей. В этом же
> месте прицеплен развевающийся флая. На задке саней, среди
> разных завитушек, изображены два маленьких языческих
> божка; по углам задка два изображения солнца. На боках
> задка контурные изображения животных с разинутой пастью.
> На колесе сидит старик . . ."[64]

The wheel figures in another procession from the Jaroslav government. Here it
is attached to the mast of a model ship and is decked out in female clothing,
thus combining the purely symbolic with the anthropomorphic representation
of Shrove: —

> "Нижний ярус обвертели рогожами конусообразно, а на
> верхнем ярусе прикрепили надетое на мачту колесо и
> покрыли его женским сарафаном . . . На колесо протянули
> веревочную лестницу и на него посадили самого ловкого
> шалуна, одетого в женское платье, с большим кокошником
> на голове и в маске."[65]

In the Simbirsk government (Ardatovskij *uezd* and others) and some parts of
the Penza government the usual procession complete with a comic Maslenica

was drawn through the streets not by real horses but by a grotesque band of mummers fantastically dressed in horse costumes.[66]

The final phase of the Shrovetide celebrations consisted of the 'seeing off' or 'sending off' of Shrove (*provody Maslenicy*). This seems to have taken one of several forms, depending upon the place and historical time of each particular example. Sometimes, especially in more modern times, Shrove would simply depart from the village insisting that it was time to leave in spite of the repeated requests of the villagers for him (or her) to stay. The Shrove games of the 19th and early 20th centuries mostly ended in this way with Shrove setting out for home, to the fair in Rostov or to the next village.[67]

The influence of the Christian festivals of Lent and Easter can be seen in the battle which sometimes completed the Shrove celebrations, ending with Maslenica's ignominious flight after her defeat by the Lenten fast (*Velikij post, post dolgij xvost*). The humour of this situation was reflected in many popular songs and folk pictures. Kuz'mina quotes an account of such an ending to a St. Petersburg Shrove in the 18th century: —

> "Проскакала она (Масленица) мимо моего зрения с перебитыми в сражении пулями и ядрами ногами на двух ухватах, как на костылях, подпираясь вместо посоха сковородником, в замасленном сарафанишке с привешенною на левом бедре сковородою, накинув на плечи нагольную шубионку, закутавши свою голову затасканным утиральником, высуня запекшейся от усталости язык, положа оной на отекшие от бывшего еио празнества губы, как помело."[68]

Of a much more intriguing nature is the custom in some parts of the country of solemnizing the passing of Shrove with a mock funeral. From Šejn, for instance, comes this account of the burial of Maslenica (*poxorony Maslenicy*): —

> "В прощенное воскресенье, т.е. в последний день масляницы, после обеда соберутся девки и бабы и совершают обряд ее похорон следующим образом: делают из соломы куклу . . . В таком виде кукла эта изображает собою масляницу. Затем одну бабу нарядят попом, наденут на нее рогожу наместо ризы и в руки дадут ей навязанный на веревке осметок — на место кадила.
> Двое из участвующих в обряде берут масляницу под руки и в сопровождении толпы, под предводительством попа пускаются в путь из одного конца деревни в другой, при пении различных песен. Когда же процессия выступает в

обратный путь, то масляницу сажают на палки вместо
носилок, накрывши ее пеленкой. Дошедши до конца
деревни, процессия останавливается. Тут куклу масляницу
раздевают, разорвут и растеплют всю. Во все время шествия
с масляницей поп, размахивая кадилом, кричит "Аллилуя",
а за ним кричит, шумит вся толпа, кто во что горазд: кто
плачет, кто воет, кто хохочет и т.д. . А когда масляницу
хоронят, то поют песни. В заключение нужно заметить что
куклу масляницу делают во многих домах на деревне а
хоронят только одну."[69]

With the destruction of Shrove we have another hint of the major theme of
Russian ritual drama, which reflects in its turn the major theme of existence
whether in the human, animal or vegetable kingdom, the problem of life,
death and rebirth. This awareness of an unending cycle is constantly repeated
both in the agricultural rituals and in the animal games which are in many
ways closely related to them.

3. *The spring and summer rituals*

After the Lenten fast began the spring and summer rituals, *Semik, Jarilo,
Kostroma* etc. There is a great deal of similarity in content among these rituals
and a certain amount of overlapping in the dates of their celebration which,
moreover, vary from place to place.

   The highlight of all spring festivals in Russia is of course the abundance of
greenery, the budding vegetation of tree and flower whose swift appearance
from under the melting snow has something of the speed and impact of a revelation. The return of spring after the long, dark months of winter brought
with it to the eyes of the Russian peasant a tremendous surge of new energy,
warmth, colour, growth, the awakening of animals, the return of the birds
from migration. The reappearance of the birds was encouraged by the making
of little clay or dough models on the Feast of Forty Martyrs (*Soroki*) on 9th
March. On the eve of this day mothers would bake pastry swallows or larks
for their children. In the morning the children of the village would all go off
together to a barn or similar place to 'summon the larks' (*zaklikat' žavoron-
kov*). Each child placed his own bird on the ground and then they cried out
all together: —

"Жаворонки, прилетите,
Студену зиму унесите,
Теплу весну принесите;
Зима нам надоела,
Весь хлеб у нас поела . . ."[70]

The sense of a resurrection in nature is well expressed in the peasant calendar of spring: —

> "On the 1st of March the *Baibak*, or Steppe Marmot, awakes from its winter's sleep, comes out of its hole and begins to utter its whistling cry. On the 4th arrives the Rook, and on the 9th the Lark. On the 17th the ice on the rivers becomes so rotten that, according to a popular expression, 'a Pike can send its tail through it'. On the 25th the Swallow comes flying from Paradise and brings with it warmth to the earth . . ."[71]

a) *Semik*

On the Thursday of the 7th week after Easter *Semik*, one of the earliest of the spring dramatic rituals, takes place.

During this time not only are the houses and streets of the villages decorated with flowers and birch branches but the birch tree itself often figures as a totem image, decked out with flowers and carried from place to place by singing and dancing youths and maidens.

Sometimes the birch tree was replaced by a human being, a young girl, the Russian equivalent of our Green George, dressed to represent the freshness of spring, garlanded with birch or maple branches and crowned with a wreath of flowers and leaves. Oddly at variance with this picture of freshness and brightness is Vsevolodskij-Gerngross' assertion that Semik is often portrayed by a girl in the guise of an old hunchback, carrying a broom. Accompanying her is Semičixa, a youth dressed like an old woman, with a bucket and stick.[72] In the town of Azov the festival of *Semik* was known as *Ripej* (*Vodit' Ripej*) and took place on the second day of Trinity. Here, the same strange old couple appeared. Sometimes even elderly women played the game *Ripej*, making of it something approaching a primitive dramatic sketch. From among their number one woman would be chosen to play a young man, another an old woman. These were supposed to be man and wife. This odd couple went into the centre of the ring formed by the players and the old woman pretended to beat her young husband. The choir asked her why she was beating him and she replied that he had thrown her over and had started chasing after young girls.[73]

These figures are in fact not only among the stock characters of the Russian folk theatre recurring throughout its history in a variety of guises, but also appear to have connections with a European tradition of extreme antiquity.

Equally strange too amidst the celebration of new life is the reappearance of the death element, for the birch tree (or doll) stripped of its finery is, like Shrove, abandoned or destroyed when the festivities are over: —

"Оканчивается это все тем, что пародирнют похороны чучела. Кладут его на носилки в гроб или без гроба, носилки четыре девушки берут на плечи, впереди идет девушка зрелых лет с распущенными волосами, в широком кафтане с широкими рукавами; она жалобно поет "Святый Боже". Позади носилок идет другая девушка, тоже с распущенными волосами, и машет вместо кадила старым лаптем на веревке. Третья девушка изображает мать Семика. Она идет за носилками и причитает, как на похоронах; за нею следует целая толпа. Чучело бросают в овраг или воиу, чем празднество и канчивается."[74]

The rest of the spring rituals were usually celebrated between April and June or more precisely between Whitsun and the beginning of the St. Peter fast (*Petrovskij post*) on the 29th June. In White Russia *Jarilo* took place very early, towards the end of April, although in most places both *Kostroma* and *Jarilo* fell in the latter half of June immediately before or after the beginning of the Fast.

b) *Kostroma*

Closest to *Semik* in content was the game *Kostroma* (known as *Kostrubon'ka* in the south of Russia and the Ukraine). Normally, the ritual followed a set pattern of preparation (making and dressing the figure), procession, and destruction (burial, drowning, etc.). In this version taken from Korinfskij *Kostroma* is played by a young girl: —

"Созывались со всей деревни, собирались в заранее облюбованное место красные девушки, шли в простом — не праздничном наряде, становились в кружок на лугу. Одной из красавиц доставался жребий изображать собою Кострому. . . . Брали—клали ее на широкую доску белодубовую, относили ее, с припевами голосистыми, на берег реки. Здесь принимались будить притворявшуюся спящею 'Кострому', поднимали ее за руки; звтем начинали купаться, обливая водой друг дружку; которая—нибудь из девушек оставалась при этом на берегу, держала лубяное лукошко и била в него кулаком, как в барабан."[75]

The day usually ended with merrymaking, the girls changing into their holiday finery.

Kostroma as a doll could be either masculine or feminine although the latter was more common. Šejn gives examples of both types. In the following example the doll is feminine (the description is from Muromskij *uezd*): —

>"Притаскивается большой пук соломы и все находящиеся тут парни и девки делают куклу на подобие женщины . . . Женщины и девушки одевают чучело в сарафан и рубашку, голову повязывают косынкою и убирают цветами, на ноги надевают башмаки и девушки и женщины кладут ее в корыто."

Then comes a description of the procession to the river, which takes the form of a mock funeral. One woman acts as the lament singer, the *plakal'ščica*: —

>"Пришедши к реке или озеру, Кострому разоблачают, снимают с нее все уборы и бросают ее в воду, при чем поют следующую песню:
>"Во поле, было в поле,
>Стояла береза . . ." "76

When a male figure is used the procedure is much the same. In Šejn's description of another ceremony from western Muromskij *uezd* the figure is dressed in male clothing. Kostroma's 'widow' follows the coffin, weeping and crying out: —

>"Батюшка Костромушка, на кого ты меня покинул, закрылись твои ясны оченки!"

When the body is flung into the river, however, she begins to dance, saying: —

>"Пойди дума прямо таки в рай, таки в рай, таки в рай!"77

As in the Christmas mummings a certain sense of impropriety was felt by some of the women and girls taking part in *Kostroma*. Šejn suggests this as a major reason for the ritual's gradual disappearance in the latter half of the 19th century. He quotes some amusing comments by a peasant woman Ekaterina Dobrynkina who provided him with ethnographical material. She imagines a conversation among a group of young women who want to play *Kostroma*. One refuses saying: —

>"— Мне хозяин говорил: грех, потому тут в песнях—те гроб поминают, слышь, на том свете за это язык вытянут, да сковороду раскаленную лизать заставят."78

26

Some interesting variations upon the death and funeral of Kostroma were found in the early spring of 1940 among the peasant women of the villages Doroževo and Domaševo (near Brjansk) which, by reason of their remoteness, retained till comparatively recently a rich folklore tradition. Several editions of the game were known in these villages, including a *xorovod* (round-dance) and a full scale dramatic spectacle with as many as a hundred participants, which was later staged in Moscow.[79] The central motif, apart from the usual illness and subsequent death of Kostroma, was a step by step demonstration of the processes of spinning and weaving: —

> "На подстилке, посреди круга (карагода) медленно (не в такт пению) движущмхся женщин и девушек, лежит на спине тяжело больная Кострома, роль которой всегда исполняет девочка. Лицо больной покрыто платком. Кострома неподвижна, молчит. Рядом с нею сидит женщина — мать Костромы или просто — 'Кума'. Быстрыми, уверенными движениями она имитирует исконно женскую работу — обработку 'прядева' (кудели) в пряжу, а затем в холст."[80]

This version of *Kostroma* was also distinguished by the addition of a number of comic scenes drawn from everyday life, making the whole performance a comparatively rich dramatic experience.

Kostroma was also known in a completely different version, played by little girls rather than their older sisters for amusement only, with few or no traces of ritualistic significance. The game takes the form of a dialogue, a series of questions and answers between Kostroma's mother or nurse, and Kostroma's young friends. The following version, again, is taken from Šejn: —[81]

> "В эту игру играют преимущественно девочки. Выбирают оне по жребью двух: одну в бабку или няньку, а другую — в больную Кострому. Нянька садится на пол, а больная ложится к ней на колени, а остальные все, взявшись за руки, ходят вокруг них и поют:

> > "Костромушка, Кострома,
> > Сударыня ты моя!
> > Состарила ты меня
> > Своим умом—разумом,
> > Своею походкою,
> > Скорою поговоркою."

Играющие	— Тук, тук у ворот!
Нянька	— Кто там?
Играющие	— Кузьма криворот.
Нянька	— Заяем?
Тграющие	— Кострома дома?
Нянька	— Нету—ти, в город уехала."

The players continue to ask if Kostroma is ready and the nurse replies with a variety of excuses: —

> — обедает
> — при смерти
> — за попами послали
> — под образами лежит
> — обмывают
> — унесли на погост

The game is concluded with Kostroma's death and funeral followed by a resurrection: —

> "Кострому хоронят и все ложатся спать недалеко от нее. Ночью Кострома встает и, ударяя по нескольку раз каждого из спящих, приговаривает: — Пеките блины, поминайте Кострому —. Спавшие вскакивают и рассказывают друг другу: — А что я видел во сне! Кострома приходила и говорила: — Пеките блины, поминайте Кострому —. Все идут на место погребения Костромы. Последняя вскакивает и гоняется за всеми до тех пор, пока не переловит их всех . . ."

An analogous game called *Jenny Jones* or *Georgina* was popular among the little girls of England and Scotland during the last century. An eyewitness account given by Alfred C. Haddon,[82] from the village of Barrington, near Cambridge, in the summer of 1896 is remarkably similar to the version given above. It too has a question and answer routine followed by the death and resurrection of Jenny.

c) *Jarilo*

In the *Jarilo* games two distinct types of figure emerge. In one of these the element of the absurd is predominant. In Voronež, for example, a crowd would gather from early morning on the town square and decide who was to be Jarilo. When this was done the chosen one was dressed in bright, multicoloured clothing. He was decorated with flowers, ribbons and bells and a coloured paper dunce's cap with cocks' feathers stuck in it was placed on his head. This procedure was followed by a procession in which drums were played and Jarilo performed various antics for the entertainment of the crowd who followed behind him.[83] In the village of Turovskoe, near Galič the game was very similar, centring round an old man, dressed in a miscellany of odd garments. The villagers gave him wine to drink and then led him to a meadow where they stood round him in a circle. The young girls and youths then approached him and bowed 'reverently'. After games and dancing the crowd accompanied Jarilo back to the village.[84] In the description given below, in addition to the grotesque old man in his rags and tatters there is also an anthropomorphic figure playing the part of Jarilo: the townspeople, as in Voronež, chose the human Jarilo collectively. When he was suitably attired they gave him

> "a small coffin to hold in which there was a doll, depicting Jarilo and made deliberately with exaggerated sexual organs. Then they set off out of town; the old man carried the coffin and the women walked beside him wailing funeral dirges and trying with gesticulations to express their grief and despair. Once in the fields they dug a grave and buried the doll in it with weeping and wailing and then immediately afterwards the games and dances, reminiscent of a pagan wake, began".[85]

The enlarged phallus is also mentioned by Afanas'ev as a specific feature of this ritual in both the Ukraine and Great Russia.

In other parts of the country, particularly in White Russia, Jarilo emerges as a beautiful youth resembling the Greek Adonis, riding upon a white horse. In his fair curls a wreath of flowers is set. His feet are bare and he carries in his left hand some ears of rye. It was believed that when he rode across the fields and meadows he helped the crops to grow and this brought joy and prosperity to the peasants.[86] Clearly there is some confusion here with the figure of St. George (*Jurev den'* – 23rd April). There was a legend among the people about how St. George, released from thirty years' imprisonment by the Emperor Diocletian rode out dressed as a knight on a white horse; in the St. George's day rites he too is always represented as a beautiful youth decked in flowers and greenery.[87]

d) The water nymphs (*Prazdnik rusalki / Petrov den'*)

Another slight variation on the main theme of the spring rituals can be found in the *Prazdnik rusalki* when the water nymphs were chased from the Russian village. This event was celebrated about the same time as *Semik* or during the week after Whitsun. The *rusalki*, who were supposedly the spirits of drowned girls, could exert an evil influence either by luring others to a watery grave or by tickling to death any man unfortunate enough to come across them. Superstitious peasants refused to bathe in the rivers at this time. The *rusalka* was usually played by one of the village girls dressed in a white dress or shift. Her hair was worn loose and uncovered and was adorned with gay spring flowers wound into a garland. In spite of her vernal appearance the *rusalka* was often shown astride a poker and holding a besom in her hands to remind people of her witchlike nature. In parts of the Kaluga government she was depicted in this fashion with her hair loose and wearing only a shift. Little children ran alongside trying to touch her garments and crying: — "Tickle me, tickle me!"[88]

Like Semik, the *rusalka* could also be represented by a birch tree or a straw model. Like Semik too, she was borne from the village amidst noise and merriment, shouting and banging, firing from guns, etc. The figure was then disposed of or 'chased away'. Among the most complete accounts of the ritual is this one given by Snegirev: —

"В Спаске Рязанском следующее за тройцыным днем воскресенье слывет "Русальным заговеньем", а понедельник "Провожанием русалок". Тогда вечером хороводы девиц и женщин с веселыми песнями сходятся с разных сторон города в назначенном месте и стоят около часа на углах улиц; каждый почти хоровод имеет чучелу в виде женщины, представляющую, по их словам, русалку. В это время составляются хороводные кружки, а в середине их бойкая женщина, с чучелою в руках, пляшет под веселую песню, делая разные кривлянья. Потом хороводы разделяются на две стороны, наступательную и оборонительную. Держащие в руках русалок защищаются несколькими женщинами от нападений других, которые стараются вырвать у них чучелы; при чем обе стороны кидают друг в друга песком и обливают водою. Вышед за город, оне говорят, что "проводили русалок". Тогда растерзывают чучелы, разбрасывают их по полю а провожавшие их девицы возвращаются в город с унынием."[89]

e) *Ivan Kupala*

The last important festival in the spring/summer cycle was the Eve of St. John the Baptist (*Ivan Kupala*) or Midsummer's Eve on 23rd June. Midsummer's

Eve was a time of strange supernatural influences, a time when the fearless and adventurous might set out at midnight to seek the flower of the exotic plant *razryv trava* (believed to be a type of flowering fern) which blooms only at this hour. With the help of the blossom, hidden treasure might be found by the man who was bold enough (like Petro in Gogol's story *The Eve of Ivan Kupalo*) to pluck it from the grasp of the demons and spirits guarding it. It was a time when the countryside was splashed with the garish glow of bonfires, in whose flickering light girls and youths danced and sang and leaped with gay bravado back and forth across the flames. The distinguishing feature of the midsummer games is indeed the bonfire, for in many other ways they closely resemble the other agricultural rituals previously examined. At *Ivan Kupala*, too, a straw figure, usually feminine, is made, dressed and decorated with flower garlands and necklaces, or instead of the dummy, a girl may play the part. Vsevolodskij-Gerngross tells us that the latter was usually dressed as a bride and that with bandaged eyes she had to distribute garlands of flowers to the other girls of the village.[90]

A typical feature of the *Ivan Kupala* festival is the appearance of a second figure alongside that of Kupala itself. This frequently consisted of a tree branch (usually willow, poplar or black maple) with flowers and ribbons intertwined among its twigs. This tree figure was known as Marena, Marenočka, Morana, Morynka, etc.

In the ceremony itself the figure, Kupala, was carried to an appointed place outside the village. A little hut or bower of tree branches and flowers was made and Kupala placed inside. Before the hut stood a table spread with a selection of food and drink. When 'Marena' also participated the doll Kupala would be laid at the foot of the tree totem.

Kupala (and Marena) usually suffered the same fate as Semik, Jarilo and the others. When the amusements round the bonfire were over the 'honoured guest' was undressed and destroyed. Groups of boys and girls would fight for possession of it and the victorious party would fling it into the river or scatter the fragments of it to the winds.

This constantly recurring destruction of the vegetation figure during the spring and summer months is at first puzzling. Yet one must suppose behind it a latent belief in or hope of resurrection and reawakening in nature the following year. Such a belief is openly expressed in some of the spring rituals. Thus, a Ukrainian version of *Kostrubon'ka* in which the central figure is portrayed as a dead youth wept over by his wife, contains a resurrection scene with the words: —

> "Ожив, ожив наш Кострубонько,
> Ожив, ожив наш голубонько."[91]

A resurrection or cure was certainly quite common for the Christmas animal masks whose function as symbols of fertility was close to that of the spring figures.

f) The harvest festivals

Somewhat apart from the spring and summer festivals stand those of late summer and autumn; apart that is in ritual significance, though basically similar in content.

After Midsummer, the attention of the villagers was increasingly drawn by the prospect of gathering in the coming harvest, which, depending on the crop and the geographical location, might take place any time between the end of July and October. This important period in the agrarian calendar was accompanied, no less than the earlier work of preparation, by a considerable amount of ritual action and celebration.

It was customary, for instance, to gather a fistful of grain stalks (in particular rye) and fold them in half with the ears head downwards. This was known as 'plaiting the beard' (*zavit' borodu*) and was intended as an offering to the pagan god of cattle Volos or, by a process of later rationalisation, to the prophet Elijah or even God himself.[92] Other ritual observances included the washing of hands, clearly an act of purification, and the prophylactic binding of the scythes with grass "so that next year none of the reapers would cut their hands". Then, before leaving the fields, the workers would bow three times to the earth with the words: —

"Нивка, нивка, отдай мою силу на другую нивку."[93]

The last sheaf from the harvest (known as the *požinal'nik* or *imeninnik*) was particularly endowed with special significance and was carefully preserved. The peasants of the Dvinick *volost'*, for instance, used to lay great store by the powers of the last sheaf of oats from the field. This was usually left unthreshed and brought into the home where it was laid beneath the icons, and carefully preserved until the 1st October. On that date (*Prazdnik Pokrova*) it was divided up among the cattle, each receiving a small piece before its proper feed. The cattle were thus strengthened, the peasants believed, to withstand the effects of any shortage of fodder during the long winter months.[94]

Snegirev gives many examples of the type of celebration which attended the 'harvest home'. One such was taken from a letter by T.K. Kaškadamova describing the course of events in the Penza and Simbirsk governments: —

"В Пензенской и Симбирской губерниях, в 'Пожинки', по окончании жнитва, весь народ сбирается в поле дожинать последние загоны и когда уже свяжут последний сноп

> (имянинник), тогда наряжают его в сарафан и кокошник, и
> с песнями несут на господский двор, где господа подчивают
> жнецов пивом и вином, поздравляя с окончанием жатвы."[95]

Sometimes it is a young girl who is the centre of attraction. In such cases a special garland was woven. The girls cast lots and by this means one of their number, the *talaka*, is chosen, dressed in a white mantle and crowned with the garland. The other reapers make themselves garlands as well; then, organising themselves into a long row, they bow three times to the east and then set off homeward, singing, with the *talaka* at their head.[96]

With the gathering in of the harvest, the last cycle of dramatic rituals connected specifically with the growth and maturation of agricultural vegetation is completed till the following spring.

4. *The dramatic significance of agricultural ritual*

These dramas in miniature remained basically tied to their ritualistic origins. Thus, even in the 19th century when the actual significance of the performances was more than half forgotten by the villagers, the strict seasonal nature of their appearance, related to the two highest peaks of pagan religious activity, Christmastide and early spring, was still largely preserved. The active hostility of the Russian Church from the eleventh and twelfth centuries up to at least the early 18th century towards all forms of popular entertainment including, of course, masking and dramatic games, clearly stems from a continued awareness of pagan antecedents. In church invectives these amusements are often prefaced by the epithets 'devilish' (*besovskoe*) and 'idolatrous' (*kumirskoe*) and those who took part in them were considered as unclean and often required to purify themselves by plunging into icy water.

It was not only the timing of the ritual dramas but also the place of action that was affected by factors outside the realm of drama as pure entertainment.

There was no special theatre or stage for the village rituals. The place of action was defined not by the need to find a situation which would allow the actors to make the best impact on those watching but by the demands of the plot itself which required now a forest, now a meadow, now a river. This was especially true of the spring and summer agricultural dramas which, because of their strong connections with nature itself and because the weather at this time of year was conducive to outdoor activities, were always performed in the open air. Animal games belonging to the winter cycle, on the other hand, were clearly better played indoors where the place of action, surrounded by onlookers had a similar function to the theatrical stage. They eventually became incorporated into the popular round of indoor winter entertainments where they were able to develop away from their ritualistic origins.

Similarly, the criteria which governed the choice of actors in these ritual dramas were not those of the modern theatre. Aesthetic and professional considerations were replaced by social and economic ones, the sexual division of labour in the primitive community being an important factor. Women took no part in hunting expeditions therefore they would not be expected to participate in hunting rituals, and for the same reason men would be excluded from rituals derived from specifically female occupations such as spinning. Moreover, the many superstitions which surrounded women, whose physiological functions were often misunderstood, denied them a part in any ceremony, especially those involving the conjuring of spirits, where their presence might have an adverse effect. It is clear that the traditional divisions of labour within the Russian village, where the men were primarily concerned with the farm animals and the women with work in the fields has left its mark on the nature of the acting body. It was rare for a woman to take the part of one of the major animal masks and the spring and summer agricultural games were, conversely, mainly the property of the female sex, although male actors were not unknown in Shrove and *Semik* processions. To a considerable extent, too, the lack of a strict division between audience and actor typical of ritual, also applies to the Russian games. At Shrove, for example, there was no limit to the amount of people permitted to join the grotesquely costumed retinue. At *Semik* and *Jarilo* large numbers of young girls would weave themselves garlands of flowers or, at *Rusal'ja*, dress up all in white to resemble the water nymphs. At *Semik* too, in some parts, it was common to make more than one doll so that small groups of women each having their own figure could take a more active part in the proceedings. The purpose for which each of these rites was performed was important not only to the few people playing the major roles, but to all of the villagers who were emotionally involved in the evolution of the 'plot' and its successful outcome.

The aim of these maskings was not directed originally towards entertaining an audience but towards producing certain specific material results and the whole visual effect of the drama was influenced by this intention. The primitive actors did not strive for a realistic but for a symbolic portrayal of the creatures and events they imitated. It was not necessary for the spring dolls to be detailed replicas of human beings, but it *was* necessary for them to be decorated with and surrounded by flowers and greenery, the emblems of the spirit they represented. It was not necessary for the bull, the goat or the horse masks to be zoologically exact, but it *was* necessary for them to be recognizable as such through some specific sign such as a pair of horns or a sheepskin covering. Similar considerations governed the choice of the properties and effects whose use nevertheless added to the spectacular nature of the ceremonies, and added to their value as entertainment. Such were the symbols of life and lust, the burning wheels of Shrove and the blazing bonfires of *Ivan Kupala*, such was the joyous yet potentially frightening cacaphony of jingling bells, raucous rattles and banging drums, the clamour of voices, beaten metal and gun fire which was an essential part of many processions, such was the ritual food placed as an offering before Kupala or Moryn'ka and shared out between the girls who came both to 'worship' and to enjoy themselves.

Even the movements and gestures of the actors remained to a certain extent governed by ritualistic principles. Thus, although the leaping of the goat and the butting of the bull became merely a source of amusement or girlish confusion the original hope of encouraging fertility and growth through these antics was not completely obscured.

The fact that the dramatic elements of these agricultural games were still clearly influenced by the exigencies of ritual even in the 19th and early 20th centuries, when the pagan faiths which created them had long since disappeared, does not mean either that the Russians did not actively enjoy taking part in them or that their dramatic instincts were in any way retarded. On the contrary they not only managed to embellish dramatically what already existed but also to draw upon their experience of ritual to create new dramatic forms. This was done in many different ways. For example, the austere nature of the destruction of the spring figure was rationalised and thereby made dramatically more immediate by the addition of funeral scenes borrowed from the Orthodox Church, some perfectly serious, others of a more flippant nature such as the parody upon the rite of *soborovanie* (here called *podzaborovanie*) which appears in the Doroževo version of *Kostroma*: —

”Невестка.	— Что мне теперь делать? А думаю теперь причастить матерю, за попом послать. (Едут за Попом. Привозят Попа.)
Одна из хоровода.	— Здорово, Кострома!
Невестка.	— Здоровенькя!
Одна из хоровода.	— Что ты делаешь?
Невестка.	— А во, привезли батюшку, хочет матерь поисповедовать.
Поп.	— Раба, кайся грехами.
Кострома.	— Как начала я грешить с конца и грешила до конца. Чужих мужиков любила. Грешная я, батюшка, хочу грехи замолить.
Поп. (причащая)	— Как звать?
Кострома.	— Хоботья.
Поп.	— Во имя овса и сена и святого Хоботья, аминь!”[97]

New nonritual characters were added: the priest, the mother, even in some cases the widow, and the emotional impact of the death was heightened by the laments of the *plakal'ščica* or professional mourner.

The potentialities for developing the humorous side of certain situations were also fully exploited and may be seen, for example, in the person of the quack doctor or wise women who were sometimes called in to cure Kostroma[98] or attend to the sick 'animals'. Even the crude goat's head became a more satisfying sight when the simple mechanism for manipulating it had been added.

Both the winter and the spring/summer ritual games, especially the latter, were essentially noisy affairs, noise being considered useful for the warding off of evil spirits. To the artificial sounds of rattling, jingling and banging were added the emotional overtones of women's voices weeping, lamenting, exulting, shrieking and laughing; but dialogue as such occurs only in those cases where the ritual itself has become rationalised and reinterpreted according to the understanding of the people who performed them, such as the funeral scenes into which responses from the Orthodox service and the laments of the mourners have been incorporated, or the comic animal revival scenes which include humorous exchanges between the owner and the doctor. Such examples represent a step forward in the creation of folk drama through the medium of ritual. This is the case, too, with the 'question and answer' structure of the speech in the game *Kostroma and her nurse* which may be said to be one of the most primitive forms of dialogue.

Some evidence of a breakdown in the ritual pattern of the rites described in this section is visible. Thus, for example, the strict participation barriers of the ritual were broken when *Kostroma* passed from the young women to become, in altered form, the property of the little girls. In Doroževo village the original actors in *Kostroma* were, according to ritual tradition, always women but by the 1940's the part of the priest, the doctor and Kostroma's husband were played by men. Similarly, the sense of spectacle or entertainment to be found in some rituals had clearly become very strong in modern times and we find in the animal games and in such well developed versions of *Kostroma* as that found in the villages of Doroževo and Domaševo a definite distinction between those performing and those watching. However, it is still true to say that the dramatic elements of both the agriculture and the animal games remained very largely bound by the principles of ritual.

NOTES

1. Raymond Firth, *Elements of social organisation* (3rd edition, London, 1961), p. 71.
2. V.I. Čičerov, *Zimnij period russkogo zemledel'českogo kalendarja XVI-XIX vv* (AN SSSR, Moscow, 1957), p. 11.
3. B.D. Grekov, "Kievskaja Rus' ", *Izbrannye trudy*, Vol. 2 (Moscow, 1959), p. 41.
4. A.N. Afanas'ev, *Poetičeskie vozzrenija slavjan na prirodu*, Vol. 1 (Moscow, 1865), p. 109.

36

5. *Infra*, pp. 83-105.
6. I.M. Snegirev, *Ruskie prostonarodnye prazdniki i suevernye obrjady*, Issue 1 (Moscow, 1837), pp. 37-38.
7. Snegirev, Issue 2 (Moscow, 1838), p. 32.
8. Snegirev, Issue 2, p. 33 and A.N. Veselovskij, *Starinnyj teatr v Evrope: Istoričeskie očerki* (Moscow, 1870), pp. 299-301.
9. *Infra*, pp. 19 and 20.
10. "Kirilovskie kudesy", P.N. Berkov (Ed.), *Russkaja narodnaja drama XVII-XX vv* (Moscow, 1953), p. 68.
11. Adam Olearius, *The voyages and travels of the ambassadors sent by Frederick Duke of Holstein, to the Great Duke of Muscovy, and the King of Persia*. Translated by G. Davies. 2 parts (London, 1662), p. 129.
12. In contrast to Western Europe, the secular drama in Russia did not develop from the liturgical drama. Along with one or two other religious ceremonies of a semidramatic nature (e.g. the *Xoždenie na osljati* on Palm Sunday or *Omovenie nog*), the *Fiery furnace* is the only example of liturgical drama in Russia of the kind which in mediaeval Europe laid the foundation of a far-reaching dramatic tradition.
13. The term *xaldej* is probably a more recent addition to an ancient custom. There is some similarity to the Halloween torches in Braemar, Scotland. See F. Marian McNeill, *The silver bough*, Vol. 3 (Glasgow, 1961), p. 20.
14. Henry Bourne, *Antiquitates vulgares* (Newcastle, 1725) republished in *Observations on popular antiquities* by John Brand (London, 1810), p. 213.
15. V.V. Selivanov, *God russkogo zemledel'ca*, p. 129; quoted by A.D. Avdeev, "Maska", *Sbornik muzeja antropologii i etnografii*, Vol. 19 (Moscow-Leningrad, 1960), p. 209.
16. V. Ju. Krupjanskaja, "Narodnyj teatr", *Russkoe narodnoe poetičeskoe tvorčestvo*, edited by P.G. Bogatyrev (Moscow, 1954), p. 389.
17. P.G. Bogatyrev, "Otčet o poezdke v balkanskie strany: No. 1 – Po Bolgarii", *Kratkie soobščenija instituta etnografii*, No. 3 (Moscow, 1947), p. 83.
18. *Infra*, pp. 10, 23, 171-172 etc.
19. Afanas'ev, *Poetičeskie vozzrenija slavjan*, Vol. 2 (Moscow, 1868), pp. 100-101.
20. A sort of half storey or *entresol* in the peasant house which could be used when the main part of the *izba* became overcrowded.
21. Avdeev, "Maska", p. 203.
22. S.V. Maksimov, *Nečistaja, nevedomaja i krestnaja sila* (St. Petersburg, 1903), p. 327.
23. *Ibid.*, pp. 343-4.
24. Čičerov, p. 222.
25. "Kobyla", V. Golovačev and B. Laščilin (Ed.), *Narodnyj teatr na Donu* (Rostov-on-Don, 1947), p. 178.
26. V.N. Vsevolodskij-Gerngross, *Igry narodov SSSR* (Moscow-Leningrad, 1933), p. 77.
27. Maksimov, p. 461.
28. Vsevolodskij-Gerngross, *Igry*, p. 70, No. 170.
29. Afanas'ev, *Poetičeskie vozzrenija slavjan*, Vol. 1, p. 635.
30. Vsevolodskij-Gerngross, *Igry*, p. 86, No. 220 (from the Kursk government).
31. V. Baxtin and D. Moldavskij (Comp.), *Russkij lubok XVII-XIX vv* (Moscow-Leningrad, 1962), No. 63.
32. Vsevolodskij-Gerngross, *Igry*, pp. 86-87, No. 220.
33. Maksimov, p. 298.
34. Giles Fletcher, *The Russe commonwealth*. Republished in *The English works of Giles Fletcher the Elder*, ed. by Lloyd E. Berry (University of Wisconsin press, Madison, 1964), pp. 297-298.
35. Siegmund von Herberstein, *Notes upon Russia*. Translated from the *Rerum Moscoviticarum commentarii* by R.H. Mayor (London, 1852), p. 137.
36. I.E. Zabelin, *Domašnij byt russkogo naroda v XVI i XVII st.*, Vol. 1: "Domašnij byt russkix carej", Part 2 (Moscow, 1915), p. 308.
37. D.A. Rovinskij, *Russkie narodnye kartinki*, Book 4 (St. Petersburg, 1881), p. 231.
38. For refs. see Famincyn, p. 122.
39. Olearius, p. 11.

40. *Drevnjaja i novaja Rossija* (1876), No. 12, pp. 418-419; quoted by Famincyn, p. 120.
41. Rovinskij, Book V, pp. 227-228.
42. Compiled by V. Baxtin and D. Moldavskij.
43. *SPburgskie vedomosti*, 1771 g., No. 54; quoted in V.N. Vsevolodskij-Gerngross, *Istorija russkogo teatra*, Vol. I (Leningrad-Moscow, 1929), p. 117.
44. Berkov, *Russkaja narodnaja drama*, p. 21.
45. Vsevolodskij-Gerngross, *Istorija russkogo teatra*, p. 116.
46. Vsevolodskij-Gerngross, *Igry*, No. 81, pp. 34-35.
47. *Ibid., loc. cit.*
48. *Infra*, p. 53.
49. Afanas'ev, *Poetičeskie vozzrenija slavjan*, Vol. 1, pp. 390-391.
50. Famincyn, p. 95.
51. P.G. Bogatyrev, *Lidové divadlo české a slovenské* (Prague, 1940), pp. 35-36.
52. P.V. Šejn, *Velikoruss v svoix pesnjax* . . . Vol. 1, Issue 1 (St. Petersburg, 1898), p. 331.
53. Veselovskij, pp. 297-298.
54. Maksimov, pp. 297-298.
55. Vsevolodskij-Gerngross, *Igry*, No. 195, pp. 77-78.
56. Avdeev, "Maska", p. 199.
57. Maksimov, p. 317.
58. According to V.I. Čičerov from 1832-1940 Shrove was celebrated in Russia 39 times between 25th Jan. and 6th Feb., 31 times between 7th and 15th Feb., and 37 times between 16th and 28th Feb.: Čičerov, p. 21.
59. Quoted by Snegirev, Issue 2 (Moscow, 1838), p. 118.
60. Snegirev, Issue 2, pp. 122-124.
61. P.O. Morozov, *Istorija russkogo teatra*, Vol. 1: "do poloviny XVIIIogo st." (St. Petersburg, 1889), p. 12.
62. A.A. Korinfskij, *Narodnaja Rus'* (Moscow, 1901), p. 160.
63. Morozov, *Istorija russkogo teatra*, p. 12.
64. A procession from the Tula government, in Vsevolodskij-Gerngross, *Istorija russkogo teatra*, pp. 161-162.
65. N.S. Tixonravov, "Načalo russkogo teatra", *Sobranie sočinenij v četyrex tomax*, Vol. 2 (Moscow, 1898), pp. 58-59.
66. Snegirev, Issue 2, p. 128.
67. V.D. Kuz'mina, *Russkij demokratičeskij teatr XVIII v* (Moscow, 1958), p. 58.
68. Kuz'mina, p. 60.
69. Šejn, Vol. 1, Issue 1, p. 333.
70. Maksimov, pp. 354-355.
71. W.R.S. Ralston, *Songs of the Russian people* (London, 1872), p. 213.
72. Vsevolodskij-Gerngross, *Istorija russkogo teatra*, p. 166.
73. S. Brajlovskij, "Prazdnik Ripej", *Živaja starina*, Issue 3 (St. Petersburg, 1891), pp. 223-224. This version was related to Brajlovskij by 80 year-old Akulina Koncurova in 1889.
74. From *Rukovodstvo dlja sel'skix pastyrej*, 1862, No. 21, p. 119: quoted in Vsevolodskij-Gerngross, *Istorija russkogo teatra*, pp. 167-168.
75. Korinfskij, p. 298.
76. Šejn, Vol. 1, Issue 1, pp. 368-370.
77. *Ibid.*, p. 370.
78. *Ibid.*, p. 368.
79. In the winter of 1940 in the *Dom aktera* and the *Sojuz kompozitorov*.
80. L.V. Kulakovskij, *Iskusstvo sela Doroževo* (Moscow, 1965), pp. 11-12.
81. Šejn, Vol. 1, Issue 1, pp. 49-50.
82. Alfred C. Haddon, *The study of man* (London, 1898), Ch. 15, pp. 412-420.
83. Afanas'ev, *Poetičeskie vozzrenija slavjan*, Vol. 3 (Moscow, 1869), pp. 726-727.
84. I.P. Saxarov, *Skazanija russkogo naroda*, Issue 2 (St. Petersburg, 1885), p. 212.
85. Afanas'ev, *loc. cit.*

38

86. Korinfskij, p. 300.
87. Afanas'ev, *Poetičeskie vozzrenija slavjan*, Vol. 1, pp. 700-706.
88. Šejn, Vol. 1, Issue 1, pp. 366-367.
89. Snegirev, Issue 4 (Moscow, 1839), pp. 10-11.
90. Vsevolodskij-Gerngross, *Istorija russkogo teatra*, p. 173.
91. A. Beleckij, *Starinnyj teatr v Rossii*, Pt. 1 (Moscow, 1923), p. 21.
92. For the above references see Vsevolodskij-Gerngross, *Istorija russkogo teatra*, pp. 121-122.
93. *Ibid., loc. cit.*
94. P.A. Dilaktorskij, "Prazdnik Pokrova u krest'jan Dvinickoj volosti", *Etnografičeskoe obozrenie* No. 4, (Moscow, 1903), p. 125.
95. Snegirev, Issue 4, p. 84.
96. Vsevolodskij-Gerngross, *Istorija russkogo teatra*, pp. 121-122.
97. Kulakovskij, *Iskusstvo sela Doroževa*, p. 24.
98. See eg. Kulakovskij, *Iskusstvo sela Doroževa*, pp. 14-24.

CHAPTER II

RITUAL DRAMA IN THE LIFE OF THE INDIVIDUAL

In the preceding chapter some dramatic games involving the village community as an entity were discussed. However, events affecting the peasants on a more personal level also played an important part in the ritual life of the village. In this respect birth, puberty, marriage and death are clearly of overriding importance and, as might be expected, were accompanied by a considerable amount of superstition and ritual ceremony. Rites accompanying the first of these events were more or less limited to purification of the mother on the one hand and prophylactic measures supposedly influencing the future health, prosperity and happiness of the newborn infant on the other. Puberty rites were certainly known in Russia particularly those concerned with the initiation of children into the secrets of certain trades such as the weaving and spinning ceremonies for Russian girls.[1]

It is possible that imitation of the actions involved in certain work processes demonstrated at female puberty rites lies at the bottom of a type of dance with actions, long popular among Russian girls, in which the mimetic movements corresponded to the text of the song. These mimetic dances (*igrovye*) are often referred to as *xorovodnye* although in fact the two groups do not necessarily correspond for the themes of the *xorovod* with its formal structure (circular, linear, figure of eight, serpentine etc.) are not always dramatic or mimetic while the *igrovye* dances do not always follow the formal pattern of the *xorovod*.

Kolpakova in her discussion of the work songs divides them into two main groups, those connected with the agrarian calendar (*kalendarnye*), depicting, for example, the sowing and tending of millet, flax or cabbages, and those unconnected with it (*vnekalendarnye*), showing actions involved in spinning and weaving, the brewing of beer, etc.[2]

Among the most typical of the first group is the dance *Len* which describes the processing of flax. Here, a 'mother' and 'daughter' are chosen to stand in the centre of the circle. The girls of the choir, who are also 'daughters', ask their mother to show them how to prepare the ground for the sowing of seed: —

"Научи меня, мати, на лен землю пахати!"

The mother performs actions to represent the ploughing of the land while her daughters imitate: —

"А вот эдак, дочи, дочушки, вот так, так, да вот эдак."

In this way they run through a whole series of symbolic gestures (weeding, gathering the ripe flax, placing it on a cart, drying it, threshing it, braking it) until the flax is finally spun and woven into fine cloth. In this dance there are two solo performers with a supporting chorus, each of whom performs individually the mimetic gestures appropriate to the various stages of the dance.[3] In the following weaving dance, however, the action is communal, the mimesis being exhibited in the various figures of the dance itself: —

"Девушки становятся в два ряда, лицом друг к другу, взявшись руками так, как это делают при гимнастике для того, чтобы сделать носилки. Пары становятся плотно друг к другу. С краев проулочка стоит по девушке. Пары изображают основу, а девушки с краев ткачиху. Одна ткачиха берет мальчика или девочку и кладет на руки первой от себя пары, та — следующей и так до другого конца. Девушка на другом конце проулочка принимает мальчика, который в этой игре изображает поперечную нитку в холсте."[4]

While the actual construction of these dances has remained the same for centuries the content, however, has always been developing and expanding, new topics continually being added, among which three main groups may be discerned. Some dances have a social theme, some are satirical, others draw upon the animal world for inspiration.

Typical of the animal theme in the *xorovod* is the *Igra v zain'ku* (the hare game) in which the soloist mimics the actions of a hare trying to escape from its captors (i.e. the circle of the choir). The game is as follows. The choir stands or sits in a circle. One youth, the 'hare', takes up his position in the centre of the ring. The choir sings to him asking him to perform certain actions: —

"Заинька, походи!
Серенькой, походи!
Вот так, вот так походи!
. . . .
Заинька, перевернись!
Серенькой, перевернись!
. . . .

Заинька, попляши!

. . . .

Заинька, топи ножкой! . . ."⁵

The soloist mimics all the actions of the song and the game ends with him kissing one of the members of the choir who takes his place in the middle, and the whole thing recommences.

Essentially, from a dramatic point of view, there is little difference between games of the type *zain'ka* and the work games. A change may be observed, however, in games like *Igumen* (The Abbot) which reflects the thread of satire running strongly through the whole of Russian literature since the seventeenth century. Some variants of this have lost the formal pattern of the round dance and have developed into more or less independent dramatic games, in which the action, however primitive, is based upon a mixture of social awareness with fantasy. In other words invention, one of the most important ingredients of true drama, takes the place of mimesis. In it the youths and girls playing choose from their number an 'abbot' while the rest play 'monks' and 'nuns'. A humorous song (*Ox, xo, xo!* / *Ja po kelečku xožu*) accompanies the game in which a young nun tells how much she would like to dance: —

"Поплясати было,
Для милых гостей
Поломать костей."

The players then all demand to be made monks and nuns and each approaches the abbot with the words: —

"Ты святой отец игумен, постриги меня пожалуй,"

upon which the abbot fulfils their request, tapping each LIGHTLY on the back with his whip. When everyone has been 'consecrated', the humorous song is sung again. Finally, the monks and nuns decide to become unfrocked and the abbot performs this ceremony by giving each a HEAVY blow with the whip.⁶

Typical of the social theme are dances dealing with love and domestic life, ranging from the more or less erotic, such as *Golubec* or *Russkaja*, to comical tales of marital dispute like *V ženu i muža* or *Varili my pivo*.

In the dance *Russkaja* a young man and a girl in the centre of the circle act out a simple love scene. With movements of the body, gestures of the arms and legs and facial expressions, they portray the youth's courtship, the girl's reluctance, the young man's desertion and attentions to another, his beloved's timid advances and declaration of love and their final reconciliation. Dances of this type offer far greater scope for dramatic talent to show itself.

In the work dances, as was seen, the actions are dictated by the subject of the dance and the girls reproduce them passively. No characterisation is involved beyond that of the arbitrary titles of 'mother' and 'daughter'. In dances like *Russkaja*, however, things are more complicated. The soloists are free within the basic outline of the simple plot to improvise, to fulfil the role according to their own inclinations and talent. They represent two distinct personalities, that of the bold, passionate *dobryj molodec* and that of the shy, modest *duša devica*, and must convey this impression through their acting. In this description from Tereščenko the youth's dance as he pays court to his beloved, —

> "... подбоченясь одной рукою, он пламенными телодвижениями выражает любовь свою: то манит к себе, то прижимает свою руку к груди, мысленно обнимает и расстается печально ..."

contrasts well with the girl's sadness at his desertion and her attempts to win him back which are expressed in the slowness and gentleness of all her movements: —

> "Она рисуется пред ним задумчивой картиною; то поднимает руки вверх, то опускает их со вздохом, и остановясь, подумав немного, складывает руки на грудь, и плывет с поникшей головою, словно горемычная лебедка, с тяжелой крутинушкой ..."[7]

Of a much simpler nature is the quarrel and reconciliation scene between husband and wife, in which the quarrel corresponding to the words of the song —

> "Малода жана нялюбитсь миня,
> Що нялюбитсь миня, ни глядзитсь на миня" —

is represented by the formation of the *xorovod* which makes a circle round the husband, leaving the wife outside it. Similarly, the reconciliation is effected by the wife's re-entry into the circle, and sealed with a kiss to the words: —

> "Идзе сойдится—паклонитца,
> Разыйдетца — пацалуитца."[8]

Although a certain amount of ritual activity was centred on the new born child or the adolescent, it was the young adult on the brink of marriage who received the greatest attention from the guardians of tradition in the Russian village. The old Russian marriage ritual, remnants of which still survive to the present day is not only the most complex of all the rituals involving the individual peasant but also the most advanced from a dramatic point of view.

1. *The marriage ritual*

It is impossible to estimate exactly the earliest date at which the marriage ritual as we think of it today was first performed on Russian territory. The ceremony known and loved in Russian village communities at least until the end of the 19th century was, rather, the result of a gradual process of accumulation and development over centuries of usage. However, from analysis of texts recorded in the 18th and 19th centuries and from eyewitness accounts it is obvious that parts of it are of extreme antiquity.

The earliest accounts of marriage customs among the East Slavs come from the Chronicles: —

"Поляне . . . имеют и брачный обычай; не идет зять за невестой, но приводят ее накануне, а на следующий день приносят за нее — что дают. А древляне жили звериным обычаем, жили по–скотски, убивали друг друга, ели все нечистое, и браков у них не бывало, но умыкали девиц у воды. А радимичи, вятичи и северяне имели общий обычай: жили в лесу, как звери, . . . И браков у них не бывало, но устраивались игрища между селами, и сходились на эти игрища, на пляски и на всякие бесовские песни и здесь умыкали себе жен по сговору с ними; имели же по две и по три жены . . ."9

Here clearly there is still no hint of the complex marriage ritual that was to emerge later, although games (*igrišča*) of various kinds certainly became a traditional part of the celebrations.

The coming of Christianity in the tenth century did not entirely put an end to the old ways of the peasants although the Church tried hard to stamp out all heathen relics and unseemly revelry at wedding ceremonies. They had little success and the popularity which wedding games and merrymaking of one form or another still enjoyed by the fifteenth to sixteenth centuries is attested by the very Church documents which denounced them. The *Stoglav*, for example, describes and censures the various entertainments to be found at the village wedding, the playing of musical instruments, the antics and songs of the mummers and *gusli* players (*gusel'niki*), all of which often seemed to obliterate the serious and sacred nature of the ceremony itself.[10] It is not really very surprising that the Russian peasants should have clung for so long

44

to those elements of tradition which brought them laughter and entertainment, but it is perhaps more startling to discover that even as late as the 17th century the old barbaric custom of marriage by capture was still practiced in some parts of Russia. Tereščenko quotes the evidence of a foreign observer: —

"Инженер Боплан, живший в Украине около 17 лет, описывает кражу девиц, совершавшуюся в его время, в половине 17 века. В Украине, во всякое воскресенье и всякий праздник, говорит Боплан, собираются после обеда к корчме казаки с женами и детьми. Мужчины и замужние женщины проводят время в питье, а юноши и девушки забавляются на лугу пляскою, под дудку . . . . Тогда казаки, по старому между ними обыкновению, похищают девиц, даже дочерей помещика. В сем случае необходимы ловкость и проворство. Похититель непременно должен ускользнуть с своею добычею, и скрываться в лесу не менее 24 часов. Этим только он спасается, иначе пропала его голова . . . Если уведенная девушка пожелает вытти за него замуж, то он обязан жениться на ней, в противном случае лишается головы. Если же девица не изъявит желания вытти за него замуж, то он свободен от смерти."[11]

The complex and extended ceremonial of the Russian marriage ritual which evolved in the Middle Ages was not by any means the exclusive property of the village communities. Descriptions of royal and aristocratic weddings in the *Drevnjaja rossijskaja vivliotika* (St. Petersburg, 1775)[12] indicate that in the late sixteenth to seventeenth centuries even among the upper circles of society, who would be the first to discard outmoded and despised forms, the old customs were still observed. The traditional roles of the matchmaker (*svaxa*) and the groom's friends (*tysjackie, družki*) were preserved as were such ritual elements as the scattering of hops over the young couple and the eating of a special porridge (*kaša*).

The eighteenth century, however, shows a different picture, for by this time the ritual was largely abandoned by the educated upper classes, although it was still retained among the peasantry. Even in the countryside, however, most of the magical or ritualistic significance was lost giving way to a formal game with set parts much of whose original meaning was no longer understood. Eventually, only the ornamental side was appreciated and the more dramatic or aesthetically pleasing sections were gradually adopted into the village repertoire where they were 'played' out of context for the amusement and enjoyment of the young people.

The ultimate stage in the development of a ritual before its complete disappearance may be said to be that of its artificial revival. The marriage ritual in Russia was entering this final phase by the early twentieth century. In Leningrad on 22. December 1923 the State Experimental Theatre (*Gosudarstvennyj Eksperimental'nyj Teatr*) made a dramatic spectacle of it,[13] and V. Ju. Krupjanskaja writing in the 1950's speaks of such performances as regular occurrences in the amateur dramatics of schools and collective farms.[14]

a) The main parts of the marriage ritual

The marriage ritual may be divided, generally speaking, into the following main sections (with variations of both a historical and a regional nature): −

(i) The match-making (*svatovstvo, sgovorki, prosvatan'e, propivanie*).

(ii) Inspection of the bride's household by the groom's relatives and vice-versa (*smotriny, smotren'e* or *osmotr ugolkov*).

(iii) Preparation for the wedding, the sewing of the trousseau and dowry linen (*prigotovlen'e k svad'be, šit'e pridannogo*).

(iv) The bath (*banja*).

(v) Party, when the bride makes merry for the last time with her girl friends (*devišnik*).

(vi) The arrival of the groom and the setting off for church (*sbory k vencu*).

(vii) The church ceremony (*venčan'e*).

(viii) The wedding feast (*svadebnyj stol, knjažnyj stol, pir*).

(ix) The wedding night (*son molodyx, bračnaja noč'*).

(x) The morning rites (*utrennie obrjady*).

(xi) Post-wedding feast (*xlebiny*).

The length of the ceremony varied considerably from place to place. According to Agreneva-Slavjanskaja[15] no more than a week must elapse, and often two or three days only, between the match-making and the celebration of the nuptials. Kolpakova's analyses of wedding rituals in the region of the Pinega River, however, indicate that a somewhat longer period was more normal − as much as a month in the rituals of the mid-nineteenth century, decreasing to a week/ten days by the beginning of the twentieth century. Thus for the town of Pinega in 1850 the following sequence was usual: −

(i) The *svatovstvo*.

(ii) During the next few days discussion of the match with relatives followed by *smotrenie*.

(iii) A time-lapse of a few days for preparations.

(iv) Thursday of the wedding week: *posidka* (bridal party).

(v) Friday: the bride visits her relatives.

  (vi) Saturday: *banja.*
  (vii) Sunday: *venčan'e.*
 (viii) Monday: the morning rites.
  (ix) A few days later the *xlebiny.*[16]

In fact Vsevolodskij-Gerngross[17] indicates that with the addition of many minor details the ceremony could be spread over as much as six weeks. Although this would seem an unusually long period it is obvious that the length of the ritual was quite flexible.

In the Russian patriarchal peasant community at least until the middle of the nineteenth century it was customary for parents to choose marriage partners for their children. If a family had a son of marriageable age and knew of a suitable bride for him, they would decide, often after consultation with close relations, to call on the girl's parents and make their intentions clear. Sometimes they preferred to delegate this job to responsible relatives or, indeed, to a professional match-maker. The choosing of the match-maker is known as *vybor svatov.* These people called on the parents of the bride to find out if their suit was acceptable and either received an answer there and then or agreed to come back in a few days.

The match-making itself was carried out in an indirect manner by use of set formulae. The match-makers pretended that they had come hunting or had some merchandise to sell and were offered hospitality by the bride's parents. Sometimes, but not usually, the bride herself was allowed to be present. The match-makers next began to compare the relative merits of the bride and groom and proceeded to discuss such details as who should pay for which expenses of the wedding, how much wine and food should be bought, the size of the bride's dowry, etc. The parents might require time to consult together and this period was known as the *duma.* When all the points had been settled the two families sealed the bargain with a reciprocal hand-clap as in business deals (*udarit'/bit' po rukam*) and prayed before the icons. Sometimes a small celebration took place (*zapoj*) and eventually the match-makers were sent home with some small gift each.

At this juncture the bride would begin her part in the ceremony by singing a lament in which she upbraided her parents for making up their minds so quickly to get rid of her, for sending her into bondage with a strange family, for taking away her freedom: —

> "Обневолили меня желанные родители за чужого чужанина, на чужую сторону. Как то будет привыкать мне к чужому чужанину, к чужим родителям, к чужой стороне? Мне уж не долго красоваться волюшкой у своих родителей, и у братцев ясных соколов. Видно я им наскучила, видно была им не работница и не заботница. Видно приустала, мои родители

меня поючи, кормючи, узки плечики одеваючи, резвы ножки
обуваючи!"[18]

Usually the two families had agreed on the marriage beforehand and the
match-making procedure was a mere formality. Often, indeed, the bride and
groom already knew each other and had themselves decided to marry, await-
ing only their parents' consent. The young people had ample opportunity to
meet and form alliances at the winter parties (*besedy*) at which the girls would
entertain the youths with homemade delicacies and where the long winter
nights would be whiled away in homemade amusements and games of all
kinds. A love token of some sort from the girl, a handkerchief or a piece of
jewellery, was taken as a sign of consent and would be produced eventually
by the match-makers. It was customary for a reciprocal inspection of the
bride's and groom's households to be made before the final decision was
taken. Finally, in some places the ceremony of *zaporučen'e* took place in
which the groom gave the bride a shawl and a ring as a token of his affection.

The time between the match-making and the church ceremony was
used for the sewing and preparation of the bride's trousseau. It was primarily
her own best friends who performed this task, coming to her home each
evening for that purpose. The bride herself made use of this period to visit
all her near relatives in the surrounding district. Each visit was accompanied
by an appropriate lament: —

"Добры конюшки поустоялись,
Колокольчики помешались,
Я приехала дочь — невольница,
Ко крылечку ко оперему
Во любимы да во гости.
У крылечка да у перена
Есть подкопы, да все подкопы . . .[19]

She might also pay visits to her own friends and they too were greeted by a
special song. Another type of lament was introduced if the bride had been
married to an 'old' groom (approaching 30!): —

"Родни—братцы чего дать меня не за ровню?
Ах, да не за ровнюшку дать замуж за старого.
Ах, да са старым мужем девка в любви жить не могу . . .[20]

If the bride's parents were dead it was now that she must visit their graves —
yet another occasion for a suitable lament.

During these days before the wedding the bride and her young friends not
only prepared the trousseau but at the same time enjoyed the excuse for or-

ganising parties and games and generally making merry. Sometimes the young
men and the groom were also permitted to attend. This prenuptial entertainment took place out of doors in summer and then wedding games of the
xorovod type were also performed.

A day or two before or, more usually, on the evening immediately preceding the wedding, there was an important gathering of the bride's girlfriends
(the *devišnik*). Here again the bride's songs were sad and bitter as she mourned
the passing of her childhood freedom. Many of these songs contain references
to the bride's single thick plait of hair, symbol of her maiden status. During
the course of the evening this was ceremonially unwound by a close friend
with the bride protesting all the while at the harsh treatment meted out to her
and trying vainly to resist. She wails: —

> "Отходилась, отгулялася
> У свово—то родимого батеньки,
> У своей у родной у маменьки:
> Отплела косушку русаю,
> Отвила ленточку алаю.
> Как и мне—то воля унимаетца,
> Красота с лица она стираетца."[21]

Often, however, the unwinding of the plait was reserved for the day of the
wedding itself as in this description from the Nižegorod government: —

> "Затем сваха расплетает косу невесты и просит подать ей
> тарелку, на которую и кладет все принадлежности девичьей
> косы, которые и отдает матери невесты со словами:
> "Свахынька прими — на девичью красу"."[22]

The bride's hair was then left loose until after the church service when it was
wound round her head in two plaits to show she was now a married woman.
At the same time a special headdress (*povojnik*) was placed on her head.

The last sad farewell of the bride and her girlfriends was often coupled
with the ceremony of 'the bath', the ritual purification of the bride in the
bath-house on the night before her wedding. A female friend or relative
(*banšcica, bajnaja istopšcica*) prepared the bath while another saw to the
bride's linen. When all was ready the girls would invite her to enter the bath-
house: —

> "Ты пойди, наша голубушка,
> Во теплую парну баеньку,
> Во белую умываленьку!
> Из лучины баня топлена

> Со колодцев вода ношена,
> Со двенадцати колодцев."[23]

During this whole ceremony the bride was expected to weep and bewail her fate, entering the bath-house only with great reluctance: —

> "У ворот банюшка стояла,
> Жарко каменка горела,
> Ай люли, люли, горела!
> Тут расплакалась Марьюшка,
> Перед батюшкой стоючи:
> 'Государь ты, мой батюшка!
> Подержи меня хоть годок,
> Подержи меня хоть другой'."[24]

Many of these songs are not merely melancholy but contain a sense of foreboding, of outrage and betrayal. In the following song from the Olonec government the bride sings of how she was startled one day by the sound of horse's hooves and the arrival not of a prospective suitor but of a purchaser to whom her relatives have shamelessly sold her into bondage: —

> "Мимо теплу да парну баенку
> Проезжал да чуж отецкой сын,
> Прошла ископыть кониная,
> Прошли сбеги лошадиные, —
> Торговал да дорогу волю,
> Как у ваших провожатыих.
> Много давал злата серебра,
> Много крупных скачных жемчугов
> Тридцать ведр да зелена вина . . . . .
>
> Как после этой поры времени
> Стали девушки разбойницы,
> Молодцы да подорожники,
> Мои дядевьица пьяницы,
> Милы братья стали бражники,
> Как силом волю обсилили
> Грабежом волю ограбили
> У теплой да парной баеньки."[25]

On the following day, the wedding day itself, the groom began to play a more active part in the proceedings. He arrived with his train (*poezd*) of relatives and close friends (the *družki*). The train was stopped at the gates of the bride's house and was sometimes asked for a ransom before being allowed to pass. It was common, however, for another, more interesting ritual to take place. The leader of the train (*tysjackij*) with one or two others would approach the gates with gun in hand as if to seize the bride by force. A verbal battle of wits ensued after which the victorious train was allowed to enter. The dramatic qualities of this encounter are well revealed in the following account from Nižegorod government given by Tereščenko: —

> "Но ворота для жениха заперты, он останавливается с поезжаными, дружка стучит в ворота, говоря: отворите! — Нельзя, отвечают ему, не сюда вам дорога; а хотите проехать, заплатите. — Сколько надобно? — А сколько вас людей? — спрашивает предворотник. — Душ двести, отвечает дружка. — По рублю с человека, да и то мало, говорит предворотник, — у нас княгиня молодая, никому не велит ездить через ее земли. — А у нас князь молодой, говорит дружка, мы люди сбройные, ворота отобьем и силой войдем. — Он начинает стучать покрепче, но предворотник товорит ему: не пущу! разве силой возьмете. Тогда дружка начинает объясняться с ним по ласковее: Эй, любезный друг! нам некогда долго ждать, нам пора ехать! Хочешь ли выпить чару зеленого? — Почему же не так, — отвечает предворотник, берет стакан с водкою и выпивает; дружка дает еще, потом еще и дотоле подает, пока не упоит. — Тогда поезжаные сами отворяют ворота; и вьезжают с шумом на двор.[26]

The groom's troubles were not yet over. Before he could take his rightful place beside his bride he had first to buy the right to do so from the bride's small brother or another little boy who was occupying this seat. The child would answer the groom with some set formula such as 'a rouble for a plait, fifty copecks for a hair'. A glass of vodka or a small gift of money settled the matter and the boy then relinquished the seat. At last the bride was dressed for the wedding and her parents blessed her, using in the ceremony bread, salt, an icon, a lighted candle and money, objects which symbolised their hopes for her happiness and security in the future. Her father then handed her over to the groom.

The next step of course was the church ceremony which will not be discussed here as it forms a purely artificial break in the folk ritual itself, which continues again afterwards.

When the train arrived at the groom's house from the church, the newly-married couple were again blessed and friends scattered grain, hops or feathers over them. Before the wedding feast a humorous little scene was sometimes enacted, in which the bride's relatives and friends with a great deal of noise pretended to beat her new mother-in-law so that she would treat her daughter-in-law well. The feast began and as the wine and vodka flowed freely songs proceeded from the serious and stately, from special addresses to the main guests, to gay wedding and dance songs, to comic songs and finally, when the men were left alone, to songs of ribald and dubious content. The bride and groom were not allowed to partake in the feasting but were fed separately on *kaša* and *kvas*. Finally, the young couple were led to the marriage bed. Sometimes a dummy in the shape of a child was placed between them and the women of the household tried to imitate the crying of a baby. A felicitous union was the subject for much rejoicing and congratulation. If, on the other hand, it was discovered that the bride was not a virgin, her mother was made to bear the shame of it, being presented with a special glass (*xudoj stakan, dyrjavaja čarka*) which did not hold the vodka.

In the morning the couple went to the bath-house to wash. The bride might then be required to perform a number of tasks (sweeping the floor, baking bread, fetching water, etc.) during which the groom's family, to the great entertainment of all present, tried to get in her way as much as possible.

Vsevolodskij-Gerngross also cites among the amusements of this time a mock trial with a death sentence pronounced on the match-makers.[27]

The whole ritual might well be rounded off a few days later by another feast, this time at the bride's home. The newly-weds would spend the night there, leaving in the morning with the bride's dowry to begin their life together.

b) Remnants of ancient beliefs and practices in the marriage ritual

Although extant accounts of the marriage ritual are of comparatively recent origin it is possible even so to detect many traces of ancient beliefs and magical practices which have lingered on, half in earnest, half in fun. Analysis of these shows that they may be divided into three main categories, with the intention of: −

  (i) purifying,
  (ii) protecting,
  (iii) inducing fertility, happiness, etc.

(i) Purifying rites

Purification before and after major events, times of crisis and change in the life of the individual, when people who were themselves vulnerable to the dangerous influences of evil spirits became a risk to the whole community, played an important part among the ritual observances of primitive societies. Such observances often involved the female members of the community whose complex biological functions were not always properly understood and for this reason feared. The complicated ceremony of the 'washing of the hands' (*razmyvanie ruk*) by a Russian peasant woman several days after giving birth is one such instance.[28]

The most important rite of purification in the marriage ritual was the ritual bathing of the bride on the night before her wedding. That the bath was felt to be a psychological turning-point for the young bride, a critical moment of transference from one state of existence to another is borne out both by the girl's behaviour and by the symbolism of the laments accompanying the ceremony. The girl expresses an extreme reluctance to enter the bath-house and throughout the washing she continues to lament and protest. She sings of the loss of her 'freedom' and her maiden status. The bath-house according to peasant superstition was the home of the *baennik* or spirit of the bath-house, a cousin of the house spirit (*domovoj*). His duty was to protect the members of the family although he could be dangerous and vindictive too if offended. Some of the wedding songs after the ritual bathing indicate an awareness of the powers of this spirit and express gratitude for his protection: —

> "Спасибо тебе, парная мыльная баенка,
> На хранении да на бережении,
> Что хранила меня, сизу косату голубушку."[29]

Instances of purification by fire are also found in the marriage ritual. In White Russia the waggon taking the young couple to the groom's house was made to pass over fire.[30] A similar custom was known in the Ukraine. Tereščenko describes how, upon their arrival at the groom's house after the wedding, the groom and his men followed by the bride were made to cross over a bonfire lit between the gateposts.[31]

(ii) Prophylactic rites

These were designed to protect the bride and groom from evil spirits, whose influence was supposed to be particularly strong at this crucial threshold stage in the relationship of the young couple.

One simple measure to protect the bride from harm was the veiling of her head and face. Similarly, the exchange of clothing between bride and groom was also designed to outwit the evil spirits.

The segregation of the bridal pair from the rest of the company at the wedding feast and the ritual eating of specially prepared food performed a like function. The barrier thus placed between them and ordinary mortals not only acts as a symbol of their altered state but also, through the strict observance of taboo reduces the possibility of interference from external forces of evil. The traditional refusal of the wedding train to pass a funeral procession on the way to church or to go near a crossroads or a graveyard stems from the same desire to protect the young couple from places where they might be particularly vulnerable to attack.

The general reluctance of the young girl throughout the whole of the ritual to participate actively was also deliberately exaggerated for an overt expression of joy at the prospect of future happiness would only have been a direct encouragement to the evil spirits to come and spoil everything right at the outset.

Sometimes the local wizard (*koldun*) was called in to give his expert advice and services. Upon entering the house he would spit three times, examine the corners of the room, blowing and spitting in each in turn. In one corner he sprinkled rye, in another some herbs or grasses and ashes in the other two. Rye was also scattered over the bride and groom. Finally the wizard would inspect the horses chosen to carry the young people to the church. During the journey he would mutter spells every time the procession passed a crossroad or through a gate.[32]

Noise of all kinds was frequently used in ritual as a means of scaring evil spirits away and in this respect the Russian marriage ritual was no exception. During the progression of the wedding train towards the church the groom's friends frequently fired guns into the air and rattles and bells were also used for the same reasons.

Many objects were considered by the Russian peasant to be effective against evil, for example, pebbles, wax, salt, onions, garlic, amber, incense and the cross. To guard against evil spirits pebbles or linseed might be sprinkled in the bride's shoes, a coin put in her stocking, an eyeless needle sewn in the hem of her skirt, a bit of wax stuck on her pectoral cross. Stones (or bread) were often twisted into a shawl and swung over the heads of the young couple as a form of blessing. In Kostroma government salt was flung into the faces of the bridal pair on their return from church "to preserve them from quarrelling".[33]

(iii) Rites designed to produce the happiness, prosperity or fertility of the newly-weds

One very interesting rite with such an intention is recorded by Nikol'skij.[34] It refers specifically to White Russia but the marriage ritual in both countries is very similar. This rite involved the bear which, as one of the most powerful totem animals of the ancient Slavs, was supposed to bring prosperity and success.[35] The young couple returning from church are met by the groom's mother dressed in a sheepskin coat turned inside out. She smears them with honey. Later, the bride and groom themselves may be dressed in sheepskin hats and coats, imitating the bear 'for good luck'. Similar customs were practised in Russia, the intention being "Как шуба мохната, так чтобы и вы, детки, были счастливы и богаты".[36]

The sheepskin coat representing a bear in wedding rites is also connected

54

with hopes of fertility. In Samuel Collins' *The Present State of Russia* (London, 1671, p. 7) there is the following reference to a wedding rite: —

> ". . . and at their coming out of church, the Pannama or Clerk throws Hops upon the Bride, and wishes her Children as thick as Hops; another with a sheepskin coat turn'd outward meets her, and prays she may have as many children as there are hairs on his coat."

Of a similar nature is the transparently symbolic action of placing an imitation baby in the bed of the newly-married couple.

(iv) Marriage by capture or sale

The above represent only a brief selection of some of the ancient magico-religious rites which were preserved for centuries in the marriage ritual. The abundance of such rites is a strong indication of the extreme antiquity of many of the component parts of the ritual. Historically too, it is possible to trace the ritual back into the distant past. There are, for example, instances which recall the practice of kidnapping one's wife, of carrying her off by force (*umykanie*).[37] A remnant of this custom can surely be seen in the symbolism according to which the groom and his train are, at least for part of the ceremony, regarded as the 'enemy' come to seize the bride away from her friends and protectors. In Listopadov's *Old Cossack Wedding*[38] the arrival of the groom's train at the bride's home the day before the wedding is described in the following terms: —

> "Действительно, из чулана несется чем дальше, тем больший и настойчивый шум песен, требований и нетерпеливых стуков в запертые двери: сегодня жених, царь—царевич, король—королевич, не только охотник на диковинного зверя, но и неприятель, осаждающий и берущий вражескую крепость. Невестина сторона играет теперь роль осажденных, защищающихся, до тех пор пока обе стороны не сойдутся на общем мирном сговоре."

There is a similar description given by Vsevolodskij-Gerngross[39] where, on the day of the wedding, a few of the groom's friends, armed, approached the bride's home which is locked and barred. Negotiations begin, involving a battle of words. Gerngross has suggested that this contest of words and wit reflected a much earlier conflict in which cunning was combined with force of arms in the effort to outwit the guardians of the desired girl.

The groom in the marriage ritual is often known as 'the hunter' and the bride as the 'hunted animal'. This again may bear reference to ancient times when a bride was regarded much in the light of a hunting trophy. Once again in the Cossack wedding,[40] a representative of the groom's party arriving at the bride's home tells how they have hunted a wild animal up to the very door: —

> "Вот и день едем и другой едем: и ляса проехали дрямучия и стяпя широкия, — ни тебе зверя, ни птицы, хоть назад поежжай! Откуда ни возьмись, братцы мои, — зверь! Не малай, не большой, — не то куница, не то лисица, не то красная девица! . . . Мы за ним! Гнались, гнались, да в басурманской—то земле и след потеряли. Ан нет! . . . У самова—то вашего двора собаки наши унюхали какия—сь то диковиннаи сляды . . . Не дозволитя ли, люди добраи, поискать у вас?"

Many of the bride's songs bewail her loss of freedom, her capture by the wicked hunter, or her parents' inhuman treatment in sending her into bondage with a strange and hostile family: —

> "Вижу, едет разоритель мой,
> Разорил мою головушку,
> Разломал мои святочики;
> Разлучает с отцом, с матерью,
> С родным братцам да с сястрицами."[41]

Of much later date are traces of marriage by direct sale. The customary giving of small gifts to the mother, brothers and sisters of the bride is probably a distant reflection of this mediaeval practice. A more obvious one is the ritual of making the groom buy his place beside the bride. The idea of a commercial undertaking comes out strongly in the old Cossack wedding again, although it is, of course, a common feature of the ceremony in other places too: —

> "Торгуйся, братец, торгуйся, —
> У—рано, рано, торгуйся,
> . . . .
> Не 'тдавай сястру дешево,
> Проси за сястрицу сто рублей,
> За русу косу—тысячу,
> За ум, за разум — сметы нет! . . ."

When the boy has already relinquished the seat they sing: —

> "Татарин братец, татарин,

56

У—рано, рано, татарин,
У—рано, мое, татарин,
Продал сястрицу задаром,
Красу девичью за пятак,
Русу косушку отдал так!"[42]

Another remnant may be the habit of clinching the match-making by the beating of hands (*rukobit'e*), as at the conclusion of a business deal.

In some places even, for example in the town of Nerext, the bride was in fact sold for money. The bride-price was known as the *kalym* — a borrowing from the Turks or Tartars.[43]

c) The marriage ritual as drama

Clearly, within the marriage ritual one finds some of the most outstanding examples of dramatic poetry in the field of ritual in Russia. The widespread use of the expression *igrat' svad'bu* indicates a general awareness of the dramatic potential of the ceremony among the people who took part in it. However, it would be dangerous to overemphasize some of the parallels which appear to exist between the marriage ritual and drama proper, for the former, no less than the agricultural rituals, was initially governed by nondramatic, nonaesthetic principles. The Russian marriage ritual came into being as a rite of passage with a specific and important sociological role to play in the lives of the people. Certain parts of the ceremony have no dramatic function whatsoever, for example, the mutual examination of home and property by the families of the bride and groom respectively (*smotriny*). There are, on the other hand, as will be seen, parts which are very definitely dramatic in form, and the dramatic potentialities of many of the methods used in the celebration of the ritual were recognised, developed and exploited through the aesthetic feelings and imagination of the folk until upon the basis of the social act, there had grown up a dramatic edifice which for sheer complexity, variety, beauty and emotive power can scarcely be rivalled in folk literature.

In the discussion of the agricultural rites as dramatic entertainment a fundamental difference between ritual and drama was seen in the composition of the acting body.[44] The same is to a large extent true of the marriage ritual although the choice of actors here is governed by a different set of factors.

The chief roles were allocated, if the word can be used here, according to the social status of certain people in relationship to the bride and groom; in other words they were filled by the bride's and groom's parents, the groom's best friend and assistant (*družka*), the bride's closest friends, her young brother and so on. The awareness of a rigid social convention in this respect was a deep-seated one among the Russian peasantry as can be seen even in the games of children. In wedding games with dolls played by the children of the village of Xolm the little girls several times disputed the allocation of roles. They argued for instance about which girls and how many should accompany the bride to the bath, and which dolls should play the part of the cook at the wedding feast, a role which should be fulfilled by the bride's married sister.[45]

Although the main criterion for active participation in the drama was therefore a social one, certain subdivisions can be found within the larger group. The acting body is found to be split always into two opposing and often hostile camps. There are three main subdivisions of this nature: firstly, the most important division between the faction supporting the bride and that supporting the groom; secondly, but allied to the first, a sexual division between males and females; and thirdly, an age division between the older and the younger generation. Taking the first division, it is clear that opposition between these two groups breaks out at the very beginning of the ritual. The match-makers represent one group, the bride's parents the other. Both extol the virtues of their own side and each searches for a solution that is advantageous to itself. Similarly, during the *smotriny* where both sides perform essentially the same act, that of examining each other's home and property, the 'separateness' of the groups is preserved, since each maintains the right to express its individual opinions and requirements. The climax of this division comes, of course, in the mock battle between, on the one hand, the gaining groom's party, who at last take active steps to gain possession of their property, and on the other the losing bride's party, forced to take a final defensive stand.

The second division is in some respects similar to the first since the groom's side is largely, although not wholly, represented by males and the bride's side by females. However, there is a difference. Where the two groups are regarded from a purely social point of view it is the male side which has the ascendancy. Where the groupings are seen from a dramatic point of view, it is clear that it is the female side which has the lion's share of the action. The significance of the whole ritual primarily affected the bride rather than the groom. It is the bride who has the burden of learning and performing the laments, of simulating emotions she may not truly feel, of playing a part from the moment the match-makers enter her parents' house till after the marriage ceremony has taken place. Whereas the groom and his male friends remain more or less passive except at specific points in the action (as in the arrival of the groom's train, the buying of the groom's seat, the battle scenes, etc.), the bride is forced to react to a constantly changing succession of situations and people, the groom's parents, her own parents, her own friends, various relatives, the groom and the groom's train, etc. Many parts of the ritual are of an almost exclusively feminine nature: for example the sewing of the dowry linen, the *deviŝnik*, to which the youths were not usually invited and particularly the

58

ritual bath from which they were rigorously excluded. Finally there comes the third division, that between the elder generation consisting primarily of the two parental pairs and the younger generation of the bride and groom and their respective friends. Although on the face of it the older generation play a relatively small role in the ritual it is nevertheless an important one. It is they, firstly through the groom's family and the match-makers and then through the consent and collaboration of the bride's parents, who set the ritual in motion. Thereafter it is they who regulate the course of events, supervise the correct fulfilment of each separate part, make sure that the young people know their role and conduct themselves in the proper manner. It is the parents who seal the bargain with a clasp of the hands at the *rukobit'e*, it is the two mothers who supervise the ritual actions designed to ensure the happiness, prosperity and fertility of the match. In a sense, then, although the marriage ritual dramatically speaking is performed by and for the young people, their social role is largely a passive one since all their actions are instigated and controlled by their parents.

Although social relationships were originally the dominant factor governing the choice of actors, other considerations eventually crept in. In Listopadov's Cossack wedding the groom's father chose his match-maker, Nikolaj Taras'evič, because he was afraid that he himself might become tonguetied and be unable to fulfil his mission properly. Nikolaj on the other hand had an easy way with words ("за словом, не полез в карман"). Here too, the groom's messenger, sent ahead of the groom to the bride's home on the day of the *rukobit'e*, also had particular qualities, since he had the difficult task on this occasion of acting as the groom's ambassador and presenting his friend in the most favourable light. The groom was therefore careful to choose a representative who was capable of doing the job conscientiously and with dignity.[46]

Particularly important of course was the role of the *družka* who organised the groom's side of the participation in the ritual and acted as a sort of master-of-ceremonies during the wedding feast and other festivities. To keep the course of the ritual running smoothly he had to be not only knowledgeable about and experienced in the traditional running of the event but also witty and lively enough to ensure the necessary atmosphere of lighthearted merriment and joy.

In such a way considerations of a nonritual character crept in. Moreover, the words and actions specific to each character in the ritual did not come naturally to them but had to be learnt like the parts in a play. The young people's parents and others with an accumulated knowledge of the ritual through years of watching and participating had to coach the bride and groom, the *družka*, the young brother, etc., to the best of their ability for the reaction of the relatives, friends and bystanders to a poor performance was much the same as that of an audience to a badly rehearsed play. Often it was the *družka* who coached the groom, giving him advice on how best to carry out all the intricate stages of the ritual, how to conduct himself at any given moment, how to react to specific situations, when to bow, when to kiss the bride, whom to address and how, in short helping to fulfil his obligations in the most satisfactory way possible.

This demand for a convincing, polished performance fell particularly upon the bride, for the extent of her apparent grief was taken as a measure of her love and esteem for her parents. Although, to a certain extent, the bride's own feelings might well correspond with those she had to exhibit there is no doubt that 'acting' also played a considerable part. The emotion, in other words, was largely simulated. This impression is given by some of the remarks to descriptions of the marriage ritual; note the following comments about the bride's actions during and after the ritual bath: —

> She sways from side to side *as if* in the depths of despair . . . *Pretending* that she doesn't want to go any further . . . then, *as if* she had guessed something, . . . she bursts into tears.[47]

Indeed Vsevolodskij-Gerngross goes so far as to say that as much as ninety per cent of the time the bride's emotion was not real.

This analogy between actors with their parts in a play and the participants in a marriage ritual can be carried a stage further. As in a play the action and the words of each part are tied to a particular character and a particular situation and the 'actor' is not usually at liberty to alter the basic text at will, but whereas in the play these rules are laid down by the imagination of the writer, in the marriage ritual they are laid down by social conventions.

Within the framework of such obligatory or set passages (corresponding to the scenes of a play), the number and nature of which varied considerably from place to place, there was plenty of scope for improvisation and free development. The same is true of the spoken or sung addresses which formed an integral part of the marriage ritual. A great variety of songs and laments to fit a multitude of situations was available to those arranging the ceremony. There were songs not only to accompany or describe the main stages of any normal ceremony but also songs for more unusual or specific occasions. Thus there were not only laments for the bride visiting her relatives for the last time before the wedding, for taking leave of her parents, for the loss of her freedom and girlhood, but also for a bride marrying an old groom or for a bride visiting the grave of her dead parents.

There were songs and toasts which could be sung in honour of any of the guests likely to be present at the wedding, the bride and groom, the parents, the young girls, the married women, and many others which could be used to prolong the merriment, and if the wedding fare itself was not very lavish there were comic songs which could be sung at the expense of the hosts.

The extreme variety of these verbal exchanges leads to another point. Most of the dramatic rituals which have been examined up till now have been conspicuously lacking in any sort of developed auditory side, apart from noise and a few songs of much later interpolation. The situation in the marriage ritual is very different for here we find a rich store of verbal exchange in which songs and the spoken word are mixed in such a way as to give an almost operatic scope to the work. The songs are not simply a commentary upon the action; they are a commentary in which the real situation (the physical appearance of the bride and groom, the interior of the bride's house, the accoutrement of the festive table, the weather and a multitude of other details) which might well be extremely uninteresting, even squalid in some cases, is transformed by artistic embroidery into a picture of extreme lyrical depth. In such terms the young girl here describes the coming of the match-makers on the day of the *rukobit'e*

> "Как сегодня, сего денечка,
> Сего денечка господня,
> День ко вечеру скороталося
> Солнце к западу двигалося.
> По закат да красна солнышка
> По пути да по дороженьке,
> Стучит, гремит копыто лошадиное,
> Заскрипели дубовы сани . . .
> . . . ."48

The ritual of the bath is similarly romanticised: —

> "Ты пойдем — да наша белая лебедушка,
> В эту в тепло — парную во баенку,
> Проторена — прочищена дороженька,
> Разостланы суконцы да одинцовые . . ."49

In other cases the original detail or event is enriched by the addition of parallel metaphors. In the following example the bride's brother is described: —

> "Братец красное мое солнышко,
> Братец свеща, да не топленая,
> Ты верба да золоченая,
> . . . ."50

Sometimes, through the extended use of symbols and imagery a play within a play develops. Such is the case when the match-makers and the bride's parents conduct the marriage bargaining as if it were a business transaction.

The match-makers have heard a certain precious article is for sale and have come to arrange terms for the sale. The bride's parents sustain the deception, pretend not to recognise the match-makers or the real reason for their presence. A similar situation develops when the groom's train acts in the manner of a hunting or military expedition eventually seizing the bride after a mock battle or chase. In some examples of the marriage ritual the whole tone of the ceremony was released from the humdrum content of peasant village life and raised to an altogether more elevated plane in which the bride and groom appear as a prince and princess: —

> "The groom's men turn to the girls with the question —
>   Есть ли в этом доме хозяин?
> Девушки — Есть!
> Дружки — Дайте нам дубового стола — поставить нашего князя под святые образа.
>
> The groom's men turn to the girls with the question —
>   — Что вы за люди?
> Девушки — Молодой княгини верные служаночки!
> Дружки — Где же княгиня? Отчего она не снаряжена и за стол не посажена?
> Девушки — Наша княгиня в парной баенке, под шелковым веничком . . ."

> Дружки начинают торговаться, чтобы служанки продали свою княгиню. Они кидают, сначала медные деньги, — девушки говорят: "Наша княгиня больше этого стоит. Выкиньте нам маленьких, да беленьких: мы баню топили, сто пар башмаков износили, косу княгине расплетали. Если у вас не сыщется золотой казны, то ваша невеста в зеленый дуб посажена, золотыми ключами замкнута."[51]

Through such artistic artifices the marriage ritual is in parts withdrawn from its functional role and approaches a step nearer to true dramatic entertainment.

Apart from the songs, speech in the marriage ritual consists mainly of brief monologues and dialogues in which the use of set formulae plays an important part. This is particularly true of some of the symbolic scenes described above where the true meaning behind the conventional phrases of the 'hunter' or 'merchant' is understood by all. Otherwise, as for example in the bargaining between the two parental groups over such details as the dowry and the ordering of the wedding feast, the dialogue would tend to spring naturally from the subject under discussion.

Although, as has been shown, there are many instances where the marriage ritual becomes truly dramatic, there are others where the normal exigencies of dramatic entertainment are outweighed by the demands of the ritual. This is true of both the time-span and the place of the action. Normally, for the sake of convenience, the time taken to enact a play is limited to a few hours, but in the marriage ritual the action may span a period of several days or even weeks, according to the social etiquette of the family groups involved. Similarly, as was the case in the agricultural rites too, the place of action is in no way chosen to facilitate audience-viewing but varies according to the needs of the ritual, from the living room of the bride's parents, to the homes of relatives in other villages, to the bath-house, to the street, to the church, to the groom's home and so on. The dress and outward appearance of the chief 'actors' was also largely dictated by social convention.

The structural pattern of the marriage ritual is largely defined by its function as a typical rite of passage. A well developed rite of passage according to Van Gennep[52] consists of three main parts: — (a) the separation, including rites in which the subject is secluded or cut off from his own group; (b) the transition with rites which facilitate the transition of the subject from one group or state to another; (c) incorporation, with the rites which underline the ties now linking the subject to his new group. The Russian marriage ritual can be said to follow this pattern. The bride is forced, from the very first, to consider herself as a doomed creature pitilessly cut off by her parents from her own group of family and contemporaries and the familiar environment. This is the main theme of her laments. The bride and groom together are placed on a level apart by the symbolic terminology in which they are addressed by the scenes of dramatic pretence which they are forced to enact. They are rarely referred to by name throughout the ceremony, particularly in the set songs and laments. The groom becomes, rather, the hunter, the bird of prey or the prince, the bride the hunted animal, or the princess who must be removed from the protection and seclusion of her palace. In the often exotic imagery of the latter concept, the exclusiveness of the young couple is particularly evident. During the scene of the ritual bath the clothing of the bride, the special girdle and headgear also serve to distinguish her from her friends. At this time too there takes place the ritual unwinding of the bride's plait, symbol of girlhood, and with its unwinding, however reluctantly, she renounces for ever her maiden status, her freedom and her past.

Among the transitional rites three important moments stand out in the Russian marriage ritual. Through three separate actions, ritual washing, defeat in battle after the groom's attack, and direct sale (her brother's sale of the seat), the bride passes over more irrevocably from possession by one group to possession by the other.

As far as rites of incorporation are concerned the bride cannot be said to have properly entered the new group, her husband's family, until after the wedding night. The household tasks which she is made to perform under the eye of her mother-in-law the day after the wedding night are clearly intended to emphasise the bride's new status as housewife and her new social position vis-à-vis the adoptive family group.

However, in spite of the enormous importance of the social and psychological functions of the marriage ritual there is no doubt that the village communities regarded it very much as a form of entertainment. That this had already happened at a comparatively early stage in its development can be seen from ecclesiastical diatribes in which it is condemned along with a variety of other dramatic and musical entertainments: —

> "В мирских свадьбах играют глумотворцы и органники и гусельники и смехотворцы и бесовские песни поют, и как к церкве венчатися поедут, священник со крестом будет, а перед ним со всеми теми играми бесовскими рыщут . . ."[53]

Not only were the dramatic and general entertainment qualities of the marriage ritual recognised and enjoyed by the Russians, they were also developed further, for upon the basis of the ritual there grew up a number of games and playlets quite independent of either ritual or social significance.

'Pretend weddings' were popular at the young people's parties. Here, an old villager recalls how the youths used to enjoy tricking people into believing that the match-makers had come: —

> "Срядятся свахами, пойдут сватать невесту, жениха с собой поведут, поедут в чужое село. У нас ведь с этих пор сватать начинают. Вот ряженых примут за сватов. Сваты приехали — сейчас самовар ставить.
> — Садитесь сватушки. —
> — Нет, вы самовар не ставьте, вы нам невесту покажите!
> А так не полагается. Они опять сажают, с самоваром возятся. Но тут, конечно, откроется, что это ряженые.
> — Ну, не сердитесь! — "[54]

Another popular game depicted the choosing of a bride or groom. The groom chooses his bride from two rows of girls but his friends begin to criticise and find fault with her. Then he chooses another who meets with general approval. Now comes the turn of the brides. One is offered a 'bent old man' for a husband but she turns her back on him. Instead she chooses a handsome young man and tells how she will love and look after him. The actions follow the words of a song.[55]

Eventually even the village children had incorporated parts of the ritual into their games. Quite small girls were familiar with the procedure and knew long parts of the text by heart. I.M. Levina was present at a children's wedding game played with dolls in 1928 in the village of Xolm (Pokšen' ga),[56] in which seven small girls took part. Each doll was given a specific part to play (bride's family, groom's family and friends). Significantly, while only the parents of the groom were represented, the bride's parents, three sisters and a brother were all included. The girls chose which roles they wanted to play and spoke and 'acted' in turn for the dolls. One place on the windowsill of the *izba* was set aside for the bride's home, and another on the table for the groom's. The ritual then began, starting with the match-making and finishing with the post nuptial games. The *xlebiny* or feast usually held on the day after the wedding was omitted because by that time it was too late in the day to play any longer. The game went according to the following pattern: —

(i) The match-making

Before setting off for the bride's house the groom's family prayed before the icons. Eventually they left, riding in a little blue carriage, drawn by a wooden horse and guided by one of the girls, Anfisa, to talk the affair over with the bride's parents. Once arrived and the formalities over the two families sat down to tea. The *samovar* was represented by a spent cartridge and the cheese cakes (*šan'gi*) by small pieces of paper.

(ii) *Nalaživan'e k bogomol'ju*

The two 'homes' were gaily decorated with odd scraps of knitted lace, sweet papers and long strips of coloured material to represent the embroidered napkins traditionally draped over the icons on special occasions. The groom's family arrived to inspect the bride's home.

(iii) *Posidki*

During this part of the game the unwinding of the bride's plait took place while the girl Asja, who was acting for her, sang a lament.

(iv) The bath

A certain amount of argument took place at this point between the girls. One of them, Katja, wanted to take all the bride's girlfriends to the bathhouse but the others insisted that only two should accompany her. Eventually it was decided not to hold the ceremony of the bath at all because the 'boys' would be looking in the window.

(v) The wedding day

The bride sang a lament describing the arrival of the groom's train and just at that moment the groom and his family were placed in the 'carriage' and taken over to the bride's *izba*. The fathers of the young couple were too young-looking according to the children, so they sewed them beards out of tow. The bride's father, now looking more appropriate to his age, was able to bless and wish the bridal pair good luck. He swung a 'silk shawl' containing a few pebbles (instead of bread) over their heads.

Next came the 'wedding feast' at which the little girls used all their in-genuity to improvise the conversation between the guests. A modern note was added by the following stage in the proceedings.

(vi) The civil ceremony

The registry office was arranged on a bench beside the stove. Two girls took the part of the secretary and president of the *ispolkom* and presented a formal questionnaire to the young couple.

The civil ceremony was followed by a religious one. All the girls were keen to have a part in this.

(vii) The church service

The 'church' was situated on a bench beneath the window. The priest chanted *Gospodi pomiluj* twice and the crowns (half a walnut shell and a stemless wineglass) traditionally used in the Orthodox service were placed on the bride and groom's head. Then they were led round the lectern while the priest continued *Položi vency na golovy ix* and the elder sister of one of the little girls chimed in with the bass responses. After the ceremony the newly-weds left in their carriage.

(viii) The feast

Again there was an argument while a cook was being chosen. Eventually, the feast began and the symbolic bowl of *kaša* (porridge) was brought in.

In the final stage of the game the girls reconstructed some of the trials undergone by the new wife in her mother-in-law's household. They scattered 'feathers' (hemlock leaves) over the floor and the doll representing the bride was supposed to sweep them up with a besom also made from a bundle of leaves.

It is difficult to decide the degree to which the children's game may be called truly dramatic, or indeed to define the theatrical genre to which it belongs. To a certain extent it might be considered as a subsidiary form of the puppet theatre, to be classed alongside the *vertep* or *Petruška*, for the girls not only dressed and prepared the dolls and spoke their parts for them as does the professional puppeteer but also manipulated them as well, making them go through the motions of praying, blessing the bride, riding in a car-riage, drinking tea and so on. However, there is a major difference in that here the dolls may be regarded simply as an extension of the girls themselves who, while obviously finding the game more fun when the action is, as it were, one stage removed from them personally, still identify themselves with the dolls, whereas in the puppet theatre a definite attempt is made to create an illusion of independent action on the part of the puppets. Neither the text nor the action involves the puppeteer personally and indeed he takes pains to hide his presence from the audience.

The game is really an example of one of those spontaneous upsurges of the desire to act and imitate which seems to be instinctive in children even more than in adults and the result is an odd mixture half-way between the real ritual and the sort of dramatic performances based on the ritual which will be discussed later in this chapter.[57] One of the most striking things about the game was the serious attitude of the children towards it and the strict attention to exactness in reproducing the appearance of the characters (as in the addition of beards to the fathers) and the décor (the elaborate decoration of the two houses), the songs, laments and church responses (albeit abridged) and social conventions (note, for example, the preponderance of *bridal* relatives when lack of dolls necessitated a choice, and the arguments about who should accompany the bride to the bath house). All these factors recall the ritual itself.

2. *From the marriage ritual to secular drama*

One of the most curious plays to have been inspired, in part at any rate, by the marriage ritual is the folk play known as *Paxomuška*.[58] This play used to be performed at village parties. At those known as *malye besedy*, when the girls gathered to spin and sew and gossip only a female cast would take part, but at the *bol'šie besedy* when boys were allowed to attend they too could join in the fun. Once the roles had been allocated, the young actors disappeared to fix their hastily improvised costumes while the remainder arranged the stage and the scenery. As this play is not widely known I consider it not inappropriate to describe the text here.

The play opens with the entrance of Paxomuška himself; he rushes in 'riding' upon a long-handled baker's shovel (*skovorodnik*). Twisting and gesticulating he dashes up to his parents and falls on his knees to ask for their blessing as he has decided to get married. His father and mother point out his weaknesses, doubt his ability to perform his duties as a husband, but at last give their blessing. Paxomuška jumps over to any girl in the audience and sits on her lap, asking in a stage whisper if she will marry him. When the girl accepts he rides back to inform his mother of the good news but she only laughs and assumes the girl must be stupid to want to marry him. Paxomuška himself is completely empty-headed, and relays what his mother has said back to the girl herself, who is understandably annoyed. A quarrel ensues. Paxomuška then courts all the girls in the audience one by one, but there is something wrong with each. One won't marry him because of his humpback, another because of lice, another because he shakes all over, another doubts his potency, another doesn't like his mother, etc. Between each scene *častuški* of dubious content are sung, such as: —

> "Нива, нива, пеньев нет,
> Хочу жениться, мочи нет.
> Выйду в поле, закричу:
> Караул . . . . . хочу!"

At last he finds Paxomixa, who agrees to marry him. His parents give their blessing and the wedding train sets off for church, Paxomuška and his bride both riding on the shovel in place of a horse. Next follows a mock wedding scene in which the priest, choir, bride, groom and relatives all play their part. The following scene is supposed to represent the wedding night. The couple stretch out, facing in opposite directions, upon a cloth on the floor. Paxo-muška searches for his 'wife''s head but can't find it.

"Mother," he shouts in mock consternation, "my wife has no head!"

"Have a good look, that can't possibly be right," she answers.

The next day Paxomuška sets off for the town to look for work, leaving instructions with his parents on how to look after his wife. His wife rows him across the lake and he leaves her with an admonition to behave herself ("Be good, don't go away anywhere, obey father and mother, don't play about with the lads"). On the other side of the lake Paxomuška finds work as a shoemaker, while his wife rows home again. Paxomuška sings, banging away with a tool: —

> "Чорт возьми
> Косые ноги
> Тятька отдал в пастухи
> Сел на камешки, заплакал —
> Куда тпрукушки ушли . . . !"

A passer-by tells him that his mother has died but this has no effect. Then he tells him his father is dying but Paxomuška is only pleased that there will be more room in the house. He sings: —

> "Разукрашены колеса,
> Едет новый тарантас,
> У меня жена хороша,
> Никому чужим не даст."

However, at the news that his wife has had a baby, he sets down his tools and goes off home. Home once again he greets his wife and asks how she has been behaving, whether she obeyed his father, did what his mother told her, did the housework. He is particularly interested in how she spent her nights. "Did you always keep the door locked? Did you stay in by yourself?" he asks. When his wife insists that she kept all his instructions he then begins to question her about the unexpected appearance of the baby. It can't be his, he points out, as he hasn't been sleeping at home. She replies that he was home the first night after the wedding, and they begin to fight. One version of the scene goes as follows: —

> Paxomuška (dragging out the child): What's this you've got here?
> Paxomixa : A baby.
> Paxomuška : Whose is it?
> Paxomixa : Mine.
> Paxomuška : Where did it come from?
> Paxomixa : The lads did it.

After this scene Paxomuška goes off in search of his father and meets another passer-by (*proxožij čelovek*). He too, it turns out, has been visiting Paxomuška's wife. The playlet ends with a violent quarrel between Paxomuška and his parents ("What were you gawping at that you weren't able to watch Paxomixa?"). He beats his parents with the baby, kills the passer-by, and ends up by thrashing all those present. The audience disperses, squealing and laughing, to the accompaniment of Paxomuška's cries of, "Don't go visiting other people's wives, don't sleep with other people's wives!"

The playlet described above is clearly crude and primitive in every sense of the word but at the same time it does have features which represent a development away from ritual towards drama proper. Ritual elements are still visible but they are not predominant. The dramatic nature of the play is embryonic but nevertheless *Paxomuška* can claim to be considered purely as a piece of dramatic entertainment. It is in fact a drama-comedy compiled solely for the amusement of peasant audiences but relying to a considerable extent both in content and methods of production upon familiar and ancient traditions of an originally nondramatic nature.

Paxomuška is constructed in two distinct halves, the second of which may well have been added at a later date. In the first half we have what is virtually a parody on certain moments in the wedding ritual, and in the second a dramatic anecdote upon the social theme of the unfaithful wife and the cuckolded husband typical of many Russian comedies and tales in the eighteenth century. Parodies upon weddings and funerals were of course a popular part of village entertainments[59] and the first half of *Paxomuška* is only one of many variants, although more developed than most.

Usually such parody scenes were very elementary in form with little more action than a few clumsy gestures by the mock priest and his deacon, the swinging of the censer and some crude comic exchanges in place of the liturgy.

In *Paxomuška*, however, there is considerably more than this. In the first place more people were present than usual, not only the priest with the bride and groom as might be expected but also relatives, the choir and the groom's men (*šafery*) all of whom had a part to play however small; an attempt was made to fill out the scene with appropriate actions. For example, the bridal ring was placed on the bride's hand by the priest, the couple were made to hold a 'candle' (a smouldering spill or splinter of wood) and bow and cross themselves at regular intervals.

These actions were rendered completely absurd by the fact that each time they began to genuflect they would somehow manage to turn a complete circle and end up facing in opposite directions. The priest waved his 'censer' (a match-box dangling on a piece of string) and led the couple three times round the lectern. The whole ceremony was accompanied by the garbled chanting of the priest. The scene ended with Paxomuška and Paxomixa kissing the cross which was made from splinters of wood bound together. Whether or not there was any truly sacrilegious intention behind the parody scenes in *Paxomuška* there is certainly an important difference between it and such purely imitatory games as the wedding for dolls discussed above; in the former there was a serious attempt to reproduce the ceremony as accurately as possible, in the latter particular moments were singled out and deliberately distorted with the intention of producing a comical effect and inducing laughter from the audience. The sexual overtones of both parts of the playlet were of course exploited for humorous purposes. These included the hints about Paxomuška's impotence during the courting scene, the crude play on the situation of the wedding night, the later adultery theme, and Paxomixa's grotesque efforts to underline her own sexual appearance. The exploitation of sex for purposes of comedy has of course been a feature of drama throughout the ages but it should be remembered that overt eroticism was also a recurrent feature of Russian agricultural ritual where its main purpose was the promotion of fertility in nature, the animals and man. Paxomixa's bosom padded out with rags to grotesque proportions is reminiscent of the exaggerated sex organs of the male dolls in many fertility rites.[60]

Connected with such crudities is the willingness of the peasant audience to find amusement in obscenities of language and in brawling on stage which is to be found not only in *Paxomuška* but in most Russian folk plays, in particular, as will be seen, in the puppet play *Petruška*.[61]

There is also a certain amount of comedy of character in *Paxomuška* although the characters themselves are neither complex nor seen in development. They are merely comical in themselves, in their stupidity, in their appearance, in their movements and gestures. Paxomuška himself is no more and no less than a further development of the stock hump-backed comic character of the Russian folk theatre, already seen in the rituals but here more clearly defined; the addition of 'fangs' (splinters of wood) to the already characteristic hump renders the similarity to the *Dossemus-Manducus* of the Atellan Theatre of Ancient Greece more striking.

The comic nature of the two main characters is emphasised by the methods used in presenting them to the audiences; by their costume, make-up, use of speech and style of acting. Here again the grotesque is predominant and subtlety is nonexistent. The humour is coarse, the voices are loud (Paxomuška's is not only loud but considerably distorted by the fangs which fill his mouth and impede speech), gestures and movement on stage deliberate and emphatic. This may be due partly to the fact that the plays of the folk repertoire were very often acted out of doors where it is more difficult, if not impossible, to render subtle nuances of voice or movement except under exceptional accoustic and theatrical conditions (as in the ancient Greek open-air theatres), and partly to the fact that unskilled actors performing for audiences equally untutored tend to exaggerate in order to achieve effects and make their meaning quite explicit.

The dramatic methods used in *Paxomuška* to present the comedy of characters and situations varies from one moment to the next.

Some attempts are made at realism. Many of the props are actual objects of everyday use borrowed for the performance, such as benches for the minor participants to sit on, the stool on which Paxomuška sits to work, the tools which he uses, the wedding ring and so on. Moreover, the actors do strive to put some feeling into their parts, to make themselves and their actions as convincing and realistic as possible. Paxomuška in particular makes every effort to act in character, bending over like a hunchback, shaking and trembling when he moves, stammering when he speaks. There are also moments in the play where realism is strangely mixed with convention. Two such instances may be seen in Paxomuška's 'riding on horseback' to court the girls and in the 'rowing of the boat' across the lake to the place where Paxomuška is to work. In a sense these are done realistically; the various motions of riding a horse are reproduced, Paxomuška cracks his whip, pretends to jog the reins and even neighs like a horse. Similarly, the 'boat', for which a bench is substituted, is actually 'rowed' across the stage by Paxomuška and Paxomixa (although in fact they propel it with their feet). The rowing and the riding are therefore not merely left to the imagination of the audience. They are seen to take place but depend for effect nevertheless upon the acceptance of certain conventions; that a real object may be replaced by a 'similar' one such as a bench for a boat, a *skovorodnik* for a horse and that real actions may be replaced by mimicry.

Contrasting with the attempts at realism is the use of symbolism. Some of the minor characters are distinguished only by some sign or clue familiar to the audience. Such is the case with the groom's men, the *šafery*, who are marked only by the ribbons worn in their hats and upon their chests.

Elements of the grotesque are, as has been seen, also present in *Paxomuška*, particularly in the appearance of the hero and heroine. These features connect the folk play with the traditions of ritual drama. Apart from the exaggerated bosom of Paxomixa, we should also note the generally grotesque and ragged appearance of the two main characters; Paxomuška's sheepskin coat is turned inside out, his boots worn on the wrong feet, his weird headgear consists of a pile of assorted hats and rags and tatters; both characters have their faces smeared with burnt soot or coal dust. Such details have no connection with the plot of the play but do on the other hand allow us to connect them with the Christmas mummers, with figures popular in spring agricultural rites and, in particular, with Semik and Semičixa or Ripej and his wife.

Paxomuška was one of the Russian folk plays usually performed indoors where an acting space with seating arrangements for the audience on benches down three sides of the room was prepared in one of the larger peasant homes. Although the time and place of action in the physical sense was thus necessarily limited, the action of the plot moves from place to place, from the 'homes' of the girls courted to Paxomuška's house, to the other side of the lake and back again. In the agricultural rituals we saw that the action could move in reality from place to place according to the demands of purely non-dramatic circumstances; in *Paxomuška*, on the other hand, the movement is restricted by purely dramatic conventions.

In discussing *Paxomuška* one is entitled to speak of audience and actors as one is not with regard to ritual drama. The plot of the play is quite independent from the working life of the villagers. Its performance or nonperformance is of no material significance to them. There are signs here of the barrier between those performing and those watching which has been typical of drama in the modern world. Yet in spite of noninvolvement, the audiences at performances of *Paxomuška* were unwilling to remain on one side of the fence; they acted as a sort of multiple director or producer, prompting those who forgot their lines and even coming on stage during performances to advise and correct the proceedings. The minor characters, such as the girls courted by Paxomuška, were not prepared beforehand but chosen at random from the audience. The audience took part in the 'responses' during the wedding liturgy and also in the brawl with which the performance ended. So there were in fact moments when actor and audience merged into one. This lack of absolute differentiation between the two remained one of the distinguishing features of the Russian folk drama, as indeed of folk drama in general.

The dramatic structure of the play is extremely simple. It can be divided into two parts, the first half consisting largely of a single repeated episode (the courtship) followed by the comic parody scenes. The second half too is episodic in character. This simplicity of structure is also reflected in the dialogue. Corresponding to the repeated episodes of the first half we find a question and answer type of dialogue typical of dramatic games such as

Kostroma but somewhat more developed. Similarly, in the second half, the sketchy substance of the plot tends to result in a series of brief, at times monosyllabic answers or responses to questions and comments. There are no monologues or developed dialogue such as is to be found in some folk plays of a higher artistic order such as *Lodka* or *Car' Maksimilian.* Certain moments such as the wedding ceremony or the wedding night must have depended for success upon skillful improvisation and would vary from performance to performance.

3. *Dramatic ritual and games connected with funerals and death*

A man's passing out of the world, no less than his coming into it, was attended in primitive societies by innumerable ritual observances, some designed to facilitate his departure from the earthly life and his entry into the world of the spirit. Such was clearly the intention behind opening the doors and removing a part of the roof or wall of the room where a dying man lay, or the custom of furnishing the deceased with various objects, a change of linen, money, toilet articles, etc., which might be of some use to him in the afterlife.[62] Similarly, in some parts of Russia there was a strange belief that the fingernails of the dead should be left uncut to facilitate their ascent up the steep glass mountain upon which heaven supposedly stood.[63] Or, again, it was customary to open the window and place upon the sill a glass of water so that the soul could wash and fly away.[64] On the other hand, there were many observances whose purpose was mainly to protect the still living from any possible adverse effects that the dead might have upon them. One may suppose that the Russian peasants' dislike of carrying out the corpse through the normal door of entry to the house was of this nature.

Descriptive material upon early Slavonic burial rites is severely limited although there are occasional references in such documents as the *Povest' vremennyx let* and eyewitness accounts in the writings of early travellers. In the Christian era, of course, the funeral service became that of the Russian Orthodox Church which has no relevance to this study. Although there is little factual material about the funeral rites themselves the many dramatic games connected with death and the burial of the dead to be found among the Russians often contain elements of obvious antiquity.

a) *Opaxivanie ot smerti*

In ignorant and isolated village communities where medical aid was either nonexistent or totally inadequate, epidemics affecting either the animal or the human population were an ever present hazard; drought too and its attendant evils of famine and disease were also dreaded. At periods of particular crisis, at the height of a cholera epidemic or during an outbreak of plague death was seen as a living being, cunning and malevolent, whose entry into the village had to be prevented at all costs. Cases of voluntary human sacrifice to achieve this end were not unknown among the Russians.[65] A less drastic remedy was the extraordinary ritual ceremony of *opaxivanie ot smerti* which, as its name implies, involved the ploughing of a symbolic furrow round the village to prevent death from entering. This custom was still being practised in the second half of the 19th century.[66]

According to Maksimov, the participation of nine widows and three virgins at least was necessary for the rite to have its full effect. The participants, who were warned of the rite's taking place beforehand, would meet secretly in a field some distance from their village, where they then stripped to their shifts. Some bound their heads with white scarves but the virgins usually loosened their hair and went bare-headed. A widow was chosen and harnessed to a plough, another took hold of the steering handle and together they would begin to plough a furrow. From this magic furrow it was supposed that the healing powers of the earth, effective even against death, would emerge.[67]

Noise to frighten away Death was a common feature. In a version described by Snegirev the women carried pokers, sickles and scythes with which they beat upon frying pans and during the ceremony they emitted wild shrieks and howls.[68]

One of the strangest aspects of the rite was the air of mystery and strict secrecy which surrounded it since the men of the village were not only excluded from active participation but were not given any information about the time and place of the meeting. Any men who were unlucky enough or foolhardy enough to be abroad on the night of the ritual ploughing and who were discovered by the women could expect to be attacked and beaten.

Although *opaxivanie* was not a seasonally fixed ritual it was nevertheless often performed on or around *Vlas'ev den'* (St. Vlasij's day) about the 11th of February and an icon of St. Vlasij was often carried at the head of the procession. Performed at this time of year the ritual ploughing had a similar function to the *provody Maslenicy*, the chasing away of death and decay from the village. During the month of February there were many other ritual observances connected with the remembrance of the dead.

b) *Umran*

An awareness of the sinister and repulsive aspects of death is to be found in the village corpse game (*Umran* or *Igra v pokojnika*). In the following version of the game, the most simple-minded village lad was first persuaded to dress up as the corpse. He was clothed all in white, his face was smeared with oatmeal flour, long fangs cut from a turnip were stuck in his mouth to make his appearance more horrific and he was placed on a bench or in a coffin. He was then tightly bound to make sure that he didn't fall off or run away.[69] Although the game was supposed to be a joke, the girls at least, some of whom were forced to kiss the 'corpse', were not amused. Maksimov reports that many were terrified, burst into tears and in some cases even fell ill after the experience.

The figure of the mock corpse was often incorporated into a more complex dramatic funeral game extremely popular among the peasantry and which could be played at any time of the year. A typical example is the following: —

> "Покойника вносят в избу на посиделки четыре человека, сзади идет поп в рогожной ризе, в камилавке из синей сахарной бумаги, с кадилом в виде глиняного горшка или рукомойника, в котором дымятся горячие уголья, мох и сухой куриный помет. Рядом с попом выступает дьячек в кафтане с косицей назади, потом плакальщица, в темном сарафане и платочке и, наконец, толпа провожающих покойника родственников, между которыми обязательно имеется мужчина в женском платье, с корзиной шанег или опекишей для поминовения усопшего. Гроб с покойником ставят среди избы и начинается кощунственное отпевание состоящее из самой отборной, что называется, 'острожной' брани, которая прерывается только всхлипыванием плакальщицы да каждением 'попа'.
> ... Кончается игра тем, что часть парней уносит покойника хоронить, а другая часть остается в избе и устраивает поминки, состоящие в том, что мужчина, наряженный девкой, оделяет девиц из своей корзины шаньгами—кусками мерзлого конского помета."[70]

c) *Mavrux* and the parody funerals

Parodies of both funerals and weddings were a common feature of the Russian folk theatre. They occurred not only as independent games but also within the framework of some nonritual plays such as *Lodka* and *Car' Maksimilian*. A parody funeral was also an important scene in the folk play *Mavrux*.

This play is really little more than a dramatised version of the wellknown song *Mal'bruk v poxod sobralsja* (*Malbrouk s'en va t'en guerre*); in it the death and burial of the general are parodied. It was popular in Russia from the second decade of the nineteenth century (the song was often used to refer to

Napoleon after the 1812 campaign) among the peasants and particularly
among the soldiers. Puškin himself, while staying at Kišinev in 1812, is reputed to have watched a variant in which the death and burial of a certain
lieutenant-colonel Adamov was portrayed.

The action of the play is limited and rudimentary. It begins with the entry
of the chief characters, the officers carrying the bier with the corpse of
Mavrux: —

"... в черных пиджачках, на плечах соломенные эполеты,
сбоку на поясах сабли, на головах шапки или шляпы с
ленточками и фигурками".[71]

These are followed by the priest and deacon who are to pronounce the
service and several other subsidiary characters.

The funeral procession is accompanied by the singing of some verses
suitably attuned to the action: —

"Маврух в походе умер
Он умер из земли
Четыре офицера покойника несут
И поют, поют, поют
Вечная ему память".

A mock funeral follows. The service is interrupted by Mavrux's miraculous
although shortlived recovery and a conversation between him and the priest
about the fate of his family ensues. After this the mock funeral continues.

This short play is interesting for several reasons apart from its use of the
mock funeral. It is, firstly, an example of a folk play constructed partly on
the basis of song dramatisation, a method which will be seen in a more advanced state in the drama *Lodka*,[72] and secondly it contains a strong military flavour. The military in Russia played an important part in the preser-
vation and dissemination of the folk theatre and the influence can be clearly
seen in a number of plays including *Mavrux*.[73]

Parody scenes of the type found in *Mavrux* were often condemned by
prerevolutionary writers as blasphemous and praised by later Soviet critics as
a strong expression of anticlerical feeling among the peasantry. There are
certainly many features in them which the church could not but regard as
disrespectful and both folk ritual and drama were clearly influenced to a
certain extent by the growth of satire in the 17th and 18th centuries and the
increasingly hostile attitude on the part of certain sections of the Russian
peasantry towards both ecclesiastical and civil authorities. The rural clergy,
often illiterate and greedy, were one of the main targets of this satirical streak.

The general appearance of the ecclesiastical characters in the parody scenes was not such as to invite respect, consisting usually of an assortment of ragged garments with a cassock made from sacking (*rogoža*). The main piece of church equipment was the censer which could be a matchbox on the end of a piece of string, or an old bast shoe (*lapot'*) or an earthenware pot filled with some evil smelling fuel, usually fowl-droppings, which was swung among the crowd of spectators to the consternation of some and the amusement of others.

The religious figures in these scenes usually showed no respect towards each other nor towards the office they performed and their speech was coarse and often obscene. In one version of *Car' Maksimilian* the priest addresses his deacon: —

> "Ну, валяй найзусть, что знаешь . . .
> Дьякон, зажаривай акафист!"[74]

In another the priest shouts "Теперь валяй 'прикинул'!" [прокимен] . . . А теперь стихеры запузыривай!"[75] The characteristics of the religious figures, both those who appear on stage and others who are mentioned in the dialogues, are by no means flattering and drunkenness seems to be the besetting sin. In the two plays mentioned above the priest and his deacon have drunk away the holy books: —

> " — Дьякон, дьякон, де большая—то книга? . . .
> — А вчера на Сенной—то что пропили?"[76]

The sources from which the comic dialogues in these scenes are drawn are full of references to drunken clergy. In both the above versions of *Car' Maksimilian* there is, for example, the tale of the trials and tribulations of the drunken sinner, in which various forms of drink are addressed in terms normally reserved for the Virgin or the Deity in prayers and other religious writings. Thus vodka (*gorelka, gorilka*) is addressed: —

> "О, преподобная мати Горилка, радуйся!"[77]

and beer, mead and vodka as follows: —

> "Слава тебе, пиву бешеному,
> Слава тебе, меду сыченому,
> Слава тебе, горелка страдательная!"[78]

The language and the manner of presentation of the church ceremonies was also parodied to a certain extent and the texts of these folk scenes are full of archaisms, Church-Slavonic and Old-Russian words and phrases or approximations to them. A long monologue by the deacon in one of Vinogradov's texts is full of such expressions: —

> "Увидах я храмину большую,
> И сидяша в ней мужи верные,
> Держаша чары вина мерные . . ."

and: —

> "Пострадала еси от гонителя мучителя винокура,
> Прошла еси огни и воды . . ."[79]

Church terminology was often used wrongly, but whether this was simply through the ignorance of the performers or for deliberate comic effect it would be difficult to say. Such distortions were *venčannaja kniga* for *venčal'-naja, prikinul* for *prokimen* and *tilikon* for *tipikon*[80] or *panafida s zakatistym* for *panixida s akafistom.*[81]

It was also quite common to reproduce the liturgical chant: —

> "Читает поп протяжно по книге, на церковный лад."[82]

However, it is by no means necessary to view the comic elements in the parody scenes as a deliberately negative feature. The coexistence of the sacred and the profane was a common element of mediaeval literature. In the miracle plays, scenes depicting the life and passion of Christ alternated with scenes of a ribald nature which indeed often closely parallelled the former in content.

The Russian folk theatre in general was a theatre of extremes and startling contrasts; life and death, the beautiful and the grotesque, joy and fear, profanity and worship were often found side by side in the same short ritual or game and what may have appeared to the outside observer as purely negative and undesirable features were often an integral part of the ritual stemming from causes quite alien to the moral standpoint of the modern observer. This is particularly true of the erotic and obscene elements to be found in many types of folk drama and particularly in the spring and winter rituals. Such elements provided a natural and healthy antidote to the decay and death of nature.

Erotic overtones are also present in the funeral games, providing an interesting link with agricultural ritual. Maksimov writes that a typical feature of the corpse game was the disarranging of the 'corpse's' garments in such a way as to embarrass the girls. Incidentally, the 'corpse' was securely tied down and unable to escape from his mortifying situation. The ending of life and the potential growth of new life are often bound together by the Slavonic imagination in a bizarre, yet meaningful relationship. Such was the case when, in the Ukraine, a dead girl was decked as if for her wedding day and the rites for the marriage ceremony and the burial of the dead were joined together. A 'groom' was chosen for her and was thereafter regarded as a widower and addressed as 'son-in-law' by the dead girl's mother.[83] The customs of linking death and marriage were not restricted to the Slavs. Among the wake games of the Irish too were mock marriages which in many ways resemble the mock funerals discussed above: —

> ". . . Two clever young wake-men dress themselves fantastically as priest and clerk, the latter carrying a linen bag filled with turf ashes, which he swings about to keep order, giving a good hit now and then, while the dust promotes a good deal of coughing amongst the crowd. But nothing irreverent is meant; for it is considered that whatever keeps up the spirits at a wake is allowable and harmless in the sight of God."[84]

Although the corpse game was usually played by adults for an adult audience the children of the village too were familiar with death and funerals and made use of their knowledge in play. The little girls of Xolm who enjoyed playing at weddings with their dolls also played at funerals with them. The dolls were buried in a box made to look like a coffin and parts of the burial service read over them plus the laments of various relatives. Of interest too are the strange fly burials found in some parts of Russia where insects were buried in miniature coffins cut from pieces of carrot or turnip.

NOTES

1. Vsevolodskij-Gerngross, *Istorija russkogo teatra*, p. 125.
2. N.P. Kolpakova, *Russkaja narodnaja bytovaja pesnja* (Moscow-Leningrad, 1962).
3. Vsevolodskij-Gerngross, *Igry*, pp. 95-97.
4. *Ibid.*, pp. 102-103.
5. Šejn, Vol. 1, Issue 1, No. 353, p. 67.
6. *Ibid.*, No. 1066, p. 315.
7. A. Tereščenko, *Byt russkogo naroda*, Part 2 (St. Petersburg, 1848), pp. 139-141.
8. Tixonravov, "Načalo russkogo teatra", p. 59.
9. *Povest' vremennyx let*, ed. by V.P. Adrianova-Peretc, Part 1 (Moscow-Leningrad, 1950), p. 211.
10. Famincyn, p. 20.
11. Tereščenko, Part 2, pp. 11-12.
12. Quoted in V.N. Vsevolodskij-Gerngross, *Russkij teatr ot istokov do serediny XVIII veka* (Moscow, 1957), p. 32.
13. Vsevolodskij-Gerngross, *Istorija russkogo teatra*, p. 190.
14. Krupjanskaja, "Narodnyj teatr", p. 386.
15. O.X. Agreneva-Slavjanskaja, *Opisanie russkoj krest'janskoj svad'by s tekstami i pesnjami*, Part 1 (Moscow, 1887), p. 9. (The texts used here were provided by Irina

Andreevna Fedosova of the Olonec government and another peasant woman from Petrozavodsk.)

16. N.P. Kolpakova, "Svadebnyj obrjad na reke Pinege", *Krest'janskoe iskusstvo SSSR: Iskusstvo severa*, Vol. 2 (Academia, Leningrad, 1928), pp. 163 and 174.
17. Vsevolodskij-Gerngross, *Russkij teatr ot istokov*, p. 14.
18. Tereščenko, Part 2, p. 208.
19. Agreneva-Slavjanskaja, p. 14.
20. *Ibid.*
21. A.M. Listopadov, *Starinnaja kazač'ja svad'ba* (Rostov-on-Don, 1947), pp. 29-30.
22. Šejn, Vol. 1, Issue 2, p. 815.
23. *Ibid.*, p. 490.
24. *Ibid.*, p. 590.
25. *Ibid.*, p. 491.
26. Tereščenko, p. 272.
27. Vsevolodskij-Gerngross, *Istorija russkogo teatra*, p. 145.
28. *Ibid.*, pp. 127-128.
29. Krupjanskaja, "Narodnyj teatr", p. 176.
30. N.M. Nikol'skij, *Proisxoždenie i istorija belorusskoj svadebnoj obrjadnosti* (Minsk, 1956), p. 99.
31. Tereščenko, Part 2, p. 589.
32. Maksimov, pp. 116-117.
33. Tereščenko, Part 2, p. 181.
34. Nikol'skij, pp. 98-99.
35. *Supra*, pp. 14-15.
36. E.G. Kagarov, "Sostav i proisxoždenie svadebnoj obrjadnosti", *Sbornik muzeja antropologii i etnografii*, No. 19 (Moscow-Leningrad, 1960), p. 176.
37. Zabelin has suggested that the Russian game *Gorelki* may have been a remnant of this ancient custom. *Goret'* meant that from a group of players standing in pairs, one had to stand apart and then run towards one couple, break them up and try to catch the girl for himself (I.E. Zabelin, *Istorija russkoj žizni s drevnejšix vremen*, Part 2 (Moscow, 1912), p. 306. It is interesting to think that the English game known as *Nuts in May* may have had a similar origin.
38. Listopadov, p. 55.
39. Vsevolodskij-Gerngross, *Istorija russkogo teatra*, pp. 141-142.
40. Listopadov, pp. 52-53.
41. *Ibid.*, p. 77.
42. *Ibid.*, pp. 86-87.
43. Tereščenko, Part 2, p. 170.
44. *Supra*, p. 33
45. *Infra*, pp. 64-65.
46. Listopadov, pp. 7 and 13.
47. Agreneva-Slavjanskaja, Part 1, pp. 42 and 44.
48. Agreneva-Slavjanskaja, Part 1, p. 8.
49. *Ibid.*, p. 41.
50. *Ibid., loc. cit.*
51. V.V. Sipovskij, "Začatki russkoj narodnoj dramy", *Istorija russkoj slovesnosti*, Part I, Issue 1 (6th ed. St. Petersburg, 1912), p. 139.
52. Arnold Van Gennep, *The rites of passage* (London, 1960), pp. 10-11.
53. The *Stoglav* (1551), ch. 41, question 16, quoted by Famincyn, p. 20.
54. Avdeev, "Maska", p. 201.
55. P.O. Morozov, "Narodnaja drama", *Istorija russkogo teatra*, ed. by V.V. Kallaš and N.E. Efros, Vol. 1 (Moscow, 1914), p. 9.
56. I.M. Levina, "Kukol'nye igry v svad'bu i 'metišče'," *Krest'janskoe iskusstvo SSSR: Iskusstvo severa*, Vol. 2 (Leningrad, 1928), pp. 201-234.
57. *Infra*, pp. 68-69 and 74-98.
58. S.S. Pisarev, and S. Suslovič, "Dosjul'naja igra-komedija *Paxomuška*," *Krest'janskoe iskusstvo SSSR: Iskusstvo severa*, Vol. 1 (Leningrad, 1927), pp. 176-185.

59. *Infra*, pp. 74-78.
60. See e.g. *Supra*, p. 28.
61. *Infra*, pp. 111 and 115.
62. Vsevolodskij-Gerngross, *Istorija russkogo teatra*, p. 151.
63. A.A. Kotljarevskij, *O pogrebal'nyx obyčajax jazyčeskix slavjan* (Moscow, 1868), p. 212.
64. *Ibid.*, p. 206.
65. Snegirev, Issue 1, p. 204.
66. Afanas'ev, *Poetičeskie vozzrenija slavjan*, Vol. 1, p. 565.
67. Maksimov, p. 261.
68. Snegirev, Issue 1, p. 204.
69. Maksimov, p. 300.
70. Maksimov, pp. 300-301.
71. N.E. Ončukov, *Severnye narodnye dramy* (St. Petersburg, 1911), p. 134.
72. *Infra*, pp. 129-131.
73. For the military influence in *Car' Maksimilian* see *Infra*, pp. 190-192 and 218-219.
74. N.N. Vinogradov, "Narodnaja drama *Car' Maksimilian*", Variant 2, *Sbornik otdelenija russkogo jazyka i slovesnosti imperatorskoj akademii nauk*, Vol. 90, No. 7 (St. Petersburg, 1914), pp. 78-79.
75. *Ibid.*, Variant 3, p. 165.
76. *Ibid.*, Variant 2, p. 78.
77. *Ibid.*, p. 79.
78. *Ibid.*, Variant 3, p. 164.
79. *Ibid., loc. cit.*
80. *Ibid.*, pp. 163 and 165.
81. *Ibid.*, Variant 2, p. 77.
82. B.V. Varneke, "Čto igraet narod," *Ežegodnik imperatorskix teatrov*, Issue 4 (St. Petersburg, 1913), p. 24.
83. Kotljarevskij, p. 232.
84. Lady Jane Francesca Speranza Wilde, *Ancient cures, charms and usages of Ireland* (London, 1890), pp. 131-132.

PART TWO

THE PUPPET THEATRE

CHAPTER III

THE *VERTEP*

Puppets of one kind or another have been known to man from an early period in history and they are certainly one of the oldest, most popular and most universal forms of public entertainment. It would be difficult to find a single country which does not have some form of puppet theatre tradition.

It is probable that puppets began first in the east and our earliest references to their existence come from Egypt (16th c. B.C.), India (11th c. B.C.) and China (1,000 B.C.). It is also probable that the original impulse towards making puppets of one sort or another came from religion. The anthropomorphic custom of making models or idols of the gods for the purposes of worship, or of men or animals for purposes of magic, is one common to all people in a primitive state of existence at whatever era. In Russia the use of wooden or straw figures to represent the spirit of vegetation is one such instance. The practice often found in ritual drama, religious processions, etc., of using an inanimate actor rather than a human one in the place of the god or spirit in question may well have evolved from a sense of reverence towards the deity or, more probably, from fear of the dangers involved in too close identification of the susceptible human spirit with powerful super-natural forces.

Once graven images had been accepted as a normal part of the ritual or religious ceremony the next obvious step would be an attempt to make them appear more lifelike, to make them simulate not only the external appearance but the movements and voice of the creature represented. Mobility was produced in a variety of ways, by hidden springs or clockwork mechanism for example, by wires or cords attached to their limbs and set in motion by a hidden manipulator.

The idea of the mobile puppet spread quickly throughout the east to Japan, Persia, Turkey, Ceylon, etc., and in time it penetrated to the ancient Greek Empire and later from there to the Roman Empire. It is probably from this latter source, rather than from Asia (although eastern influences obviously played a part) that the European puppet theatre tradition stems. The ancient Greeks used mobile statues in their religious festivals similar to those of the ancient Egyptians.

The type of puppet manipulated by an internal system of coils, springs, weights and levers no doubt gave rise eventually to the ingenious 'working model' puppets in which a scene such as a battle would be acted out by machine driven figures. Known as *avtomaty* in Russia, these puppets were very popular there in the 18th century, appearing regularly in the fairgrounds and public squares and owned mostly by Germans who were very skilled in this craft. In 1759, we are told, a French machinist, Pierre Dumoulin, turned up in Moscow with just such a working model: —

> "Представляющая ландшафт, в котором видны будут
> многие движущиеся изображения дорожных людей и возов
> и многие работные люди, которые упражняются в разных
> вещах так натурально как бы живые . . ."[1]

The large, unwieldy, yet as one can well imagine, effective mobile statues of the gods known in the ancient world like the Greek automaton of Bacchus at a feast given by Ptolemy, or the Philadelphus statue of Apollo in the temple of Heliopolis[2] did not die out with the coming of Christianity to the Roman world for the Christian church adopted the idea to enhance its own religious festivals. Indeed, the word *marionette* was first used for the popular mobile statues of the Virgin Mary. String manipulated puppets such as the marionettes became known throughout Europe and Asia as well, and because of their virtually unlimited potentialities could, in the hands of a skilful manipulator, reach great heights of artistic grace and expression.

The highly sophisticated marionettes which we know today in Europe are, however, a comparatively recent development. Cruder examples of an earlier type were also known: such were the Italian *fantochini*, carved wooden dolls made to move by means of a string attached at one end to the puppeteer's legs and at the other to the waists of the dolls. When the puppeteer moved his knees the dolls, which were fixed to a wooden stick, danced and jogged about.

Marionettes were also known in Russia, making their first appearance in all probability in the early 18th century, although it is often difficult to decide from the wording of the evidence, to exactly what type of puppet contemporary documents refer. It is certain, however, that marionettes were known in both Moscow and St. Petersburg by the late 18th century, in court circles and among the general public. Thus we know, from a description of St. Petersburg published in 1779,[3] that marionette performances took place there from 1749 and that special buildings were set aside for them such as the *Komediantskij dom* built in 1745, and the *Komediantskij ambar* built near the *Sinij Most* (Blue bridge). In 1761 a Dutch puppetmaster, Serger, put on a month of marionette plays in Moscow: —

> "Ежедневно, кроме субботы, штуки свои с Цицероновою

головою и другие новые показывать будет, если хоть 10 или 12 человек зрителей будет. Сверх же того, будут у него представляемы разные комедии, например, О Докторе Фаусте и пр., большими двухаршинными куклами, которые будут разговаривать и проч."[4]

It seems probable that many of the bills for puppet shows relating to the thirties of the 18th century, although not specifically quoted as such, were for marionettes, as their repertoire, which included a number of plays adapted from the academic stage (*škol'nyj teatr*) was similar to that of the west European marionette theatres; in the repertoire were plays on religious themes, hagiographical tales and several adaptations from the romantic stories popular in the 18th century, *Don Juan*, etc.

The marionette companies were, in the beginning at least, of foreign origin, Italian, German or French, although the Russians themselves eventually developed the art too. Saltykov-Ščedrin has an interesting story about a Russian marionette maker in the 1840s whose dolls (which included a *kolležskij asessor* or civil servant of the 8th grade, a peasant and a *gourmand* in the costume of an 18th century *petit maître*) and repertoire appear to have been drawn from the characters and themes of everyday life. Among the plays performed were *Nakazannyj gordec* and *Nerassuditel'nyj vydumščik ili Sdelaj milost' ostanovis'*.[5] The marionette theatre, however, did not attain any lasting popularity among the ordinary people, nor can it be said to have become an integral part of the Russian folk theatre.

Following the custom of the ancient world the mediaeval European church made use of puppet figures to represent characters from the Holy Scriptures, the Holy Family itself, the saints and martyrs; mobile statues, *papoires*, were used to portray sacred figures in processions throughout mediaeval France, in Orléans, Poitiers, Amiens and other towns. Possibly the most popular of the scenes thus shown and certainly the most widespread was the Christmas crib with the Holy Family, the oxen and the ass in the stable, the shepherds with their sheep and the wise men with their gifts. It is to these Christmas nativity scenes, combined with certain features of the mediaeval stage proper, that we should look for the origin of a type of puppet show which, as opposed to the marionettes, attained a high degree of popularity throughout Eastern Europe, particularly in Poland, the Ukraine and, later on, in Russia (mainly, but not exclusively, the south west) itself. This puppet theatre, known as the *szopka*, *betlejka* and *vertep* in Poland, White Russia, and the Ukraine and Great Russia respectively, contained puppets of an extremely simple nature. They were rigid, crudely carved and dressed figures which were moved horizontally or diagonally along the slatted floor of their little stage by means of the rod to which they were attached. Such puppets were known in Russia as *steržnevye* or rod puppets. A similar, although more complicated system, was known also in Italy. The following description is to be found in the 18th century *Storia i ragione d'ogni poesia*, by Quadrio: —[6]

> "Let a high stage be arranged, such as is used in an ordinary theatre, provided with scenes of the usual size. Place on the stage a few wooden boards grooved in channels, which are to serve as slots within which figures about two feet or more in height, and made of papier mâché, representing various characters, are to stand or travel. These figures are then to be moved from one end of the channel to the other, as required, by means of concealed counterweights, some of which hang by a wire attached to the shoulders of each figure, and are intended to serve the purpose of manipulating the figures and arranging them in various graceful and appropriate attitudes; these counterweights are worked by men hidden under the stage, or in some other convenient place."

The exact place and time of origin of the Christmas crib with its *tableau vivant*, to which the *vertep* partly owes its origin is not known. According to Ivan Franko, the Ukrainian scholar and historian of the theatre, it was probably first introduced in Italy — in Rome at the church of Santa Maria Maggiore, founded by Liberius. Here there was a special chapel which on Christmas Day held the crib with dolls for Jesus, Mary, Joseph and the other participants in the Nativity scenes. It is suggested that this crib in the 9th century formed the model which other churches eventually copied.[7]

The Christmas crib spread throughout Europe and was known not only in Germany, Italy, France and England but eventually in Eastern Europe as well, in Czechoslovakia, Poland and the Ukraine. The Franciscan monastic order seems to have played an important part in the development of the crib for after Pope Innocent had banished it in 1210 along with all clerical participation in plays, it was St. Francis who reintroduced the custom in his monastery and it was probably the Franciscans who brought the *szopka* to Poland in the 14th century.

After the Reformation, when the crib was frowned on in the churches, it became customary for seminarists to carry it about from place to place, showing it to people in the villages, explaining the contents and receiving in return some small reward. At Christmastide in Lower Austria, for instance, up to the middle of the 19th century, a church sexton together with some boys from his parish, dressed in scarlet hassocks, used to carry a box known as *die Christschau* from house to house. When the front wall of the box was removed it revealed a landscape with shepherds, huntsmen, the Three Kings and, in the background, the Nativity scene itself. Above the crib hung a star and angels. The boys performed as a choir, singing Christmas hymns corresponding to the various stages of the Nativity, while the sexton explained to the onlookers everything that could be seen in the box.[8]

The same custom was observed in Slavonic countries; in Czechoslovakia, for example, where the youngsters of the villages used to spend their evenings during the Christmas period up to the New Year taking a crib round from house to house. In the crib would be "the newly born Saviour, in front of Him, Joseph and Mary, behind, a bull and a donkey. The crib was made from paper or wood and firmly fixed on a wooden stick".[9] Between this static crib with its explanatory text and the *vertep* with its scarcely mobile puppets and primitive monologues and dialogues the distance is not very great.

Opinions differ as to the exact date of the emergence of the *vertep* theatre in the Slavonic countries.[10] Vladimir Peretc suggests the beginning of the 16th century for Poland,[11] and it is possible that it made its début in the Ukraine not long after, for the oldest known *vertep* box, seen by the Polish ethnographer Izopol'skij in Staviŝĉi bore the date 1591. By the early 18th century it had penetrated as far as Siberia where it was introduced by the Archbishop of Tobol'sk, Filofej Ljaŝĉinskij, himself a former pupil of the Kievan academy, and supported no doubt by some of his choir boys, also natives of the Ukraine. These dates can of course only be regarded as approximate. Vsevolodskij-Gerngross recollected seeing a primitive *vertep* performance as late as the 1920s but by that time such sights must have been very rare, for its widespread existence and popularity was already seriously undermined by the middle of the 19th century. By the late 1870s-1880s G.P. Galagan was writing of it as a rarity.[12]

The actual theatrical box in which the play was performed varied little through Eastern Europe as can be seen from the following descriptions from White Russia, the Ukraine and Great Russia respectively: –

a) The White Russian *betlejka.*

> "It is a box with little windows or sometimes without any, having instead quite simply a front wall which can be raised. The floor is covered with hare's fur so that the slits along which the puppeteer leads his wooden dolls, dressed in their gaily coloured scraps of cloth, are hidden. The 'set' inside the theatre is the same as in the Polish *szopka* only sometimes the back wall of the upper stage is made to look like an iconostasis. The *betlejka* or *jaselki* is accompanied by musicians playing on the violin or pipes. The performance begins with the entrance of a puppet depicting a sacristan, who lights the candles; the lads accompanying the *betlejka* sing a Christmas hymn."[13]

b) The Ukrainian *vertep* (recorded 8th Jan., 1928, from A. Volovik by members of the Xorol Regional Studies group). The *vertep* in the description is a box divided into two levels. Its measurements are — height, 1.5 metres, depth, 36 cm. and width, 0.75 metres. It is: —

> ". . . solidly and carefully constructed and painted blue and green. The floor of both stages [i.e. upper and lower] has slits so that the puppets may be moved across it. The floors and slits are covered over with hare's fur. On both stages on the left hand side there are doors through which the puppets make their exits and entrances. On the upper stage are fixed the immobile figures of the Virgin, Joseph and the crib with Christ . . . On the lower stage there is only a throne for Herod. In the back wall there are two pairs of holes for the puppeteer's eyes. In front there was a cloth screen so that the puppeteer would not be visible while manipulating the puppets."[14]

c) The Great Russian *vertep*.

> "The marionette theatre [the term is used loosely here] is a rectangular shaped box about an *aršin* and a quarter wide,[15] three-quarters of an *aršin* in depth and about one in height. The front wall can be opened and when it is let down hides the various manipulations carried out under cover by the skilful hands of the owner of the *vertep*; the roof of the *vertep* has been decorated with a 'horse'[16] and other carvings. Strong paper of the sort used in bookbinding (*perepletnaja bumaga*) and folk pictures depicting the various 'ages of man' have been stuck on the outside of the theatre. The interior is richly decorated. Gold and silver paper, foil of different colours and spangles have been stuck over the walls and ceiling. Several small coloured lamps to light the stage during evening performances have been hung at the sides and top. The floor is covered with black fur to hide the movements of the marionettes on their wires along the slits cut in various directions. At both the right and left side of the stage a door has been cut. In the middle of the back wall stands King Herod's painted throne, raised by a few steps above the level of the floor. Near the throne, on both sides of it, stand three immobile figures, warriors in full armour. This is the royal suite. In the right hand corner there is a crib with the new born Christ and a star shining above it. A red calico curtain is drawn to mark the beginning and end of each performance."[17]

From these descriptions it can be seen that the fundamental shape and design of the *vertep* remained more or less constant although ornamentation was left to the fancy of the individual puppeteer.

The dolls belonging to the box were normally carved out of a single piece of wood and could be between 10 and 30 centimetres high. The more talented *vertep* owners might carve their own dolls, while others bought them or ordered them from a local carpenter. Sometimes the features of the dolls were skilfully carved too, and hair, beards and moustaches would be added from bits of wool. In less pretentious *verteps* all features including hair, might simply be painted on. The dolls were immobile in the sense that they were not jointed and they could not move from one part of the stage to another except along the slits provided in the floor of the stage. Only one leg, normally, was visible, the other being replaced by the rod by means of which the puppeteer manipulated them. The dolls were often cleverly dressed in costumes corresponding to their character, nationality or calling.

The division of the box into an upper and lower section corresponded to the division of the play into a religious and a secular part. Generally speaking, the religious scenes, those of the Christmas story, took place on the upper stage, while the comic scenes which followed, and which had little or no organic connection with the preceding text, were on the lower. Sometimes, however, the upper stage would be reserved only for the Nativity itself, while everything else including the scenes with Herod was relegated to the ground floor.

Although the two-tiered *vertep* was the most usual form, there were instances of a three-tiered box being used. It is probable that in such cases the lower and upper floors were used for the action of the puppets while the middle one was designed to hide the various springs and other works inside the box.

The play itself, as is usual in the oral tradition, is to be found in a great number of different versions. The basic scenes which occur are: the appearance of the angels telling of Christ's birth; the adoration of the Infant by the Three Kings, the Wise Men, Shepherds, etc.; Herod's massacre of the little children; a scene between Herod and Rachel, whose baby is killed by a soldier; Herod visited by Death, and the Devil dragging him off to hell. However, some texts are considerably more detailed than this. In one Siberian variant there is the scene of the baptism of the believers by John the Baptist, in another text there occurs the angel's announcement of Christ's birth to the shepherds watching their flocks in the fields.

For this scene there appear on the upper stage two angels in white clothing, carrying lighted candles in their hands. After they have bowed to all sides one angel approaches the side door and says: —

> "— Востаните, пастырие, и бдите зело,
> яко се приспело Рождество Спасово . . .

A little later the two shepherds themselves can be heard: —

> — Грицьку!
> — А що Прицьку?
> — Вставай хутенько,
> Да выберем ягня,
> Да притко пидемо ген-ген на гору,
> Може ще й мы поспиемо в пору." . . .[18]

There is too a scene of the Annunciation, in a performance described by Selivanov, which he saw at a friend's house on 30th January, 1880, near Kupjansk, Staroverovskaja *volost'*.[19]

In several versions the Three Wise Men or the Three Kings on their way to worship the Infant Jesus are stopped and questioned by Herod, who makes them promise to tell of the child's whereabouts. This simplified version comes from a Great Russian text: —

The Kings sing:

> — Шедше трие цари
> Ко Христу с ударом (со дары),
> Ирод им предвластен,
> Куда идут спросити.

Here they *speak*:

> Идем к рожденному,
> Идем поклониться.

They *sing* again:

> — Идем поклониться,
> Пред царем явиться;
> Аще поклонюся,
> Пред царем смирюся . . .[20]

In other versions Herod, worried by the news he has received, seeks advice from his Jewish counsellors and in some texts this opportunity is used to incorporate several comic scenes with the Jew, a character whose very unpopularity in real life made him one of the favourite stock comic figures of the Polish, Ukrainian and southern Russian popular theatre. Although more usual in the Ukraine *vertep*, such a scene is in fact also to be found in a Siberian composite text in which Herod consults his ancient scribes.[21]

Apart from the adoration of the Infant by the Wise Men and shepherds, there are some variants where David and Aaron and other Old Testament characters come and pay their respects as in the Ukrainian *vertep* from Slavuta.[22]

After the Adoration, in the Biblical text, the Three Kings are warned by an angel to return to their own land by another way instead of going back to Herod as they had promised, and this scene too can be found in the *vertep*: —

An angel comes out to them through the right hand door and says:

> — Идите иным путем,
> К Ироду не ходите.
> Ирод смущает,
> Волхвов созывает,
> Младенцев избивает . . ."[23]

E.A. Avdeeva writes of a Siberian *vertep* with the Flight into Egypt as one of its scenes, along with the Nativity, appearance of the angels and the worship of the Wise Men.[24] A strange confusion of the imagination has led to the insertion in some instances of a character called Herodiada whose dancing, like Salome's, so entrances Herod that he orders John the Baptist's head to be chopped off and brought to her on a dish.[25]

After the massacre of the children and Rachel's vain appeal to Herod to spare her son, the religious half of the drama usually ends with Herod being struck down by Death and dragged off to Hell by the Devil. Herod is, however, sometimes further punished by being presented with his own son's head (one of the slaughtered children) served up on a dish.[26] In Vinogradov's Great Russian text Herod is given a last chance to repent of his sins by a Polish priest who comes to warn him of the torments that await him: —

> — Поментуй, поментуй,
> На том то свете — бездна,
> Смола, дяготь,
> Будешь питати. Амент! . . .[27]

Sometimes, in the Siberian vertep, a final scene was added, consisting of the funeral of Herod in which the coffin was borne by generals in full uniform with medals and military sashes;[28] and thus ended in triumph the religious part of the *vertep* drama.

The exact origin of the religious text of the play is shrouded in mystery. It is probable that it was at some early stage adapted for the puppet theatre from one of the innumerable texts on the Nativity in existence in mediaeval Europe, or it may even have been specially written for the puppets on the model of plays already known.

There seems little point, however, in trying to specify an exact play of origin for the *vertep*, as Žiteckij for instance tries to do in his introduction to Galagan's *Malorusskij vertep*, pointing out the strong similarities between the Ukrainian *vertep* text and both Mitrofan Dovgalevskij's *Komičeskoe dejstvo na Roždestvo Xristovo* (1736) and Dmitri Rostovskij's *Komedija na Rozdestvo Xristovo* (1702) since the inevitable mass of influences, repetitions and borrowings among an infinite variety of plays on the same narrow subject would prove almost impossible to disentangle.

In mediaeval Europe certain parts of the liturgy, particularly the Christmas and Easter services, were rendered more explicit by the presence of a *tableau* in the church. This embryonic leaning towards dramatisation of the religious service was further enhanced by the inherent theatricality of certain parts of the liturgy. It is not difficult to imagine how the mediaeval clerics proceeded from the simple crib with its corresponding explanation read from the Bible to embellishing the service with dialogue based upon the religious text, they themselves, suitably dressed, taking over the part of the main characters from the wooden figures. In the course of time the congregations of the churches, the laity as well as the clergy, were allowed to participate in the dramatic scenes. They came to church dressed as shepherds and kings. They helped to rock the Infant's cradle. Minor roles like soldiers, midwives and pedlars were added to give the action more life, and these were played (possibly to prevent loss of dignity on the part of the clergy) by laymen. These characters introduced improvised speech, often of a humorous and colourful nature, and comic scenes, or scenes drawn from the everyday life of the people mingled with the conventional Biblical part.

When these performances were eventually banished from the churches onto the public squares in the middle of the 12th century, the mediaeval theatre proper was born.

One of the most important factors in the development of the drama from the church service was the insertion of appropriate religious verses or *tropes*, some already in dialogue form, as a sort of aesthetic decoration, into the main body of the liturgy. *Tropes* or *virši* played a considerable role too in the development of the *vertep* drama.

These religious verses or Christmas hymns contained the same basic text as the *vertep* although not usually in dialogue form. Close to the *vertep* for instance are the *virši, Vesela svitu novina* beginning with the announcement of the angels to the shepherds and continuing with the description of the Nativity scene, the massacre of the children, and so on; the *virši* beginning "Днесь прийдіте увидите бога в яслях нашого" in which the content is basically the same also contain a certain amount of dialogue;

> "Иде войсько к Иродові/Дае знати самому:
> — Нема Христа у крулевстві/И пів-паньстві жадному.
> Діти тяли, кровь илляли
> Для росказу твоего —"[29]

More specific references to the influence of religious songs are made by Ivan Franko, who points out some of the borrowings in Vinogradov's Great Russian *vertep* text; the angel's song at the beginning for example (*Devo dnes', presuščestvennogo raždaet*, p. 365), was taken from a hymn by the Byzantine poet Romanos, which later became incorporated into the church service. The second shepherd's song (*Nova radost' stala*, p. 365) is a well known old song appearing in a hymnbook of 1790, while the words of the Polish priest "О Ироде, о кручниги, за твоя превеликая злости приидет гибель" (p. 371), are apparently a corrupt translation of a Polish hymn "*O Herodzie Okrutniku, wielka to wina.*"[30]

Some editions of the *vertep* in fact remain very close to the original conception of the liturgical drama as a *tableau vivant* accompanied by appropriate Biblical readings or by choral commentary. In Franko's *vertep* from Slavuta, for instance, there is no live dialogue between the characters who appear on stage. Instead, as each one makes his appearance and carries out the required movements the choir sings a descriptive hymn. So, as David appears in the second scene to worship the Infant, they sing: —

> "Ты, Давыде славный, Пророче и Цару,
> На все струны ударяешь
> Хрыста восхваляешь . . .";

when the Three Kings enter with their gifts: —

> "Шедше трые Цары
> Ко Хрысту со дары.
> Ирод их пригласил,
> Куда идут, он спросил . . .";

and while Rachel's child is being destroyed the choir sings: —

> "Восплачте чада ради Ирода, бо наступаеть
> Время страшное, бо Ирод мечь свой на вас готуеть . . ."[31]

There are also texts, however, where choral participation is completely absent. This omission must have become a common feature of the *vertep* by the end of the 19th century when, often in the hands of professional puppeteers, and no longer an integral part of village life, it could not count as previously upon the presence of informed and trained volunteers ready to occupy this role. But for the most part the choir was an essential feature of performances, and there are many examples (Galagan's *Malorusskij vertep* is quite typical) of the combination of choral participation with spoken dialogue, the speech of the characters in the first half of the drama being interspersed with hymns and

that of those in the second half with gayer humorous songs. It was not unusual for these songs and the dances which were another feature of the
second section to have a musical accompaniment, on the *bandura* or other
popular instruments.

The legacy of the western mediaeval religious theatre is evident not only
in the textual side of the *vertep* but also in the structural side. The division
of the box into two floors may well be a reflection of the structure of the
mediaeval stage where heaven or paradise was often represented on a higher
level than the earth, whereas devils were wont to appear suddenly from
below through a special trapdoor on the stage. Such trick devices were
known in the *vertep* also and in several variants Herod's corpse is dragged off
to Hell by the Devil through a trapdoor.[32]

It is interesting to note that while the religious text of the *vertep* remains
essentially the same in Poland, White Russia and Great Russia the secular text
which follows is extremely varied depending largely upon regional history,
traditions and ways of life. This divergence applies both to the plot and to the
language. Most texts are a strange and unbalanced mixture of a variety of
linguistic elements, but in the secular part of the drama it is essentially the
local vernacular which is predominant. In the religious section, however,
where much of the dialogue and commentary has a common origin in church
hymns and *tropes*, the regional differences are not so marked because of the
importance of Church Slavonic elements. If, for example, we compare the
opening hymn, "Нова радость стала", as it appears in Vinogradov's Great
Russian *vertep* and Markovskij's Baturino *vertep* we can see that both are
basically the same although in the former the Church Slavonic elements are
fused with what is recognisably Great Russian, and in the latter with Ukrainian
phonetic features: —

(a) Vinogradov's text: —
    "Нова радость стала,
    Яко в небо хвала,
    Над вертепом звезда ясна,
    Светла возсияла.
    Пастушки идут с ягняткам,
    Перед малыим дитятком
    На колени упадали,
    Христа прославляли;
    ' Молим, просим, Христе-Царю
    Небесный Государю,
    Даруй лето счастливое
    Всему Господину!' "[33]

(b) The Baturinskij text: —
    "Нова рада стала,
    Яко з неба слава. ˙
    Над вертепом звизда ясна
    Свиту возсіяла
    Ось Хрыстос родывся,
    З дивы воплотывся.
    Пастушки з ягнятком
    Перед тым дытятком
    На колинах упадають
    Хрыста прославляють.
    Просым тебе, царю,
    Небесный сохвалю,
    Даруй лето щаслывое
    Сему господарю."[34]

Another interesting linguistic feature of the *vertep* is that even in the religious section, dialogue in the vernacular between people of lowly origin could also be found interspersed among the hymns and the often garbled attempts at literary speech of the other characters, just as in the European mediaeval religious drama the ribald conversations of midwives, soldiers, stallkeepers and others mingled with the religious text. Such is the conversation between the two shepherds mentioned above (p. 90), from Galagan's *Malorusskij vertep*. The unfamiliar and difficult language of the religious parts of the text must have added considerably to the problem of remembering and accurately reproducing the drama for performers were often barely, if at all, literate. Distortions verging on the incomprehensible are frequently to be found, such as "В церкви центры инфует" instead of "церкви оферует" in the Slavuta *vertep*,[35] similarly, the distorted lines: –

> "Шедше трие цари
> Ко Христу с ударом,
> Ирод им предвластен,
> Куда идут спросити,"

as they appear in one text[36] may be compared with the version: –

> "Шедше трие цари ко Христу со дари,
> Ирод их пригласи, куда идуть – испроси . . ."

in another.[37]

The relative stability of the characters and scenes to be found in the religious half of the drama also contrasts with regional fluctuations in the second half. The Cossack hero of the Ukrainian *vertep*, for example, does not occupy the same position in the Great Russian or White Russian puppet theatre. In fact, once this character became an historical anachronism he was replaced in many texts by the boastful Napoleon; the cowardly Polish *pan* of the UKRAINIAN plays is no longer the same as his prototype in the Polish *szopka*; ethnographical types popular in Poland do not occur in the Ukraine and vice-versa; similarly, in Vinogradov's Great Russian text popular Ukrainian characters have been replaced by two shepherdesses from the region of the Valdaj Mountains near Novgorod, the home territory of the Russian *vertepniki* from whom the text was taken.

The secular part of the play consists of a series of scenes based on the antics of characters from the popular repertoire and features of everyday life. The humour of these scenes is always primitive and often crude, but there can be no doubt as to their popularity. In the preface to his text Vinogradov, for instance, points out the wholehearted laughter of a peasant audience on board a Volga steamer and compares it with the affected condescension of the few intellectuals present.[38]

In these scenes we are presented with a stream of different characters, some of a national or local nature. In the Polish *szopka* we find the Mazurs (Poles living in Eastern Prussia) and the couple from Krakow; the *krakovjak* is dressed in the picturesque costume of his native land, a peacock's feather stuck in his hat which is set at a jaunty angle.[39]

There are characters from countries bordering on Poland like the lady from Vienna, the Lithuanian or the Hungarian. Then follows a whole series of minor figures, usually in pairs, the old man and old woman, a couple of Spaniards, a monk with a young girl, soldiers (such as an Uhlan or a Hussar), all with their partners. These figures generally have no speaking part, they are there for the sake of spectacle, to fill in the blanks of what could be, in the hands of a not very talented *vertepnik*, a rather uninspiring show. The action involving these characters consisted usually of the exchange of a few kisses and a gay dance accompanied by an accordionist or *bandura* player.

In both the *szopka* and the *vertep*, however, there are several characters around whom the action of the comic section principally revolves. In the Polish *szopka*, for example, we find the haughty Polish *pan* (*šljaxtič* or *gospodar*) who is represented satirically in much the same way as the *barin* of the Russian folk plays.[40] The Polish *pan* also occurs in the Ukrainian *vertep* and it is interesting to note the subtle change in emphasis in his character which has taken place during the transition. He is no longer simply the tyrannical master but the epitome of all that the Ukrainians hated about the Poles, who were characterised in their eyes by loudmouthed bragging, cruelty, cowardice and religious heresy. Scurrilous Cossack anecdotes about the Poles were still current at the end of the 19th century. An old Cossack, Ivan Ignatevič Rossolode, who was familiar with the life of the *zaporož'e* from the talk he heard around him in boyhood, related many such tales to D.I. Evarnickij. Typical is the story of how a group of young Poles were lazing about one day and boasting to the girls about their prowess in killing Cossacks. Even the old men playing cards were dreaming about how they might kill one, two, three or even four hundred Cossacks. Just then the war music of the Cossack's banging drums and rattling tambourines is heard and the Poles scatter in all directions as fast as their legs will carry them.[41]

It is exactly this mood which the *vertep* reflects. The great hero of the Ukrainian puppet theatre is the *zaporožec* or Cossack. In fact he forms the focal point of the action in the second half of the drama since much of the comedy stems from his adventures and encounters with the other characters, the Jew, the gypsy, and others. Three distinct versions of this national hero can be distinguished: the earlier *zaporožec*, the freedom-loving soldier, half brigand, half warrior; the *gajdamak*, a partisan soldier guarding the frontier and whose energies and antipathies were mainly directed against the Poles; and finally, the simple Cossack, a figure whose positive national characteristics still lingered in the folk memory, although in later times when the *raison d'être* of the Cossack ferocity was beginning to fade the character became debased and only negative qualities remained — boastfulness, over-fondness for drink and indiscriminate violence. As might be expected, it is the *gajdamak*, enemy of the Poles and national hero, who predominates in the Ukrainian *vertep*, whereas the Cossack character who appears from time to time in the Polish *szopka* is little more than a local brigand. This aspect of the Cossack may be seen in the comic scene between Cossacks and Jews in plays from Krakow and Sedletsk respectively described by Franko.[42]

An indication of the important place of the Cossack in the imagination of the people is the fact that this puppet was generally considerably larger than the others. It is easy to recognise him by his appearance and dress, which is colourful and flamboyant. He usually wears baggy trousers of scarlet or other brightly coloured material and a *župan* (a loose upper garment worn by Ukrainians and Poles). In some cases the latter may even be decorated with gold lace for a more splendid effect. He is depicted as dark of countenance with the typical long, drooping moustaches of the Cossack and a fierce expression on his face. His head was often shaven with a long, single lock of hair (*čuprina*) left in the front.

There are many scenes in the Ukrainian *vertep* in which the Cossack is represented as the champion of Ukrainian orthodoxy and nationalism. Typical are certain scenes in Galagan's text, where the Cossack, after the ignominious flight of the Polish *pan*, begins a long monologue: —[43]

> "Ґа, на! махнув,
> Мов паньскій хортяга,
> Або опареный пес! . . ."

In this monologue he describes the essential features of the fierce, free life of the *zaporož'e*, his pleasures, mainly drink: —

> "Случалось мині и не раз
> В степу варить пиво!",

his antipathies, his occupations, his battles against the Poles and his laments for the passing of this way of life: —

> "Так то бачу, що уже
> Не добра літ наших година:
> Скоро цвіте и вьяне,
> Як у полі билина."

The Cossack is an invincible folk hero and in subsequent scenes he overcomes a whole host of enemies, the *šinkarka* (tavern keeper) Feska, who demands payment for all the liquor he has consumed; the gypsy wise woman, who under cover of curing him of snake bite tries to cast an evil spell on him; the Jew who tries to strangle him as he lies in a drunken stupor; the uniate priest who tries to convert him to Catholicism. Throughout, he shouts and blusters, swears and makes a great show of his fierceness and hatred of the enemies of Cossacks, Orthodoxy and the ordinary people.

Eventually the vulgar pugnaciousness and self-importance of the Cossack itself became an object of ridicule. In Malinka's text, *Živoj vertep*, a voice is heard off stage during one of his bragging monologues accusing him: —

"Брешы як пес."[44]

The main antihero or scapegoat of the *vertep* is undoubtedly the Jew, who occurs both in the religious and the secular part of the drama. It is to his Jewish scribe or counsellor that Herod turns for advice and information. The Jew appears to misunderstand Herod's questions and is threatened with punishment. Similarly, in the *vertep* from Slavuta a Jew, instead of doing reverence to the Infant, spits on Him and is beaten by a peasant with a flail. It is, however, in the comic scenes that the imagination of the folk runs riot and the Jew, with all his stereotyped, so-called national characteristics — avarice, cowardice, cunning — and dressed in his national costume which set him apart from the local population, is made fun of in a great variety of situations, especially by the swaggering Cossack. He is often represented as a merchant or tavern keeper importunately demanding payment for large quantities of goods or drink requisitioned by Cossack bands.

The Jewish religion, too, was a source of hatred and mockery and popular literature is full of jokes at the expense of the Jewish mode of worship. In some variants the Jew was called upon to 'say his prayers' for the amusement of the audience. Thus, in a play of 1898,[45] after he has refused to believe that God would allow His Son to be born in a stable, he is ordered by Herod's minister: —

"Видправ шабас."

The Jew obliges, uttering instead of prayers a long passage of comical nonsense.

Another character familiar on the *vertep* stage is the gypsy, a brightly dressed character in boots, baggy trousers and a gay shirt, distinguished by the horsewhip which he holds in one hand or tucked into his broad belt. The gypsy was, on the one hand, heartily disliked by the peasants for his dishonesty and laziness, yet on the other admired for his cunning and ability to outwit a fool.

In some less developed texts the gypsy has no proper character. He is merely one of the many who pay homage to the newborn Christ. In the

Slavuta variant, for instance, he enters with a stubborn ram which only calms down when it draws level with the crib.[46]

The gypsy was a well known figure in southern Russia and fulfilled a variety of functions. It was often a gypsy who led the performing bear around and he was a familiar sight at the local fairs where the men dealt in horses and the women told fortunes. In the Baturino variant[47] are preserved all the details of a sale between the gypsy and the Cossack from the initial bargaining to the ceremony of sealing the transaction. Unfortunately, after all the gypsy's oaths as to the excellent qualities of the horse, it throws and kills the Cossack as he tries to ride off on it. In the same text (pp. 177-178) there is an instance of the gypsy wise woman at work when she is called in to cure the Cossack of snake bite. The old woman's spells are really in the form of a curse but the Cossack recovers in spite of her and refuses to pay the three rouble fee. Although the gypsy often gets the better of his dupe, he can himself become an object of derision, for on the whole the gypsy rivalled the Jew as a butt for much unkind humour and mockery in many examples of Ukrainian wit. In the following scene not only is he unable to sell his horse, which throws him into the bargain, but on his return to the encampment in the hope of some supper he is presented instead with some dreadful brew: —

> "Кидала, мій миленькій, цибулю й петрушку,
> А ще для свого господаря
> Кусок сала из комаря!"[48]

It is clear from the above survey that there was little or no connection between the religious and secular parts of the *vertep* unlike the early mediaeval religious theatre where the secular scenes alternated with the religious ones. Such secular scenes, originally subsidiary to the main action, arose inevitably when minor characters and the lay actors who played them took their place alongside the more important Biblical figures of the drama. As a logical development from the improvised speeches of soldiers, midwives, merchants, perfume sellers and bystanders they were often of a crude nature. It is possible that the wide range of characters appearing in the secular scenes of the puppet drama may have arisen in a similar way, or, alternatively, may have evolved from the long chain of 'speechless' worshippers at the crib such as the gypsy who came with his ram to pay homage to the Infant. Such characters, already familiar to the people from other forms of popular literature may eventually have lost their original connection with the crib and taken on an independent role in the secular half of the drama.

It was this secular side of the *vertep* which was condemned by the clergy throughout the Ukraine and Russia and which hastened its eventual decline. The clergy tried to insist upon the complete separation of the two elements, a departure from the more tolerant practice of the mediaeval stage. This artificial segregation often meant that one half or the other was not played at all, according to the wishes of the audience. At fairgrounds, for example, the religious text was entirely banned by the authorities, for fear of blasphemy. The church on the whole had a considerable amount of influence upon the fate of the *vertep*, especially in White Russia where by the 19th century it was severely suppressed. At one point it was even banned in Siberia by the bishop of Irkutsk (a White Russian, incidentally) because of the unseemly nature of the comic scenes. The later history of this type of puppet theatre is in fact more or less the history of its secularisation, the fate indeed of the whole of the mediaeval religious theatre, for gradually "the comic scenes attracted the people's attention a little too much and in them they forgot the serious purpose of the play which was to show the birth of the true Messiah. After all, they believed in it fervently and were not sorry to take their part in the joys of this world even while they sang of the Nativity."[49] In many of the extant texts no religious content is to be found at all, in others it is reduced to the bare minimum or the details so forgotten that the text has become distorted and scarcely recognisable. Such a fate has befallen the *vertep* described by Pekarskij.[50] Here, after numerous comic scenes, Herod finally steps forth to threaten the world with destruction but instead is himself destroyed along with his Jewish favourite and his wife Rebecca!

With time, too, the possession and showing of the *vertep* puppets, often in the early days the task of wandering seminarists (*bursaki*), trying to earn a little cash for their studies, became less of an ecclesiastical prerogative. Soon the youths of the village began to take the show round themselves at Christmas and finally it was exploited by professional *raešniki* or puppeteers who would travel the countryside showing their puppets at fairgrounds and markets to gain a meagre living. One recollects in this context the two men encountered by Vinogradov on a Volga steamer. Both these puppet theatre owners were from the Novgorod government. Each year they would set off with their theatre to different parts of the country. Previously, each used to go his own way but eventually they had decided to try their luck together in the Kostroma, Jaroslav and Nižegorod governments, as it had become dangerous to travel about Russia alone. They were generally welcomed at the towns and villages they called at but they did not earn much and the police often used to harry them. Particularly popular with strolling entertainers of all kinds was the big fair at Nižegorod and it was there they had decided to end their theatrical tour.[51]

The seasonal nature of the *vertep* eventually changed too. Originally shown only during the Christmas period it was gradually accepted for its entertainment rather than its didactic value and thereafter could be seen at any time during the year when enough people were gathered together with the leisure and inclination to watch it. Its popularity as a form of entertainment became so great that in Siberia, for example, a special house was set aside for per-

formances which were advertised by lighting a lantern above the house gate
on the evening of the show.

Although to modern eyes the *vertep* drama seems a crude and unsophisticated form of entertainment, a considerable amount of care and ingenuity
was often put into the presentation of the show. The box itself had to be as
spectacular as possible in order to attract the crowds, and enthusiastic puppeteers found many different ways of decorating it and adding their own
touches of individuality.

At its simplest the little theatre needed to be no more than a large oblong
box, roughly split into two sections by a dividing partition. The fourth side
of the box, closed while travelling, was merely unclipped and opened down
during performances. However, the architectural possibilities of the travelling
theatre were often more fully exploited. In some cases attempts were made
to enhance the theatrical appearance of the *vertep* either by simply bordering
the edges of the two floors with a strip of broad serrated braid to give a
closed in, stagelike effect or indeed by providing the stage with a curtain as in
the live theatre. The Great Russian *vertep* described by Vinogradov for instance has such a curtain.[52] Some of the *verteps* reflected their religious
origins in a churchlike exterior. This was particularly the case with the Polish
szopka which could be most elaborate, even to the extent of stained glass
windows fashioned from small pieces of coloured cellophane paper.

Other *vertep* theatres were built in the shape of houses. A model of this
type now on show in the museum of Sergej Obrazcov's Puppet Theatre in
Moscow shows the extent to which the simple box-structure could be imagin-
atively developed. In appearance it resembles an elaborate mansion with the
upper and lower stages in the form of pillared and balustraded balconies or
verandahs. An ingenious way of stressing the national characteristics of the
Great Russian as opposed to the Ukrainian type can be seen in the theatre
described by Vinogradov where the roof of the box was decorated with the
'horse' carving typical of Russian peasant architecture.[53] The exterior walls
of the box were usually gaily painted and decorated with patterns cut from
coloured and tinsel paper, spangles and stars or perhaps with pictures of a
religious and moral tone, while the inside of the stage was either painted or
lined with gold, silver or coloured paper. The floors of the stage were often
covered with some sort of fur whose pile effectively hid the slits along which
the dolls had to move. Scenery was necessarily kept to a bare minimum. The
upper storey was characterised by the usually immobile *tableau* of the Holy
Family with the crib, while on the lower stage Herod's throne, flanked on
either side by the doors through which the puppets made their entrances and
exits, formed the only decoration. Some properties were used, mainly as
symbols which helped to identify the various characters. Thus the shepherds
were portrayed with their crooks, sometimes with pan pipes and carrying or
accompanied by a few lambs, the *zaporožec* with his mace, the Jew with a

barrel of liquor under his arm, Herod with the royal insignia and his body-guard with their spears, Death with her scythe. The *vertepnik* was able to follow the action through special eyeholes placed inconspicuously in the back wall of the box. Performances were brightly lit by small candles or coloured lanterns.

The dolls and the costumes too were often skilfully made. The characters who appear in the drama may be divided roughly into three categories: Biblical (the Holy Family, Herod, etc.), supernatural (Death, the Devil, angels), and contemporary (comprising ethnic and religious groupings who appear in the second half of the show). The principles governing the choice of dress of the first and third groups differ considerably. The Holy Family, Herod and the Three Kings are dressed sumptuously, regally, in robes and mantles decorated with gold embroidery or lace. Herod, the Kings and Joseph are usually crowned. Typical of Joseph's costume is that of the figure in a 19th century Ukrainian *vertep* in Obrazcov's Puppet Museum. He is dressed in a long, dark-blue robe decorated with gilded stars and wearing a golden crown. The Virgin usually wears the traditional blue with white as in the version from Slavuta, where she wears a white veil and a blue robe trimmed at the neck and down the front with gold lace, over a white shift,[54] or in the Sokirenec version where a blue robe with silver brocade collar and trimmings is worn under a transparent white mantle and the head is covered with a veil fringed with silver. Here too even the Infant is wrapped in silver brocade sewn with gold lace.[55] Regal scarlet and purple are the colours associated with King Herod, and his dress, like that of the preceding characters, is always bright and decorative. In one variant he wears a blue jacket, red trousers and a red cloak,[56] or in the Sokirenec variant, a scarlet chasuble edged with gold lace worn over a gold brocade *podrjasnik* or cassock.[57]

However, there are exceptions to the general style of costume in the first section of the drama. Rachel and the shepherds, for instance, wear ordinary Russian or Ukrainian peasant costume, or, in the case of the latter, the characteristic shepherds' garb of the region represented; one group of shepherds were shown, "with long forelocks or *čuby* and moustaches, in short sheepskin jackets and leather sandals . . ."[58]

The appearance of the warriors of Herod's bodyguard, who are seen only in the religious half of the drama, shows hesitation between the 'ancient' and the 'modern' style of costume. There are texts where their dress of gilded helmets and shields with silver or gold armour is in keeping with that of the rest of the Biblical characters. There are others, however, where the dress clearly reflects military fashions long after the *vertep* had become established in the Ukraine and Russia, as in one Siberian *vertep* where the generals who bear out Herod's coffin are clothed in full military uniform with cordon across the breast, such as was worn in the 19th century. As will be shown later,[59] this was the traditional way of representing the knights in the Russian folk theatre in general and this is no doubt a sign of influence from that direction. Clearly, the whole military tone of Herod's funeral in this variant has been influenced by the playlet *Mavrux*, in which a military funeral was an important element.[60] Similarly, in performances of *King Herod*, a folk play derived from the puppet *vertep* but with live actors, in which there is strong contamination from the Russian folk play *Car' Maksimilian*, one finds the soldiers' costumes are nearly always of the 'modern' type.

Angels in the *vertep* are dressed in white, some with wings and some without. Death is also in white, a figure traditionally in the form of a skeleton with painted lines to show up the structure of the bones and a skull-like head with sunken eyes and nose; a white shroud sometimes covers her shoulders and in her hand she bears the scythe with which Herod is struck down for his sins. In Vinogradov's text Death was a skeleton cut from a picture and stuck on to a piece of cardboard.[61] By contrast, the devils who leap out to drag Herod off to Hell are predominantly black creatures daubed here and there with scarlet (on the stomach, the nostrils, eyes and ears). Some have the black or gilded wings of the fallen angel, others are more conventional with tail and horns and many are covered with fur or hair.

In the secular half of the drama with its kaleidoscope of characters emphasis was laid mainly upon a realistic representation of specific historical, national, regional, religious or professional types, each immediately recognisable from his distinctive costume. Such were the *krakovjak* in his national costume;[62] the Polish *pan*, "одетый в кунтуш с рукавами на вылете. На голове у него конфедератка";[63] the Cossack in his characteristic baggy trousers (*šarovary*) worn with a broad sash, tall boots and long, loose-fitting *župan* (red trousers with blue *župan* and pink belt in the Sokirenec variant,[64] or blue trousers and red *župan* with a grey hat in the Baturino variant).[65] It is interesting to compare his appearance with the historical description of the Cossack given by D.I. Evarnickij: —

> "They put a tall hat on their heads . . . Then they put on a *kaftan* which reached down to their knees and was red with buttons. The *kaftan* was first buttoned and then bound with a belt . . . The belts could be of various colours, green, red, blue, brown . . . Over this outfit the Cossack wore the *čerkeska* or *župan*. This was a loose-fitting and long garment reaching right to the ankles, with wide sleeves . . . The *čerkeska* was a different colour from the *kaftan*; if the *kaftan* was red, then the *čerkeska* was light or dark blue . . . To the costume there was added a pair of wide loose-fitting trousers made of cloth, nankeen or leather . . ."[66]

This description, which includes many other details of the Cossack's festive rather than everyday dress, is much more elaborate than that of the puppet, yet the essentials are the same.

The Jew, both in the religious half of the drama where he appears in the role of counsellor to Herod and in the secular half where he becomes a target for the mockery of the Cossack, is usually presented in recognisably Jewish costume. The two Jews in Vinogradov's Great Russian variant are dressed: — "В длинных черных лапсердаках, в белых штанах, на голове ермолки желтого цвета".[67] Several church figures occur at various moments in the action of the *vertep*; a sexton used to ring the little bell which announced the beginning of a performance, a priest warned Herod of his coming punishment in Hell and tried to convert the Jew to Christianity. These were dressed, with slight variations according to rank and sect (the Polish catholic priest in Vinogradov's text, for example, carries a rosary), in normal ecclesiastical garb.

On the whole, the religious characters in the first half of the drama have retained in their appearance the typical features of their west European forerunners. Neither the Virgin Mary nor Joseph in their sumptuous robes resemble the traditional figures of Russian iconography in which the Virgin is shown usually with an upper garment of red or violet over a lower robe of dark blue or dark green, while Joseph, an old man with a small, rounded grey beard is invariably dressed in an extremely modest fashion, placed to one side of the central action and often asleep. In the secular and comic parts of the play, however, each nationality felt free to embroider upon the action, adding to the plot, language, characters and costumes some of the distinctive features of the tastes and ideas of their own region. In this respect it is interesting to note that the Devil of the Ukrainian and Russian *vertep*, who in many variants plays a comic role, looks very similar to the devils of Russian folklore as, for example, in Maksimov's description, . . . "with their offspring the jolly, lively baby devils who look just like their parents, *black* and *hairy, covered with fur*, with two sharp horns on the top of their heads and a long tail."[68]

The puppets of the *vertep* theatre were carefully and attractively distinguished not only by their external appearance, but also to a certain extent by their manner of speech. Most puppeteers were not content with merely reeling off the speeches in a monotonous and unchanging voice, but made every effort to endow the puppets' words with character and national and regional variety. In Galagan's play, for instance, changing tone of voice or emotion in the speeches of the sexton, Herod, Rachel and the uniate priest are attested respectively by the following remarks in the text: —

"Тонким горловым голосом говорит . . .",
"Он говорит голосом важным, речью официальною . . .",
"Рахиль начинает рыдать . . .",
"Униатский поп дрожащим голосом смиренно отвечает ему."[69]

The speech of Poles, Hungarians and other nationals who appear in the puppet play is marked by lexical or phonetic peculiarities, ecclesiastical characters often use bookish or biblical phraseology; the speech of the Jew is sprinkled with Yiddish expressions and that of the gypsy with occasional incomprehensible words which may or may not have originally been authentic Romany. Language was used in this way not only for realistic effect but often too, particularly in the case of the two last mentioned characters, in order to poke fun at them.

The *vertep* had a considerable amount of influence upon the live folk theatre tradition. A Christmas drama entitled *Tron, Car' Irod* or *Muškurata*, popular in the Ukraine, southern Russia and White Russia and performed by groups of boys and youths up to the first decade of this century closely resembled the action of the puppet play. There was the same division into a religious and a secular plot, the participation of a choir and the singing of hymns. In its manner of presentation, however, *Tron* is clearly indebted to the acting methods and certain stylistic features of the live folk theatre in general and to the most important play in its repertoire, *Car' Maksimilian*, in particular. The forms of command and reply between Herod and his warriors are close to those used by Car' Maksimilian and his fieldmarshal; military uniforms more or less contemporary to the players and highly characteristic of *Car' Maksimilian*, but not, as has been seen, of the *vertep* appear frequently in the Christmas play. In one version Herod, for example, is dressed as follows: —

> "В солдатском мундире, поверх которого накинута красная мантия; он подпоясан широким кушаком, оклеенным золоченой бумагой; через левое плечо повешена цветная бумажная орденская лента, а через правое — шашка на портупее обклеенной золотой бумагой; на голове картонная корона, обклеенная золоченой бумагой, на руках белые перчатки."[70]

Contamination between the texts of the Herod and the Maksimilian plays was common; scenes and characters passed, often with no logical explanation from one to the other and composite texts combining the action of the two plays were also known. So, in one variant of *Car' Irod*[71] Herod pleads with Death for an extra year or month of life in a scene which has certainly been borrowed from *Car' Maksimilian* where Anika the Warrior has a similar encounter with Death.[72] In one version of *Car' Maksimilian* on the other hand one finds the incongruous intrusion from the Christmas play of Rachel, whose child is murdered by Anika upon the orders of Maksimilian.[73]

An intermediate stage between the puppet and the live theatre was also known. In it the religious parts were mainly shown through the traditional medium of the puppet theatre itself while the rest of the action was performed by live actors.[74]

NOTES

1. V.N. Peretc, "Kukol'nyj teatr na Rusi", *Ežegodnik imperatorskix teatrov* (Season 1894-5), Supplement, Part 1 (St. Petersburg, 1895), p. 94.

2. Charles Magnin, *Histoire des marionettes en Europe* (Paris, 1852), pp. 11 and 12.

3. Peretc, "Kukol'nyj teatr", p. 94.

4. *Ibid.*, p. 95.

5. N. Ščedrin, "Igrušečnogo dela ljudiški", *Sobranie sočinenij*, Vol. 10 (Moscow, 1951), pp. 368-379.

6. Vol. 3, Part 2 (Milan, 1744), pp. 245-248; quoted by George Speaight in *The History of the English puppet theatre* (London, 1955), pp. 36-37.

7. I. Franko, "Do istoriji ukrajins'kogo vertepa XVIII v.", *Zapiski naukovogo tovaristva imeni Ševčenka*, Vol. 71 (L'vov, 1906), p. 37.

8. Peretc, "Kukol'nyj teatr", p. 126.

9. Karel Jaromir Erben, *Prostonarodni ceské pisné* (Prague, 1864), pp. 43-45; quoted by Peretc, "Kukol'nyj teatr", p. 128.

10. In the Ukraine there was a rather charming explanation of the *vertep*'s original appearance, a story which told how a certain Polish king was intending to marry a princess from a distant land. As he wanted to acquaint her with the faith and customs of his own country he ordered a crib to be made and a performance of the Christmas story together with scenes from the life of his people: Morozov, *Istorija russkogo teatra*, p. 75.

11. Peretc, *loc. cit.*

12. G.P. Galagan, "Malorusskij vertep", *Kievskaja starina*, Book 10 (Kiev, 1882), p. 9.

13. Peretc, "Kukol'nyj teatr", pp. 133-134.

14. Jevgen Markovskij, "Ukrajins'kij vertep", *Materijali z ukrajins'koji narodn'oji drami*, Vol. 1 (Kiev, 1929), p. 187.

15. One *aršin* = 0.711 metres or 28" approx.

16. *Kon'* – typical carving on Russian village rooftops.

17. Vinogradov, "Velikorusskij vertep", pp. 362-363.

18. Galagan, "Malorusskij vertep", p. 11.

19. A. Selivanov, "Vertep v Kupjanskom uezde Xar'kovskoj gub.", *Kievskaja starina*, Vol. 8, No. 3 (March) (Kiev, 1884), p. 513.

20. Vinogradov, "Velikorusskij vertep", p. 366.

21. Peretc, "Kukol'nyj teatr", pp. 154-155.

22. Markovskij, p. 123.

23. Vinogradov, "Velikorusskij vertep", p. 367.

24. E.A. Avdeeva, *Zapiski i zamečanija o Sibiri* (Moscow, 1837), p. 57.

25. Tereščenko, Part 7, pp. 70-71.

26. Franko, Vol. 73, p. 47.

27. Vinogradov, "Velikorusskij vertep", p. 371.

28. B. Žerebcov, "Teatr v staroj Sibiri", *Zapiski gosudarstvennogo instituta teatral'nogo iskusstva* (Moscow – Leningrad, 1940), p. 131.

29. P.P. Čubinskij, "Materialy i izsledovanija: narodnyj dnevnik", ed. by N.I. Kostomarov, *Trudy etnografičesko-statističeskoj ekspedicii v zapadno-russkij kraj*, Vol. 3 (St. Petersburg, 1872), pp. 373 and 378.

30. Franko, Vol. 73, p. 60.

31. Markovskij, pp. 145, 146, 147.

32. See e.g. Vinogradov, "Velikorusskij vertep", p. 373.

33. Vinogradov, "Velikorusskij vertep", pp. 365-366.

34. Markovskij, p. 171.

35. *Ibid.*, p. 144.

36. Vinogradov, "Velikorusskij vertep", p. 366.

37. Galagan, "Malorusskij vertep", p. 12.

38. "Beside the sincere joy and hearty, unfeigned laughter of the simple folk their ironic sniggers and condescending shrugging of the shoulders were particularly unpleasantly noticeable" (see Vinogradov, "Velikorusskij vertep", p. 361).

39. P.P. Pekarskij, *Misterii i starinnyj teatr v Rossii* (St. Petersburg, 1857), p. 11.

40. *Infra* pp. 143-148.
41. D.I. Evarnickij, *Zaporož'e v ostatkax stariny i predanijax naroda*, Part 2 (St. Petersburg, 1888), p. 11.
42. Franko, Vol. 72, pp. 54-57.
43. Galagan, "Malorusskij vertep", pp. 22-26.
44. A.N. Malinka, "K istorii narodnogo teatra: *Živoj vertep*", *Etnografičeskoe obozrenie*, Vol. 35, No. 4 (Moscow, 1897), p. 40.
45. Franko, Vol. 73, p. 49.
46. Markovskij, p. 149.
47. *Ibid.*, pp. 180-181.
48. Galagan, "Malorusskij vertep", p. 20.
49. Gustave Cohen, *Histoire de la mise en scène dans le théâtre religieux français du moyen âge* (Paris, 1951), p. 62.
50. Pekarskij, p. 11.
51. Vinogradov, "Velikorusskij vertep", pp. 361-362.
52. For description see *Supra.*, p. 88.
53. *Ibid.*
54. Markovskij, p. 118.
55. *Ibid.*, p. 14.
56. Vinogradov, "Velikorusskij vertep", p. 363.
57. Markovskij, p. 15.
58. Galagan, "Malorusskij vertep", p. 11.
59. *Infra*, pp. 197-201.
60. *Supra*, pp. 74-75.
61. Vinogradov, "Velikorusskij vertep", p. 364.
62. *Supra*, p. 96.
63. Galagan, "Malorusskij vertep", p. 20.
64. Markovskij, p. 19.
65. *Ibid.*, p. 163.
66. Evarnickij, Part 2, pp. 21-24.
67. See Vinogradov, "Velikorusskij vertep", p. 364.
68. Maksimov, p. 7.
69. Galagan, "Malorusskij vertep", pp. 10, 12, 13, 33.
70. I.N. Eremin, "Drama – igra *Car' Irod*", *Trudy otdela drevne - russkoj literatury*, Vol. 4 (Moscow – Leningrad, 1940), p. 233.
71. Eremin, "Drama – igra *Car' Irod*", p. 229.
72. *Infra* pp. 164-167.
73. Vinogradov, "Narodnaja drama *Car' Maksimil'jan*", Variant 4, p. 187.
74. Franko, Vol. 73, p. 43.

CHAPTER IV

PETRUŠKA

Apart from the *vertep* with its crudely-made rod puppets and its partly religious plot there was another type of puppet theatre immensely popular in Russia for hundreds of years, which although differing from the *vertep* in many important features still has enough in common with it to make both appear part of an essentially similar tradition.

Petruška, the only extant play of the old glove puppet repertoire of the Russian puppet theatre, in fact probably appeared in Russia not long after the *vertep* itself in the 17th century. By the 18th to early 19th centuries its popularity had attained its highest level and by the second half of the 19th century, although it never completely died out and, indeed, helped to lay the foundation of the modern puppet theatre within the Soviet Union, it was, like most other forms of folk entertainment, gradually disappearing.

The construction of the puppets of the Petruška plays differs considerably from those of the *vertep*. The body of these glove puppets consists of a loose costume fitted over the hand like a glove, and is manipulated by three fingers, one entering the neck of the hollow body and the other two the empty sleeves. The heads of these puppets are usually made out of light wood or *papier mâché*, the former being carved into shape, the latter moulded and the features painted on. The puppets have little wooden or cloth hands, often only roughly shaped, but no legs as they are rarely visible below the waist. The exception to this is Petruška himself who, like our Mr. Punch, is fond of dangling his legs over the edge of the stage where he perches to 'converse' with the audience.

One of the earliest accounts of this type of theatre comes from Adam Olearius, the Dutch ambassador to Russia in the 17th century, who gives us both a written description and a drawing of a puppet performance, which he witnessed during his tour of duty: —

"... Those who lead Bears about, Juglers and Puppet-players, who erect a stage in a moment, by the means of a coverlet, which, being ty'ed about their wast, is brought over their heads, and within it show their Puppets, representing their brutalities and sodomies, make sport to the children, who are thereby induc'd to quit all sentiments of shame and honesty."[1]

From the drawing it is clear that these are glove puppets which were already well known in Western Europe before the 17th century. Although Olearius does not specify it is probable that the play he saw was *Petruška.* Two of the puppets closely resemble Petruška himself and the horse he buys from a gypsy. The stage upon which the performance is taking place is not, however, of the type which would normally be familiar to present day or even 19th century Russian audiences. The sacklike garment which hides the puppeteer's head, arms and trunk from the onlookers is open at the upper end, which is strengthened by some sort of frame so that his hands are free to manipulate the dolls in the space above his head. Eremin[2] suggests that this construction was borrowed from the German *Spielemänner* in the 16th and 17th centuries. Although this may be so a similar type of stage was also widespread in the East. It was used, for instance, by the Sarts, who called it *kol-čadyr*, for their puppet plays, *kol-kurčak*, which were in many ways similar to *Petruška.*[3] The skirt was usually made of a bright red or striped material, also popular for Petruška stages of the more familiar type. The skirt-theatre was also known in Uzbekistan and an excellent example of it has been preserved in the Obrazcov Puppet Museum together with the hero of the Uzbek puppet theatre Palvan Kečel' and his lifesized wife with her long black pigtails and head carved out of a melon. It was also known among the Chinese where the puppeteer, set on a small platform for greater visibility, was enveloped in a large shroud of blue calico from his shoulders right down to his ankles where it was gathered tightly together. His 'theatre' was a box lowered over his head and he manipulated the puppets with his raised hands hidden under the puppet's clothes.[4] This presents a picture remarkably similar to that in Olearius' drawing.

This type of stage did not completely die out in Russia as can be seen from the following description of a puppet show given by the popular puppeteer Kondakov among the Don Cossacks in the late 19th century. The arrangement here is if anything even more primitive than that of the Olearius drawing: —

"В соседней с горницей комнате на пол расстилали большую полсть. На нее садился водитель. Его покрывали редким пологом, так, чтобы можно было следить за движением кукол и зрителей. Руки водителя просовывались через полог, на них надевались куклы. После приготовления четверо дюжих казаков брали полсть за углы и вносили водителя в горницу где он начинал свое представление. По окончании сцены его снова выносили."[5]

Eventually, however, the box theatre more or less replaced the earlier kind. This consisted of a tall, rectangular wooden frame, covered with brightly coloured material. An opening for the 'stage' was made in one side of the structure and the puppeteer standing inside the box could manipulate the puppets so that they appeared to be walking about on it. Sometimes these stages were quite elaborate with a proper curtain, wings and backcloth. This type of stage was common all over Europe as well as in the East. Obrazcov describes a typical Chinese street theatre which is basically the same as the familiar western box theatre except that the stage resembles the exterior of a Chinese pavilion.[6]

The distinctive features of Petruška's dress were his tall, tasselled dunce's cap and his bright red shirt. The other puppets were dressed more or less according to their profession or calling, the gypsy with a whip stuck in his belt, the Jew in national costume, the doctor with tophat and huge spectacles, the soldier in uniform.

The scenes, comic and tragicomic, played out on this simple stage were many and varied, involving a wide range of characters from popular literature and the contemporary scene, the common link being the hero Petruška who vanquished all his enemies one by one.

Among the common scenes are the following. Firstly, that in which Petruška introduces and dances with his fiancée (Varja, Mar'ja Ivanovna, Katja, Pelageja, etc.). This scene is often followed by one in which the gypsy, typically represented as an unscrupulous horsedealer, tries to sell Petruška a decrepit old nag, describing it in such a way as to make its faults seem like virtues. Of course as soon as Petruška has paid for the animal and tries to ride it, the horse promptly rears and flings him to the ground. This occasions another scene with the doctor, which is typical of many analogous scenes in other genres of the folk theatre: —[7]

> "Начинается осмотр Петрушки: доктор ищет больного места, тыкает Петрушку пальцем и спрашивает: 'Тут?' А Петрушка все время кричит: 'Повыше! Пониже! Крошечку повыше!' И вдруг неожиданно вскакивает и колотит доктора. Доктор скрывается."[8]

Two other very common scenes are those in which Petruška meets the local policeman (*kvartal'nyj*) and the soldier. In the former, the policeman has come to arrest him because of all the people he has killed or thrashed. But Petruška usually has no difficulty in disposing of this enemy in like fashion. Danger threatens again when the soldier appears to enlist him (*zabrat' ego v soldaty*). Petruška, however, is not long in finding a way out of this situation: —

"Капрал приносил ружье и принимался обучать Петрушку военному артикулу.

— Слушай как я скажу: раз, два, три — так и пали! . . . командовал капрал.

— Запалю, запалю! . . . голосил Петрушка, обняв руками ружье.

— Ра-а-аз! . . . командовал капрал.

— Ра-а-аз! . . . гнусавил Петрушка.

— Два-а-а! . . . командовал капрал.

— Два-а-а! . . . передразнивал Петрушка.

— Три-и-и! . . . выкрикивал капрал.

— Четыре! Пять! Шесть! Семь! Восемь! Девять! Десять! — восторженно отсчитывал Петрушка, избивая капрала, который спасался бегством."[9]

In spite of his bravado and early successes over his enemies Petruška cannot escape paying the penalty for all his sins, and is dragged off to Hell in the last scene by the Devil or his assistant, a large, ferocious black dog (*pes – barbos*). Maksim Gor'kij, writing of Petruška, indicates that he was in the end usually victorious over all his foes including even the Devil and Death itself, but this edition of the play is no longer extant in Russia. Gorkij is probably quite correct in his assertion, however, as such a scene occurs in the puppet theatre of other European nations. For example, both the Czechoslovak Kašparek and the English Mr. Punch summarily despatch their final enemy (the Devil and Jack Ketch the executioner respectively) who comes to hang them as a punishment for the many crimes they have committed. Both make their would-be executioner demonstrate how to wear the noose and by taking advantage of their stupidity hang them instead.[10]

Apart from those just mentioned above, the different versions of *Petruška* contain a large variety of other scenes and characters. Eremin, for example, tells us of scenes with the Jew, a stupid, cowardly fellow in Jewish costume, who tries to reclaim the money he has lent Petruška and in return for his efforts is chased off to Hell by the Devil. He also tells us of Petruška's bosom friend and drinking companion, Filimoška, who is dressed as a dandy. Another interesting character who sometimes appeared was the *star'evščik*, or rag dealer.[11] Alekseev-Jakovlev also tells how a puppeteer in Nižnij Novgorod showed him a puppet dressed as a deacon (*d'jačok*) who was supposed to call Petruška to repentance. This figure was not normally used for fear of the censor. Most of the time he lay quietly in a bag, wrapped up in a rag waiting for an opportunity to appear before a small circle of spectators, when the puppeteer was asked for special command performances.[12] Other religious characters which sometimes appeared in *Petruška* were nuns (*černički*) who came to bear away the coffins of his victims.

It was no doubt such unofficial representations of the clergy upon the stage of the puppet theatre which so disgusted Prince Dolgorukij who describes in his travel diary a performance of puppet plays which he saw on his journey from Moscow to his estate in Nižnij in 1813: –

> "Куклы между тем щелкают гѵбами, а зрители хохочут, и очень счастливы. Всегда мне странно казалось, что на подобных игрищах представляют монаха и делают из него посмешище. Кукольной комедии не бывает без рясы."[13]

Also to be found are the wineseller (*celoval'nik*), the musician, usually a Frenchman, the German and various other nationalities, including Turks and Arabs.

The procession of characters and series of humorous episodes described above form the basic framework of the Petruška plays, the raw material which each puppeteer manipulated to create the success or failure of individual performances. Like every work of folk literature *Petruška* consists of two parts, one of which is more or less static and the other offering a free reign to the artistic imagination. The individual puppeteer had to embroider upon the static framework and the success of each performance largely depended upon such features as quickwitted and lively use of language, the ability to gain the sympathy of the audience towards the hero, the introduction of topical themes, events and, if possible, characters to hold the interest of and suit the mood of the particular audience and the day. He also had to draw the audience into an intimate triangular relationship between themselves, himself and the puppets. This was done in several ways. For instance, right at the beginning of the performance it was *Petruška's* custom to address the audience as old friends, to establish contact: –

> "Вот и я пришел вас позабавить, с праздником поздравить! . . . Здорово, ребятишки, здорово, парнишки! . . . Бонжур, славные девушки, быстроглазые вострушки! . . . Бонжур и вам, нарумяненные старушки — держите ушки на макушке!"[14]

Members of the audience, sometimes specially planted, were encouraged to answer back. This odd relationship between live audience and puppets was further heightened by the important role of the musician who accompanied the various dances and comic songs but who was also used in the play for other purposes. He was used as a messenger when the need arose, for instance when a doctor was needed to attend to Petruška after his fall from the horse. He is also Petruška's confidant. Petruška discusses with him such matters as his intention to get married and asks his advice about how much he should pay the gypsy for the horse. In fact the musician forms a link between the world of the puppet and the world of the live audience.

The topical themes and references to local characters were usually of a critical or satirical nature and an awareness of the audience's identification with the often violent sentiments expressed by Petruška no doubt contributed to the play's unpopularity with the authorities.

The origins of *Petruška* in Russia are obscure. Eremin considers that he was brought to Russia from the West, and that his first home there was either in the central or the northern governments. From here the play's popularity spread rapidly over the whole country, to the Ukraine as well as to Siberia and even Taškent.[15] Even Petruška's name has been the subject of much controversy. It bears a certain resemblance to its western European counterparts (Punch, Polichinelle, Pulcinella) and could easily have been chosen simply as a suitable Russian equivalent. Some scholars, however, suggest that Petruška has a more specific origin than this. Vsevolodskij-Gerngross for example, thinks that a favourite jester of Anna Ioannovna, Pietro Miro (known in the Russian folk pictures as Petrillo, Pedrillo, Petruxa, etc.) may have given his name to the puppet.[16] In southern Russia and the Ukraine Petruška very often appeared under the pseudonym of Van'ka Ratatuj or Ratjutju. The meaning of this title is unclear. Berkov has the idea that it might come from the Ukrainian phrase *ratuj-tuj* (Help! Police!).[17] It is also a possibility, however, that the word comes from the French *ratatouille* (a sort of vegetable stew), in which case the Russian Van'ka (Ivan, John) would be a cousin to west European popular comic figures also named after foods, such as the French Jean Boudin, the English Jack Pudding, the Dutch and German Hans Wurst and Jan Pickelherring who often became assimilated into the puppet shows of these countries.

Suggestions that Petruška came to Russia from western Europe may well be correct since although he was popular and admired as a particularly national hero all over Russia, neither his appearance nor his character nor his actions are exclusive to that country. Petruška, Punch, Polichinelle, Kašparek, call him what you will, belonged to no nation in particular but to all in general and wherever he appeared he was greeted by the joy and enthusiasm of his audience: –

> "Observe the audience is in pain
> While Punch is hid behind the scene,
> But when they hear his rusty voice,
> With what impatience they rejoice."[18]

In appearance Petruška corresponds to his European counterparts whose most typical features are the hump-back (in some cases two can be seen, one at the back and another at the front), hooked nose, squeaky voice, cudgel or bell, tall, pointed hat and baggy trousers. Even when Petruška appears in Russian dress with shiny black boots and a Russian shirt, the general impression remains the same.

In character too the resemblance is close. The German writer Lessing after watching performances with the puppet Hans Wurst wrote the following about his character: —

> "Altogether he is a bit simple, but not without cunning. He is a coward but at the same time a dare-devil. He is fond of drinking, eating, having a good time and chasing women. He bows before no authority, either civil or ecclesiastical."[19]

This could easily be a description of Petruška himself, in whose character it would be difficult to find a single good feature. Like Hans Wurst and indeed Mr. Punch or Polichinelle, one of the first things that strikes one about him is his love of violence which breaks out at every suitable opportunity. This violence is used not only against the traditional Russian and Ukrainian antipathetic characters such as the Jew, gypsy and charlatan doctor, but eventually against any creature who happens to cross his path, especially if that character is unable to defend himself. In many cases Petruška is no more than a bully and hooligan, using violence for its own sake or to get out of an awkward situation. In one version, after he has summarily dealt with the soldier he is confronted by the latter's old father who bewails his son's fate, but Petruška kills him too. In another, his old friend and drinking companion Filimoška turns up and asks Petruška to 'treat' him for old times' sake. But Petruška merely belabours him with his cudgel. Like Hans Wurst and Mr. Punch, Petruška is violently disposed towards anyone in authority, whether civil, military or ecclesiastic. Although keen enough to belabour those weaker than himself Petruška is at heart a coward and sometimes his bravado and effrontery break down. Thus, after he has killed the German he pretends to be quite indifferent but after a while becomes apprehensive. He tries to hide and then finally sits down and apparently in the deepest despair begins to sing a sorrowful little song: —

> "Пропала моя головушка,
> С колпачком и с кисточкой . . .[20]

Then, of course, the sudden appearance of the ferocious dog scares him half out of his wits: —

> "Ой музыкант, заступись, пожалуйста, — гнусаво вопил Петрушка. — Прощай, ребята! Прощай, жисть молодецкая! Уй — юй — юй! . . ."[21]

But in spite of his cowardice, his greed and his dishonesty Petruška has a very high opinion of himself and is inordinately vain and cocksure.

There is nothing at all subtle about Petruška and much that is crude and stupid, but as he is a great opportunist he can be quite cunning when it is to his own advantage. He is a terrible womaniser too, and although he usually intends to marry (mainly in order to have a comfortable life) in some variants a less desirable attitude is revealed. Rovinskij describes a version known as *Petruška's Wedding*, in which Petruška anticipates his wedding day and the final scenes of which women were not allowed to attend!

Not only does Petruška himself resemble his western European counterparts but the plots of the Russian plays and those of France, England and other countries also have much in common. Many have an equivalent to Petruška's 'fiancée'. Mr. Punch has his Judy, Polichinelle his Dame Gigogne or Jacqueline. As in *Petruška*, the west European plays follow a pattern of violent encounters, each designed to emphasize the hero's cunning and bravado in outwitting a succession of enemies. These characters often have local significance and variations occur from country to country or indeed from one puppeteer to another. The killing of the 'baby' is a scene typical of the English plays but is rarely found elsewhere. Mr. Punch may run foul of a whole host of characters, Scaramouche, who accuses him of ill-treating his dog Toby, Judy his wife, the doctor, a servant in foreign livery whose master complains of the noise Punch is making, an old blind man who asks in vain for alms, a police constable, Jack Ketch the hangman, the beadle, the undertaker, and the Devil himself. Similarly, the French Polichinelle may test his strength on the *commissaire*, an apothecary, his neighbours, archers, devils, etc. In this way although the basic plot remains the same each country puts something of its own characteristics into the text, and this of course is equally true of *Petruška*.

Many scenes found in *Petruška* can be shown to have close equivalents in western puppet plays. Of this kind is the scene between Petruška and the quack doctor. Variations upon this scene occur throughout Europe and it is certainly one of those most basic to the plot.[22] Most striking in its similarity to the Russian equivalent is this scene from a text related by the old Italian puppeteer Piccini in George Cruikshank's *Punch and Judy*: —[23]

> "Enter Doctor.
> Doctor: Where are you hurt? Is it here? (touching his head).
> Punch: No, lower.
> Doctor: Here, then? (going downwards).
> Punch: No, lower still.
> Doctor: Then is your handsome leg broken?
> Punch: No, higher (as the Doctor leans over his legs to examine them, Punch kicks him in the eye).

The doctor begins to belabour him as he thinks this a fitting medicine. But Punch soon gets the better of him and hits him till he falls down dead."[24]

Petruška's comic scene with the horse occurs too in some versions of *Punch*. In Piccini's version again, Punch enters leading a horse, but it runs away as he tries to mount. When he does manage to climb on it throws him and Punch calls for a doctor.

The familiar, brightly coloured or striped box stage in which Petruška performs was as familiar to English, French or Italian audiences as it was to the Russians. Petruška's habit of chatting with the audience or with the musician, fiddler or accordionist who accompanied the show was also a common feature. Petruška's distinctive, high pitched squeaky voice was also produced in much the same way over the whole continent, by using a strange instrument known as a swazzle in England, which was inserted in the mouth to distort the natural speech of the puppeteer: —

"It is a small, flat instrument, made of two curved pieces of metal about the size of a knee buckle, bound together with black thread. Between these there was a plate of some substance which he (the puppeteer Mayhew) said was a secret."[25]

This material was in fact just thin tape. In order to produce its characteristic sound the swazzle was first soaked in water and then placed in the mouth between the tongue and the upper palate. The pitch could be altered by loosening or tightening the tape.

In the preface to a MS copy of *Petruška* from Tixanov's collection, printed for the first time by Berkov, the writer describes his first attempt to use such an instrument: —

"Заложив этот снаряд за тыльную часть языка, почти у самого 'язычка', комедиант произносит слова каким-то странным ничего общего с человеческим голосом не имеющим, тоном. Говор в этот снаряд очень труден. Я, по крайней-мере, несмотря на все свои усилия, не мог ничего произнесть. Каждая попытка сопровождалась судорожными движениями горла, и являлся позыв к рвоте."[26]

Although the similarities between the Russian Petruška and Punch, Polichinelle and the others are quite clear, one cannot completely rule out the possibility of some eastern influence on the Russian puppet as well, for a figure resembling Petruška can also be found in the puppet theatres of many eastern countries. There is, for example, the Turkish puppet hero Karaghioz (known also in Greece, Roumania and the Balkans) or Palvan-Kečel' popular among the Sarts and in Uzbekistan. In the ancient Indian puppet theatre too there was a Punch-like figure, in Persia Kandal Paxlavan. All these characters are in basic appearance and behaviour similar to Petruška. At a folk festival in Singapore in the 1880s a Russian visitor witnessed a performance of the Chinese puppet theatre which amazed him by its similarity to his native *Petruška*. The hero of the performance was, naturally, dressed as a Chinese and the basic scenes, although close to those of the Russian plays, clearly reflected the Chinese background, but the longer the Russians watched, the more convinced they became that the Chinese clown and his Russian brother were one and the same.[27]

As has been seen, Petruška had much in common with the traditional secular puppet theatre of the west, but on the other hand it can be shown to have considerable affinities too with the non-religious parts of the south Russian *vertep*. The two forms of puppet theatre certainly influenced each other a great deal during the long course of their coexistence on Russian and Ukrainian territory. The appearance in *Petruška* of the Jew and the Gypsy, typically south Russian characters, is probably due to the *vertep*, whereas conversely the comic scene between the Cossack and his old horse in Russian variants of the *vertep* may have come from *Petruška* since, as was seen, this scene is common to the Petruška/Punch tradition whereas it was not common in the Polish *szopka* from which the *vertep* was descended. The structure of both *Petruška* and the secular half of the *vertep* is basically the same with a series of semihumorous scenes of an episodic nature containing similar characters and situations loosely strung together by the coordinating role of the hero. The character of the Cossack,[28] hero of the *vertep* underwent radical changes during the latter part of his existence and it is surely due to more than mere coincidence that the later Cossack so much resembles Petruška. In spite of the difference in their origins, the one being the product of a process of historical evolution and the other yet one more representative of that class of hunch-back clowns who appear so frequently in the folk theatre and ritual of Europe, many common features can be seen. Like Petruška the Cossack is fond of eating, drinking and chasing the girls. Both are mean and unwilling to pay for their own pleasures and when thwarted both react with violence and cruelty even against the weak and defenceless. Both are characters larger than life and Petruška, like the Cossack, is often bigger than the other puppets.

It is an odd paradox that the two major characters of both the northern and the southern Russian folk theatre should display these negative characteristics which separate them from other popular heroes of folk literature. Even in the plays *Barin* and *Lodka* where, as will be seen,[29] violent moods play an important part, anger is generally directed against specific economic or social conditions. But in the *vertep* and *Petruška* it is turned not only against the traditional enemies — whether they be Poles, Catholics, the police or Jews —

but against all who cross the path of the hero. In this they bear no resemblance to the other folk heroes, for in Russian folk literature it is a general principle that good triumphs over evil. The bold knightly heroes of the *byliny* use their great strength and gifts not only to defend their native land from the scourge of the enemy but also to protect the helpless. They support order and authority against anarchy and internecine struggles as well as against the inroads of the external enemy, the Tartar.

Those who use their strength and power for evil purposes are generally condemned and punished just as Herod is dragged off to Hell and Anika, who boasts too much of his skill and begins to seek battles merely in order to prove his own superiority, is struck down by a righteous death.

In the major play of the folk theatre repertoire, *Car' Maksimilian*, the hero is the meek, persecuted Adol'f and not his father who tortures and executes him for his faith.

Although Petruška is sometimes seized by a ferocious black dog or the Devil himself, the sympathies of the audience nevertheless remained with him, and the creators of the play, in a refusal to admit the defeat or humiliation of their hero were forced to insert the final scene of his triumph over even these enemies.

The comparative lateness of the appearance of *Petruška* and the *vertep* in the Ukraine and Russia must be partly responsible for this paradox. The philosophy and attitudes of the masses for whom these two forms of entertainment flourished from the 17th to 19th centuries were no longer the same as those which gave birth to the bulk of the *skazki* and *byliny*. At this stage these two heroes were symbolic of something which the ordinary Russian people admired and hungered for, total freedom of movement, self-expression and action. Too long frustrated and restrained by the social conditions of the time, their own natural instincts, soured and distorted, became reflected in the ferocity and cruelty of the Cossack and Petruška. These characters, full of an almost pagan *joie de vivre*, have no enemies who cannot be conquered by a blow from a stick. They are completely unbound by any of the moral or social laws or penalties which governed the lives of ordinary people and therefore could not but appeal to audiences who were only too conscious of their own legal and social limitations.

But whatever the true reason, there can be no doubt that Petruška remained throughout the 18th and 19th centuries one of the most indispensable and popular attractions of the fairground, adding his own distinctive squeaky voice to the general hubbub: —

"Неясный гул носится в воздухе. Громкий говор народа, крики торговцев, зазывающих публику, звуки оркестров, шарманок, писк деревянных петрушек, выскакивающих из-за ширм, стрельба в балаганах, песни на каруселях — все слилось во-едино."[30]

Petruška's place in the affections of the ordinary people is amply attested by
Ščeglov: —

"Посмотрите, пожалуйста, как все лица сразу просияли и
какой дружный взрыв детски-радостного смеха вызывает
его обычное шутливое приветствие: 'Здравствуйте, господа!
Старый знакомый пришел!' . . . Все это старо, как мир, но
все это вызывает, как всегда, оглушительные раскаты смеха
у праздничной простонародной толпы." [31]

Although, as has been shown, the Russian puppet theatre consisted mainly of
performances by rod, glove or string puppets, other forms were also to be
found. The shadow theatre for example, although primarily an eastern
phenomenon was also known in Russia and other countries of Europe.

A primitive type of shadow theatre was owned and operated by the popular
puppeteer, Čiž, from the town of Toropec, during the 60's of the 19th
century. There, the shadows of the simple paper puppets were cast onto a
sheet by the light of a candle. The audience was composed mainly of women
and young children whose tastes were not at all sophisticated. A typical performance would consist of a parade of various animals followed by scenes
from the common fund of folk anecdotes or popular literature and including
characters used by all creators of the folk theatre: the quack doctor, who
cures his patients in a most unorthodox manner and transforms old women
into young girls; duels between warriors; the satirical dialogues between
servant and master; a mock funeral resembling that of Mavrux; gypsy songs
and dances. The show was brought to a conclusion by the appearance of the
monk who announced: —

"Вот вам чернец, и всей комедии конец."

The *vertep* was also known in a shadow theatre version in the Voronež
government.[32] In the second half of the 19th century the traditional puppets
were often replaced with figures cut from paper, fixed to a revolving spindle
which passed vertically through a box. With the proper lighting effects, the
turning spindle revealed an endless procession of shadows.

Another popular feature of fairground entertainment during the 18th and
19th centuries, which may be considered as a very primitive type of puppet
theatre, was the *raek*. Although this appeared usually as an independent fairground amusement whose owners, the *raešniki*, enjoyed a considerable reputation for quickwitted humour, it was also sometimes used as an additional
attraction to the popular theatre shows (*balagan*) when the *raešnik* was placed
at the doors to attract the crowds and cajole them into entering. The *raek*
itself consisted of a large box provided at the front with peepholes covered

with magnifying glass through which the spectators could watch, for the sum of a few copecks, a series of pictures slowly revolved by the turning of a handle. This picture show was accompanied by a running commentary in *raešnyj stix*, the traditional verse of the fairground comics (*balagannye dedy*), which described the contents. There was little attempt to put feeling or expression into these monologues, which were pronounced very quickly and in a monotonous tone of voice in the traditional manner of many kinds of folk declamatory literature.

Much of the humour and interest of the *raek* in fact depended upon the improvisatory wit of the comic rather than upon the artistic merits of the pictures which, although brightly coloured and eye-catching, were often crudely drawn with little sense of accuracy or perspective. In content the pictures covered a wide range of topics wandering far from the original scenes of life in Paradise (*Raj*) and the fall of Adam and Eve which gave the show its name. Most frequent were those depicting famous characters (Peter the Great, Napoleon, Russian generals) and events either from history or from the contemporary political scene: —

> "А это, извольте смотреть — рассматривать, глядеть и разглядывать, как на Хотинском поле из Петросьского дворца сам анпиратор Лександр Николаич выезжает в Москву на каранацыю: антилерия, кавалерия по правую сторону, а пехота по левую",[33] or: —
>
> "А вот извольте видеть, город Берлин! . . .
> Живет в нем Бисмарк — господин,
> Его политика богата,
> Только интригами таровата! . . .[34]

Equally popular were pictures with views of the capitals and chief towns of Europe; Paris, where rich Russians could dissipate a fortune overnight; Rome with its *Papa, zagrebistaja lapa*; Berlin which housed the unpopular Bismarck. Many of the monologues reveal a distinctly chauvinistic attitude towards the customs and peoples of other lands. Other subjects included characters and themes from popular literature and anecdotes, the more interesting 'sights' of Russian cities and towns and scenes from everyday life often with satirical overtones, in which fat merchants, overdressed ladies and dissolute dandies came in for attack. Indeed the satirical nature of many of the monologues attracted the suspicions of the authorities and the *raešniki* were subject to police repression, particularly towards the end of the 19th century.

It is interesting to remember that all the types of puppet theatre mentioned above from the simple shadow-theatre to the more sophisticated *vertep* and *Petruška* coexisted with one of the most primitive forms of puppet theatre, the use of dolls in the agricultural rites. The construction of such

122

figures did not progress beyond a rudimentary stage. As they were regarded as symbols rather than specific characters their appearance and dress was restricted to suit the requirements of the puppets' material role in the ritual. As this role was a purely passive one ending in burial or destruction there was no need to make the figures in any way lifelike, or to make them mobile or vocal. There is a vast gulf between this use of puppet figures and the puppet theatre proper, whose aims and results were entirely different, representing like the true theatre a microcosm of aspects of real life, however subject these were to the traditions and conventions of the art form. Yet, at the same time, both in a way represent no more than opposite ends of the same ladder of dramatic evolution.

NOTES

1. Olearius, Book 3, p. 81.
2. Igor' Eremin and Orest Cexnovicer, *Teatr Petruški* (Moscow – Leningrad, 1927), p. 56.
3. N. Martinovič, "Zametki o narodnom kukol'nom teatre sartov", *Kazanskij muzejnyj vestnik*, Nos. 1-2 (Kazan', 1921), p. 15.
4. Magnin, pp. 39-40.
5. Golovačev and Laščilin, p. 181.
6. S. Obrazcov, *Teatr kitajskogo naroda* (Moscow, 1957), p. 250.
7. *Infra*, pp. 172-175, 180-181.
8. A. Alferov and A. Gruzinskij (Ed.), "Narodnye dramy", *Dopetrovskaja literatura i narodnaja poezija* (Moscow, 1912), pp. 363-364.
9. Alekseev-Jakovlev, pp. 60-62.
10. See P.G. Bogatyrev, *Češskij kukol'nyj i russkij narodnyj teatr* (Berlin – Petersburg, 1923), p. 13; and Philip John Stead, *Mr. Punch* (London, 1950), p. 142.
11. Alekseev-Jakovlev, p. 59.
12. *Ibid.*, p. 62.
13. Kn. Dolgorukij, "Materialy otečestvennye – žurnal putešestvija iz Moskvy v Nižnij Knjazja Dolgorukogo", *Čtenija v imperatorskom obščestve istorii i drevnostej rossijskix*, Book 1, Part 2 (Moscow, 1870), p. 31.
14. Alekseev-Jakovlev, p. 59.
15. Eremin, *Teatr Petruški*, pp. 49-50.
16. V.N. Vsevolodskij-Gerngross, *Russkaja ustnaja narodnaja drama* (Moscow, 1959), p. 123.
17. Berkov, *Russkaja narodnaja drama*, p. 329.
18. Jonathan Swift, "Mad Mullinex and Timothy", *The poems of Jonathan Swift* ed. by Harold Williams, Vol. 3 (Oxford, 1938), p. 776.
19. Quoted in Eremin, *Teatr Petruški*, pp. 42-43.
20. Alferov and Gruzinskij, "Narodnye dramy", pp. 373-374.
21. Alekseev-Jakovlev, p. 62.
22. Among the many illustrations of the Italian Pulcinella, as a live actor and a puppet, in A.G. Bragaglia's book *Pulcinella*, is one showing him lying ill on a bed of straw, surrounded by his family while the Doctor, wearing large spectacles, writes out a prescription for him. A.G. Bragaglia, *Pulcinella* (Rome, 1953), p. 299.
23. George Cruikshank, *Punch and Judy* (London, 1873), p. 81.
24. For similar scenes with the comic doctor see *Infra*, pp. 172-174.
25. Speaight, pp. 212-213.
26. Quoted in Berkov, *Russkaja narodnaja drama*, p. 329.

27. V. Krestovskij, "Iskusstvo na dal'nem vostoke", *Xudožestvennyj žurnal* (1881), No. 2, pp. 264-265, quoted in Peretc, "Kukol'nyj teatr", pp. 171-172.
28. *Supra*, pp. 96-98.
29. *Infra*, pp. 134-136 and 147-148.
30. From a newspaper account of the 1890s in A.V. Lejfert, *Balagany* (Petrograd, 1922), p. 61.
31. Ivan Ščeglov, "Sel'skaja jarmarka i Petruška Uksusov", *Narod i teatr* (St. Petersburg, 1911), pp. 122 and 123.
32. Veselovskij, p. 399.
33. Berkov, *Russkaja narodnaja drama*, p. 124.
34. Alekseev-Jakovlev, p. 55.

PART THREE

NONRITUAL DRAMA

CHAPTER V

THE SHIP

One of the plays discussed in Chapter II, that is *Mavrux*,[1] was in part constructed on the basis of song dramatisation. This method of forming independent playlets or scenes within the framework of larger plays was a common
one in the Russian folk theatre. One of the most popular plays of the nonritual theatre repertoire, *Lodka* (*The Ship*),[2] originally evolved in just this way.

Each play in this cycle may be composed of a variety of different scenes
but they are all linked together thematically as plays about brigands and
structurally by the dramatisation of the song *Vniz po matuške po Volge*,
which occurs in most of them and which provided a basis for the addition of
other elements.

The play *Lodka* was one of the most widespread forms of folk drama in
19th century Russia and variants of it can be found in almost every part of
the country from Archangel in the far north to the Ukraine in the south,
from Kazan' and the Urals in the east to Černigov in the south-west. V. Ju.
Krupjanskaja suggests that the original home of the play was to be found in
central European Russia, in the areas around Moscow and more particularly
in those areas which had for long been associated with Russia's textile indus-
try, the governments of Moscow, Jaroslavl', Tver' and Vladimir.[3] From here
it gradually spread in all directions, to Petersburg and its immediate vicinity,
east to the Urals and south to the Ukraine and the preserves of the Don Cossacks.

The existence of *Lodka* in the north was attested by Ončukov, who includes several versions of it (from the Onega and Archangel districts) in his
anthology of folk drama from the north.[4] It gained particular popularity,
however, among the Cossacks of the Don and the Urals which is not be
wondered at considering the historical background of these regions and their
connections with such half brigand, half partisan heroes as Ermak and Stepan
Razin who also appear as characters in some variants of the play.

The upper Don region had a flourishing folk theatre tradition in which
variants of *Lodka* played a prominent part. Plays such as *Sud Atamana Bur'i,
Ermak, Ataman Čurkin, Konec sem'i Preklonskix*,[5] however, reflect later
historical events rather than the original period of the play's existence. In the

128

Urals the play was known particularly at Ekaterinburg and in the region round Perm', for example in the villages of Levšino, Verxnie Mully, and Nasadko. Thus in the village of Levšino: —

> "Собирали чуть ли не со всего села лошадей, до 60-70 голов, их подпейвали водкой, чтобы они 'не смотрели сентябрем', запрягали гусем в большую лодку, в которую садились участники спектакля. Они так ехали по всей деревне, пели песни, гребя по воздуху веслами; атаман стоял на корме подбоченившись, брюхом вперед. Доехав до площади, останавливались, затем ставили спектакль."[6]

Similarly, in the village of Vatlašovo: —

> "При въезде в село навстречу сбегались масса народу. Он шел и стоял по обеим сторонам кортежа, участники которого распевали свои песни и гребли по воздуху веслами; не редко озорничали, задирая веслами подолы у стоящих и бежавших близко зрительниц."[7]

This type of processional ship was not on the whole common, however, and by its structure and the behaviour of those concerned reminds one of the Shrove procession which no doubt influenced it.

Although, as can be seen from the above accounts, *Lodka* was popular among the peasantry and the semi-military, semi-agriculturalist community of the Don it was by no means restricted to a milieu of this type. Indeed, if Krupjanskaja's suggestion is correct, it is to an urban rather than an agricultural milieu that we must look for the original home of the drama. That *Lodka* was as popular among the urban proletariat as the peasantry is attested by numerous documents. In the town of Varnavin (Kostroma government) up till the 1905 Revolution it was performed by young artisans as well as peasants. The young players in the town were even patronised by some of the important government officials and other wealthy citizens for whom the playing of the mummers was a popular part of the rather indolent life many of them led.[8] In the Urals too, workers as well as peasants took part. In the village of Sosnovskoe in the 1890s a shoemakers' workshop was set up to improve standards of technique. In the evenings this workshop became a sort of club where among other things the local artisans used to watch and perform in popular plays, including *Lodka*.[9]

The large number of variations to be found in the text of *Lodka* and its popularity among different layers of society can be partly accounted for by the simplicity of the original skeleton which could so easily be expanded according to the whims, knowledge or background of the participators.

The well known song *Vniz po matuške po Volge*, which should be considered as the foundation of *Lodka*, was first published in Čulkov's 1773 song book. The music to it, a fast, gay rhythm, did not appear till 1778 in Trutovskij's collection. It has been suggested that this merchant song was not itself a true folk song but the work of an unknown poet, based upon some earlier authentic folk work.[10] The song as we know it suffered numerous changes in its career from the eighteenth century to the present day. The fast rhythm of the original gradually slowed down. By the time of the L'vov-Prač edition first published in 1790 it was already considerably slower, being included in the section of *protjažnye pesni* (slow songs). Moreover, although the song was originally connected with merchant-life: —

"На корме сидит хозяин;
Сам хозяин во наряде,
Во коришневом кафтане,
В пирюсеневом камзоле,
В алом шелковом платочке,
В черном бархатном картузе . . .",[11]

it gradually became assimilated into the large body of brigand songs about the Volga, thus entirely changing its character.

In its most primitive and earliest form then, *Lodka* consisted simply of a group of men pretending to row a ship down the Volga while singing *Vniz po matuške* and pretending to obey the orders of the captain, the merchant who owned the ship, seated in the bows. Of this type is Izmajlov's eye-witness description, dating to between 1814 and 1819: —

"Ярославские студенты вздумали сыграть бурлацкую 'Лодку'. Один нарядился лоцманом, другой рулевой. Двенадцать человек сели на пол за гребцов; заиграли гусли, скрипки и гитары, запели 'Вниз по матушке . . .', все сдвинулись в кружок . . . Лоцман, одетый в вывороченный тулуп, в уродливой шапке, стоял на пороге при самом входе в большую комнату, почти в дверях и командовал."[12]

In spite of later distortions and additions elements of this simple form can be found in most extant versions of the play; in some it is retained intact as the central scene of a larger drama as in the following extract where the manoeuvres of the actors are described in detail: —

"Все кроме атамана садятся овалом, как бы вдоль бортов Лодки, а в середине, скрестив руки, становится атаман. Все разбойники одной стороны становятся на одно, а другой —

130

на другое колено. Стоящие справа опускают вбок правую
руку, а слева — левую. Другой рукой, плавно размахиваясь,
все враз ударяют по ладони опущенной руки, подражая
всплескам воды при огребании веслом."[13]

Played in this way the scene resembles the symbolic, mimetic gestures of the
xorovod games. Gradually, the interpretation of both the song and the
dramatic game changed and as *Lodka* developed into a fully fledged drama it
attracted more and more elements from robber literature both oral and
written.

Dramatically speaking, the next stage in the development of *Lodka* from
its primitive beginnings as a mimetic game may be seen in the addition of a
dialogue between the captain, now known as the *ataman* (chief) and his
assistant or *esaul*. After introducing himself: —

"Не шум шумит, не гром гремит
Сильный атаман со своей шайкой валит,"

he summons the *esaul*, gives him a telescope and asks him to spy out the
land: —

"Вот тебе моя подзорная труба
Стой прямей, гляди верней
На все четыре стороны
Не увидишь ли где пеньев, кореньев, ровных мест
Как бы нам добрым молодцам на мель не сесть!
Судна не проломить
Души не погубить."

The *esaul* reports what he sees: —

"В горах черви, в воде черти,
В городах сучки, полицейские крючки;
В деревнях богатые мужички —
Нигде нам добрым молодцам разгуляться не дадут."

The play then ends with the singing of the *ataman*'s favourite song, *Vniz po
matuške po Volge.*[14]

It is more usual, however, as well as more dramatic for the dialogue to be
interpolated between the beginning and end of the song. In such cases, the
opening lines of the song set the scene and introduce the robbers and this is
followed by the conversation between the *ataman* and *esaul*. The scene closes
with the singing of the final verses: —

> — "И мы грянемте ребята,
> Вниз по матушке по Волге,
> Ко Аленину подворью,
> Ко Ивановой здоровью,"

as the rowers, miming the words of the song, turn towards the shore, the nearby village and local hostelry. Sometimes the woman briefly mentioned in the song (Alena, Elena, Nastas'ja, etc.) also becomes a character in the play, as for instance in *Mašen'ka* where the robbers, after their arrival at the inn are warned by Nastja that the police are looking for them.[15] This, however, is an imaginative detail which does not occur in many versions.

Gradually, as the texts of *Lodka* grew more sophisticated and more scenes were added the original episode became less like a dramatised song and more integrated into the general framework of the plot. In Sipovskij's version of *Lodka*, for example, the song is woven quite skilfully into the dramatic structure. Here, the crew are seen sailing down the Volga and the *esaul* is scanning the river. Suddenly, a voice singing the robber song *Sredi lesov dremučix razbojnički idut* is heard in the distance. The *ataman* is angry that his territory has been invaded and sends the *esaul* on shore to find out the culprit. In the following scene, the singer, who turns out to be a certain Sergeant-Major Ivan Pjatakov, is brought back to the ship after a struggle, tells the story of his life in a long monologue and is admitted to the robber band. After this the interrupted dialogue between the *ataman* and the *esaul* scanning the river is continued until the latter notices a large village on the bank. The *ataman* is hungry and so, quite logically, the rowers turn towards the shore singing the closing lines of the song.[16]

The third phase in the development of *Lodka* ventures beyond mime and elementary dialogue into the realm of fantasy and imagination, one of the most necessary elements in the creation of real drama. Many of the later versions of *Lodka* contain a large number of scenes and different characters and attempts have been made to introduce a simple plot. The material for these additions has been drawn over the years from a large variety of sources, among the most important of which were certainly the songs, legends and tales which grew up around the folk heroes Ermak, Stepan Razin and others of their kind.

Little is known about the Cossack Ermak before he made his historical début in 1581 as the leader of a small band of outlaws and partisans fighting against the Siberian Prince Kučum. Tradition has it that he received a royal pardon for his misdeeds as a reward for his conquest of Siberia. However little is known of him factually his reputed exploits certainly fired the popular imagination and a rich folk tradition was built up around him. The historical songs (*istoričeskie pesni*), for instance, trace the whole course of Ermak's career, factual or legendary, from his appointment as *ataman* by the Cossacks

or, in some versions, by the sailors of the Caspian fleet, his taking of Kazan'
(legend has it that it was Ermak's idea to mine the foundations of the city),
his meeting with Ivan the Terrible, his Siberian campaign.

The Ermak of the historical songs appears as the leader of a band of out-
lawed brigands who ply the river Volga in search of ships to plunder. They
regard the Volga as their own special territory where they lead an uneasy,
nomadic existence moving from one camp to another along the river bank in
constant fear of pursuit and capture: —

> "Как проходит, братцы, лето теплое,
> Настает, братцы, зима холодная,
> А где-то мы, братцы, зимовать будем?
> На Яик нам пойтить — переход велик,
> А за Волгу пойтить — нам ворами слыть,
> Нам ворами слыть, быть половленными,
> По разным по тюрьмам порассоженными,
> А мне Ермаку, быть повешену."[17]

They consider any ships, whatever their type or nationality, as fair game.
Their main concern is the hope of rich booty and the excitement and danger
of a pitched battle in which the *ataman*, Ermak, always shows himself to be a
fearless leader: —

> "А бегут тут по морю
> Славны гости турецкие
> Со товары заморскими.
> А увидели казаки
> Те корабли червленые
> И бросали казаки
> На двенадцать кораблей.
> В три пушечки гунули,
> А ружьем вдруг грянули . . ."[18]

The life which Ermak and his followers lead is certainly a precarious one,
although it has its charms: —

> "Пропьемся мы, мазуры,
> Промотаемся,
> Мы во косточки, во карты
> Проиграемся,"[19]

the greatest of these being the absolute freedom and independence which the
robbers enjoy: —

"Как на Волге-реке, да на Камышинке
Казаки живут, братцы, люди вольные."[20]

Ermak, the *ataman*, not only leads his men in battle, he is also somewhat of a patriarchal figure who has to worry about the welfare of the men who follow him. In the historical song *Ermak v kazač'em krugu* it is he who foresees the difficulties of the onset of winter, and takes steps to safeguard the other robbers. He is the father and provider of his company, — "Кормилец наш батюшка Ермак Тимофеевич."

It is clear from careful study of the texts of *Lodka* and its variants that this type of robber literature has left its mark upon them although it is difficult to unearth these elements from under the mass of later influences.

The robber band from a play entitled *Šljupka* for instance, shows some evidence of the Ermak cycle. Here the nomadic, freedom-loving life of the robbers on the Volga is underlined: —

"Фу, какая здесь прекрасная долина
Для нас скитающих людей!
Хочу здесь остановиться с буйной шайкой со своей,"

as well as their gay, if severe mode of life: —

"Хочу пить, гулять и веселиться,
Грабить добрых людей.
Чем мне жить в лесу,
Лучше я буду жить здесь.
Чем мне жить там,
Лучше я буду при матушке Волге-реке Атаман."[21]

In contrast to this in another variant the plight of the robbers as hunted men seems to echo the plaint of Ermak and his followers: —

"Леса мои, лесочки,
Кусты мои, кусточки,
Все повыжженные и повырубленные,
Все друзья мои и товарищи
Повыловленные.
Остался я один молодец при реке Волге."[22]

The chief occupation of the robbers in *Lodka* is also that of attacking and looting ships on the river Volga. As one of them proclaims: —

"Я есть слуга того, кто вмиг по матушке-Волге летает, ко-

134

рабли, корветы разбивает, и тем богатство наживает."[23]

Similarly, the *ataman*, like Ermak, is both leader and father of his men: —

"Так как я стал при старости лет,
И сдаю тебе свою шайку молодцов,
Удальцов, славных песельников,
Пой, корми, обувай и одевай."[24]

Certain constructions and formulae, too, found in *Lodka* may have arisen under the influence of the Ermak historical songs. Compare, for instance, the *ataman*'s order (which appears in numerous variants) to prepare a boat: —

"Поди и построй мне легкую шлюпку,
С гребцами, с молодцами,
С удалыми песенниками
Чтобы она вмиг по матушке Волге летела
Из-под носу белая пена кипела,"[25]

with the equivalent order from Ermak: —

"— Эй вы делайте лодочки-коломенки,
Забивайте вы кочета еловые,
Накладайте бабайчки сосновые,
. . . .
Мы пригрянемте, братцы, вверх по Волге по реке . . ."[26]

Ermak himself actually figures as a character in some texts, indeed *Ermak* is one of the title variants of the play. Two such plays occur in Golovačev and Laščilin's *Narodnyj teatr na Donu*, but in both these the hero is far removed from the prototype of the historical songs. An interesting version, strongly biased towards the exploits of Ermak, is the recently published *Drama o Ermake*,[27] which includes several scenes of a pseudo-historical nature, Ermak's victory over Matmetkul, general of Xan Kučum, the *esaul*'s journey to Moscow to ask for a free pardon in exchange for the liberation of Siberia, his audience with Ivan the Terrible, Ermak's next campaign against the Tartars at the request of the ambassador of Buxara, premonition of disaster and the report of Ermak's disappearance.

From the late seventeenth to the nineteenth century the increasing hardship of the peasants under the continuous oppression of the landed aristocracy led to an atmosphere of unrest and often open hatred among the peasantry with sporadic revolts and uprisings of varying intensity, reaching peaks in 1667-71 and 1773-75 with the wars under the leadership of Stepan Razin and Pugačev respectively. Both wars were typified by merciless treatment of all representatives of the ruling or privileged classes, from the rich landed aristocracy to local squires, from shopkeepers to representatives of the imperial administration, from officers of the royal forces to members of the priesthood, but it was Stepan Razin, in particular, who became the figurehead of popular antifeudal feeling and the hero of innumerable songs and tales. He was even accredited with supernatural powers.

It is probably to Razin and the type of popular literature which he inspired that we owe the violent elements which are to be found in certain incidents in *Lodka* and in the character of some of the *atamans* of these texts.

The most apparent result of this type of influence can be seen in the distorted ending of the dramatised song *Vniz po matuške po Volge* in which, originally, the crew turned towards the shore for refreshment and relaxation at the local inn. In many variants of *Lodka* this has been replaced by a scene in which a village or an estate is sighted by the *esaul*. The robbers land and the ensuing conflict between them and the landowner, rich innkeeper or merchant, on whom they billet themselves is depicted with varying degrees of violence. In the following extract the *esaul* has been sent to investigate the landowner: —

```
"Эсаул:       — Тебя-то нам и надо!
               Рад ли ты нам
               Дорогим гостям?
Помещик:     — Рад!
Эсаул:       — А как рад?
Помещик:     — Как чертям!
Эсаул (грозно): — Ка-ак? Повтори!
Помещик (дрожащим голосом): — Как милым друзьям."
```

After this the whole band arrives to be entertained: —

```
"Атаман:      — Деньги есть?
Помещик:     — Нет!
Атаман:      — Врешь, есть!
Помещик:     — Тебе говорю — нет!
Атаман (обращаясь к шайке, кричит): — Эй, молодцы, жги,
               пали богатого помещика!"[28]
```

A scuffle ensues and on this note the play ends.

A strong antifeudal note can also be felt in *Ataman*: —

"Толстый барин с крестьянами грудь берет,

А добрый молодец свинцовы пули льет."

and: —

"На торгу купец ворочает,
Добрый молодец булатный нож точит."[29]

However, this antipathy, whatever its origins, was no doubt strengthened, developed and crystallised by the growing political consciousness of the masses and the political activities of those leading them in the late nineteenth and early twentieth centuries.

The vivid impression left on the minds of the people by Stepan Razin is emphasised by Česalin who points out that even at the beginning of the twentieth century songs and legends about Razin could still be heard in many parts of the country, in the Saratov, Nižegorod and Smolensk governments, for instance, or around Lake Pečora, even among the modern factory songs of the urban workers in the Vladimir government.[30] That many scholars believed the folk play *Lodka* to belong to this tradition is apparent in descriptions like that of Professor Šljapkin who, in a footnote to his edition of Griboedov's works, refers to a performance of *Lodka* which he saw near St. Petersburg as a "complete account of Razin's campaign along the Volga".[31]

Within the texts of *Lodka* are several interesting references which seem to point towards Stepan Razin personally. Among the legends about Stepan Razin are many which accredited him with gifts of magic. It was generally held, for instance, that no ordinary bullet could kill him and that, like the heroes of the magical tales, he had special powers which enabled him to evade his enemies. This corresponds to some of the remarks made about the *ataman* in *Lodka*. In one version, relating his adventures and imprisonment (a distorted version of Puškin's poem *Brat'ja razbojniki*) he adds: —

"Но меня доброго молодца
Не могли удержать за каменными стенами,
За железными замками.
Я на стене лодку написал и оттуда убежал."[32]

In another, he ridicules the *esaul*'s doubts about the possibility of capturing a heavily armed ship: —

"— Фу, чорт возьми! Ты сам знаешь, что я мелкие пули духом отдуваю, а крупные ядра в руки принимаю."[33]

Indeed Razin was so heartily disliked by the church both for his strange reputation and for treasonable activities that it pronounced anathema on him which was still repeated in church services during the nineteenth century. Perhaps it is with this in mind that the Hussar addresses the *ataman* in *Mašen'ka* as: —

"Волшебник, супостат, изверг ада, чортов брат."[34]

Apart from these, in some cases rather vague references, there are of course several versions of *Lodka* in which Razin and his exploits are actually depicted. Such a play under the title *Stepan Razin* appears in Golovačev and Laščilin's *Narodnyj teatr na Donu*. This play was noted down in 1937 in Stalingrad *oblast'* from two old Cossack women. In this play we find the incident, often related in songs about Razin, of Stepan and the beautiful Tartar girl who is his mistress. Razin's men, jealous of his attention to her and afraid that their leader will become softened by her influence and lead them to disaster, begin to upbraid and mock him. Razin in reply, after his famous address to the river Volga, throws his mistress into the water as a gift.[35]

Golovačev and Laščilin also mention an interesting version from the Urals which ends with Razin fleeing from his enemies to perish in the waters of the Ural River.

In spite of the fact that one can occasionally distinguish incidents connected with a specific historical figure it is certainly true that a great deal of confusion developed, as a result, no doubt, of the similarity between the careers of Ermak, Razin and other peasant heroes and the mass of legends that grew up around them, so that exploits of the one were sometimes attributed to the other and even their names were interchanged. Moreover, the popularity of songs and tales about them led to the creation of much pseudo folk literature about robbers which eventually became attached to the original cycles. The resulting confusion can be seen, for instance, in the historical song *Ermak u Ivana Groznogo*: —[36]

"У Ермака Тимофеича, самого набольшего изо всех станишников, были много удалых товарищей, верных помощников; правою рукою у него был Стенька Разин, а за Стенькою Разиным Ванька Каин, Иван Мазепа, Гришка Отрепьев."

A similarly confused gathering of historical and fictitious characters from different periods of time can be seen in *Šajka razbojnikov*[37] when the *ataman* calls out the names of his followers, Sten'ka Razin, Van'ka Kain, Griška Otrep'ev, Karikatura, etc.

Robbers and brigands whose actions in eighteenth and nineteenth century Russia were often linked with the movements of social unrest and protest became a popular theme not only of Russian folklore but also of Russian artistic literature and popular literature (*lubočnaja literatura*) in which setting the heroes and leaders of the robber bands were idealised and romanticised, robbing the rich to succour the poor, like Robin Hood. Such is the *ataman* in *Drama o Ermake*: —

> "Он убит при том сраженье
> Как пошли на окруженье,
> Штобы золото забрать
> И крестьянам все отдать."[38]

The imagination of Russian poets, Puškin with his *Dubrovskij* and *Brat'ja razbojniki*, not to mention his deep interest in Pugačev and the legends and stories surrounding him; Lermontov with his *Vadim*, were fired by the deeds and way of life of the freedom loving brigands. However, borrowings of this nature did not merely constitute a onesided enrichment of Russian artistic writings through themes taken from the life and literature of the folk. It was very much a mutual phenomenon in which both sides profited from the knowledge and creativity of the other. The actors and producers of the folk theatre, always eager to embellish their plays did not only make use of material from other forms of folk literature, but also borrowed extensively from literary sources. Songs like *Sredi lesov dremučix*[39] and *Čto zatumanilas' zoren'ka jasnaja*[40] were not originally folksongs but poems which were later adopted into the folk repertoire and became an integral part of *Lodka*. The first, which describes the death and funeral of a robber chief, was traditionally sung, with actions corresponding to the words (carrying out the corpse upon crossed swords, digging the grave, etc.), after the death of any member of the robber band in *Lodka*, the second was usually associated with the unhappy fate of the girl caught by the robbers in some versions of the play.

Among the earliest and most important literary influences upon *Lodka* Vsevolodskij-Gerngross accounts Puškin's unfinished poem *Razbojniki*. He notes the similarity between the opening scene of the poem in which the robbers capture a merchant ship and the *ataman* seizes the captain's daughter for his concubine, and the scene occurring in several versions of *Lodka* in which the robbers bring in a captive girl who was travelling to Astraxan with her father. The father is killed and the *ataman* demands possession of the girl. However, the links between the two works seem very slender and it is difficult to imagine how the authors of *Lodka* managed to get hold of the unfinished outline of a poem known only to a few of Puškin's friends and subsequently destroyed. It is much more likely that both Puškin and the authors of *Lodka* were drawing upon a similar knowledge of folk and popular literature on the subject. What is undeniable, however, is the influence of Puškin's complete robber poem *Brat'ja razbojniki*, based upon an actual event, about which Puškin had read. Parts of this poem, which has suffered numerous distortions

as a result of oral transmission, occur in many versions of *Lodka*.[41] The robber theme inspired not only some of Russia's greatest poets but also many
less well known writers and during the nineteenth century a welter of short
stories and novels appeared in the popular press. From these stories come the
names of some of the members of the robber bands in *Lodka*, for example,
Medvež'ja Lapa (from *Ljubov' atamana Prokla – Medvež'ej Lapy, ili Volžskie
razbojniki*), Sorvi-Golova (from the story *Ataman razbojnikov Sorvi-Golova*),
and Zarezov (possibly a reference to the Zarezko of *Xutorok bliz reki
Unži*).[42]

The importance of this type of popular literature upon the later formation
of the plot of *Lodka* can be seen in one scene in particular. Basically, this
scene consists of the capture of a girl by the robbers as she wanders through
the forest singing: – "Я вечор в лужках гуляла, грусть хотела разогнать";
the *ataman* offers her rich gifts if she will become his wife or mistress: –

> "У меня есть для тебя
> Кофточка золотом шитая,
> Шуба на лисьем меху.
> Будешь ходить ты бархатом одетая
> И спать на лебяжьем пуху,"[43]

but she refuses; there follows her imprisonment or death. There are numerous
variations on this scene, some of which indicate a confusion of disparate
sources. The girl in question is known by different names, Marija, Mašen'ka,
Raisa, Sofija, Ksenja, and her background varies from version to version; she
is a priest's daughter,[44] a prince's daughter,[45] or from a *bojar*'s family: –

> "Я села Царского,
> Рода боярского;
> Мать моя Даря,
> Зовут меня Марья."[46]

The most significant variation here is perhaps in the text of the *Drama o
Ermake* where a sharper and more modern note is heard. Here the girl is the
daughter of a washerwoman who feeds her family by washing clothes for the
children of rich folk.[47] The girl in several versions is not found in the forest
but captured while travelling with her father, a merchant: –

> "По чистому полю едет карета,
> В этой карете сидит девица,
> Распевает, словно райская птица."[48]

This is the incident in which Vsevolodskij-Gerngross saw the link with Puškin's

Razbojniki. A further regular addition to this scene, probably, indeed, part of the original, is the search for the missing girl by her brother or fiancé, usually an officer who is later killed by the *ataman* in a duel. Among the most detailed scenes of this type and one revealing by its style and language its closeness to a popular literary rather than folk source, is to be found in Česalin's *Lodka*.[49] The scene opens with the officer coming upon his beloved, Sofija, in the forest on her father's estate. After a brief exchange of amorous sentiments they part and Sofija is captured. Shortly afterwards the officer returns to look for her: —

> "— О божественная София, куда ты сокрылась? Или хладная могила сокрыла тебя, или сие адские чудовища похитили тебя."

At this point he too is captured by the robbers and shot. In the verbose, although naively expressed language of this scene: —

> "— Как пленительно ваши взоры проницают грудь мою,"

the exclamatory, ecstatic tone: —

> "— О божественная София!", "— О восторг, о очарование!",

one hears an echo of the sentimental novels of the late eighteenth century. One feels that such a scene would not be too out of place, for instance, in Karamzin's *Natal'ja, bojarskaja doč*. Another theme, clearly of literary origin, is that centring on the fortunes of a family of impoverished landowners, the Preklonskij's. This theme is found particularly in Golovačev and Laščilin's collection from the Don (in *Ataman Burja, Ermak, Konec sem'i Preklonskix*). In the third of these plays the drunkard and reprobate landowner Preklonskij is discovered, in spite of his attempt to escape disguised as a monk, and forced to join the robber band. In other versions, however, we see only the later part of the story in which the old man, degraded and forced to serve the robbers, is offered a captive girl as a wife. He recognises a medallion round her neck and realises that she is his long-lost daughter: —

> "— Ва, да, ба! Дочь моя, кровь моя. А атаман хочет не ней женить меня."[50]

The pathos of such scenes is heightened by judicious use of sentimental ballads and romances such as the song by which the girl betrays her presence to the robbers, *Ja večor v lužkax guljala*, or the ballad *Ty kuda moj drug stremiš'sja*, sung by the officer and choir for the benefit of his fiancée just before they are captured in the first scene of Volkov's *Car' Maksimil'jan*.

NOTES

1. *Supra*, pp. 74-75.
2. The general title *Lodka* has been used in this chapter for purposes of convenience. It encompasses a large group of plays and dramatic scenes (about 40 known texts) bearing a variety of titles: *Šajka razbojnikov, Šljupka, Ermak, Ataman Burja, Mašen'ka, Mogila Marii*, etc.
3. V. Ju. Krupjanskaja, "Narodnaja drama *Lodka*, ee genezis i literaturnaja istorija", *Kratkie soobščenija instituta etnografii akademii nauk SSSR*, No. 3 (Moscow, 1947), p. 71.
4. Ončukov, *Severnye narodnye dramy*.
5. See e.g. Golovačev and Laščilin's anthology.
6. V.P. Birjukov, *Dorevoljucionnyj fol'klor na Urale* (Sverdlovsk, 1936), p. 59.
7. *Ibid.*, p. 60.
8. T.M. Akimova, "Narodnaja drama v novyx zapisjax: *Car' Maksimilian, Učenye zapiski Saratovskogo gosudarstvennogo universiteta*, Vol. 20, philological issue (Saratov, 1948).
9. Birjukov, *Dorevoljucionnyj fol'klor*, p. 60.
10. Vsevolodskij-Gerngross, *Russkij teatr ot istokov*, p. 73.
11. N.A. L'vov, and I. Prač (Comp.), *Russkie narodnye pesni* (St. Petersburg, 1896), p. 81.
12. A.E. Izmajlov, *Vzgljad na sobstvennuju prošedšuju* (Moscow, 1860), quoted by Vsevolodskij-Gerngross, *Russkaja ustnaja narodnaja drama*, pp. 66-67.
13. "*Šajka razbojnikov*", Variant 2, Birjukov, *Dorevoljucionnyj fol'klor*, p. 48.
14. N.M. Lopatin (Comp.), *Polnyj narodnyj pesennik* (Moscow, 1885), p. 100.
15. V.N. Dobrovol'skij, "*Mašen'ka*: materialy dlja istorii narodnogo teatra", *Etnografičeskoe obozrenie*, Book 46, No. 3 (Moscow, 1900), p. 121.
16. "*Lodka*", in Berkov, *Russkaja narodnaja drama*, pp. 146-149. This text is reprinted from V.V. Sipovskij, *Istoričeskaja xrestomatija po istorii russkoj slovesnosti*, Vol. 1, Issue 1 (5th ed., St. Petersburg, 1911), pp. 239-242.
17. "*Vjzatie Ermakom Kazani*", B.N. Putilov and B.M. Dobrovol'skij (Ed.), *Istoričeskie pesni XIII-XVI vv.* (Moscow – Leningrad, 1960), p. 529.
18. "*Kazaki ubivajut carskogo posla*", *Ibid.*, No. 356, p. 520.
19. "*Ermak v kazač'em krugu*", *Ibid.*, No. 331, p. 506.
20. *Ibid., loc. cit.* .
21. "*Šljupka*", Ončukov, *Severnye narodnye dramy*, pp. 75-76.
22. P.N. Berkov, "Odna iz starejšix zapisej *Carja Maksimiliana i Šajki razbojnikov*", *Russkij fol'klor: Materialy i issledovanija* (A publication of the Institute of Russian literature, Academy of Sciences USSR), No. 4 (Moscow – Leningrad, 1958), p. 366.
23. "*Šljupka*", Ončukov, *Severnye narodnye dramy*, p. 85.
24. *Ibid.*, p. 81.
25. "*Šajka razbojnikov*", Berkov, *Russkij fol'klor*, p. 366.
26. "*Ermak u Ivana Groznogo*", Putilov and Dobrovol'skij, *Istoričeskie pesni*, No. 364, p. 533.
27. I.A. Moxirev, "Vjatsko-poljanskij variant narodnoj dramy *Ermak*", *Učenye zapiski kafedry literatury kirovskogo gosudarstvennogo pedagogičeskogo instituta*, Issue 20 (Kirov, 1965). The text of the play is on pp. 251-264.
28. "*Lodka*", Berkov, *Russkaja narodnaja drama*, p. 149.
29. Baron N.V. Drizen, "*Ataman*", *Materialy k istorii russkogo teatra*, Supplement 2 (Moscow, 1905), p. 280.
30. S. Česalin, "Novaja zapis' *Lodki*", *Etnografičeskoe obozrenie*, Books 86-87, Nos. 3-4 (Moscow, 1910), p. 102.
31. Quoted by Vsevolodskij-Gerngross, *Russkaja ustnaja narodnaja drama*, p. 69.
32. "*Šljupka*", Variant 1, Ončukov, *Severnye narodnye dramy*, p. 71.
33. "*Šajka razbojnikov*", Variant 1, Birjukov, *Dorevoljucionnyj fol'klor*, p. 43.
34. Dobrovol'skij, p. 120.
35. See pp. 66-67.
36. Putilov and Dobrovol'skij, *Istoričeskie pesni*, No. 369, p. 541.
37. "*Šajka razbojnikov*", Berkov, *Russkij fol'klor*, p. 373.

142

38. Moxirev, "Vjatsko-poljanskij variant", p. 253.
39. From F.B. Miller's *Pogrebenie razbojnika* (1st pb. 1846).
40. See A.F. Vel'tman, *"Pesnja razbojnikov"* in the long poem *Muromskie lesa* (1831).
41. See e.g. *"Šajka razbojnikov"*, Berkov, *Russkij fol'klor*, p. 367; *"Lodka"*, Berkov, *Russkaja narodnaja drama*, p. 147; *"Šljupka"*, Variant 1, Ončukov, *Severnye narodnye dramy*, p. 71.
42. Berkov, *Russkaja narodnaja drama*, pp. 333-334.
43. *"Šajka razbojnikov"*, Variant 1, Birjukov, *Dorevoljucionnyj fol'klor*, p. 44.
44. R.M. Volkov, "Narodnaja drama *Car' Maksimil'jan"*, *Russkij filologičeskij vestnik*, Vol. 68 (Warsaw, 1912), p. 325.
45. Česalin, "Novaja zapis' *Lodki"*, p. 113.
46. Dobrovol'skij, *"Mašen'ka"*, p. 120.
47. Moxirev, "Vjatsko-poljanskij variant", p. 257.
48. *"Šajka razbojnikov"*, Variant 1, Birjukov, *Dorevoljucionnyj fol'klor*, p. 44.
49. Česalin, "Novaja zapis' *Lodki"*, pp. 114 and 113.
50. *"Šljupka"*, Variant 1, Ončukov, *Severnye narodnye dramy*, p. 85.

CHAPTER VI

1. *The barin* (*The master*)

In the previous chapter the presence in some scenes of the play *Lodka* of an antipathetic, even violent attitude towards the local landowner was discussed. This was not merely an isolated case for in the eighteenth and nineteenth centuries the landed aristocracy in Russia was a recurring subject of satire not only in folk literature but also in the MS stories and anecdotes which circulated among the folk and in the repertoire of amateur urban theatre groups as well as in the main stream of Russian literature. The conflict between a greedy, ignorant or oppressive landowner and a quickwitted peasant was a common theme. It is to be found, for example, in such tales as *Skazki o derevne Kiselixe* in which a cunning peasant outwits the local landlord and helps to feed the serfs who are dying of hunger and neglect; or in the *Skazka o nekoem gospodine* in which the landlord questions his bailiff about the progress of his estate.[1]

Variations upon this theme based upon a mixture of borrowings from folk and other types of popular literature entered the repertoire of the folk theatre too, some as early as the eighteenth century and others during the nineteenth century when continuing deterioration in the fortunes of the peasants and many of the smaller landowners provided new elements of satire. Among the simplest examples of this theme in the folk theatre and standing somewhat apart from the others is the game *Igra v barina*, popular among the young folk of the villages. The action consists of the following; the coachman who accompanies the *barin* approaches the lads in the audience and asks which of them want to get married. Those who do must then ask permission of their master (possibly a remnant of feudal practices). He, being deaf, does not understand immediately as in place of *ženit'sja* (to marry) he hears *telit'sja* (to drop a calf) and *jagnit'sja* (to drop a lamb). When each lad has chosen his girl the latter are presented, much against their will, to the *barin* who tries to kiss them.

The fun of the game consists partly in the outlandish and intimidating appearance of the *barin*: —

"Человек необыкновенной толщины, в высокой шапке, с лицом, густо вымазанным сажей, и с длинным чубуком в руках."

He is made to look as stupid and gross as possible and always tries to rub the soot and dirt on his face onto the girls who come to kiss him. His coachman too provides amusement by riding round on a stick, lashing out not only at the 'horse' but at any girls in the audience who cross his path.[2]

One of the most common forms taken by plays on this theme is that of a satirical duologue between two characters, the landowner dressed in somewhat soiled finery and his bailiff or *starosta* in rags. The conversation is based upon questions from the *barin* about his estates (since he has not been near the place for years his own knowledge is of course abysmal) and the bailiff's ironical answers. Taking advantage of his master's deafness and stupidity the bailiff, in a series of paradoxical statements, describes the terrible conditions prevailing on the estate, the poor crops, lack of agricultural implements, the poverty of the peasants. Here are some typical extracts from such a duologue: —

"Барин: — Ну расскажи, дядя староста, откуда ты?
Староста: — С вашей новой деревни.
Барин: — Ну, как в деревне мужики поживают?
Староста: — Порато дородно поживают: с ножки на ножку попрыгивают, у семи дворов один топор . . . .
. . . .
Барин: — У наших крестьян и посев большой бывает?
Староста: — Порато большой.
Барин: — А как большой?
Староста: — В полосу зерно, в борозду друго, и посев весь.
Барин: — . . . А эдак у них урожай хороший бывает?
Староста: — Порато большой, боерин-батюшко.
Барин: — А как велик?
Староста: — Колос от колоса — не слышно человеческого голоса."[3]

It is probable that these dialogues had a factual basis since it was common practice for a visiting landowner to summon his bailiff who would present him with an official description of the progress of work on the estate. We find examples of this practice in Russian literature. In Turgenev's story *Burmistr*, for example, Arkadij Pavlič visiting his village Šipilovka after a long absence asks the bailiff about the state of the crop, the yield and a variety of other points about the running of the estate with which he was completely out of touch. Although in fact all these things are in order the *barin*'s lack of interest in the affairs of his villagers is brought out in another way. The villagers are oppressed by the tyranny of the *burmistr* Sofron: —

> " — Да что ж они на него не жалуются?
> — Экста! Барину-то что за нужда! Недоимок не бывает, так ему что? . . ."[4]

The indifference of many absentee landlords to the fate of their lands or peasants was also expressed in folk tales and anecdotes. In Afanas'ev's collection of folk anecdotes there is one from the Ukraine which tells of the visit of an absentee landlord who has been away so long that his villagers no longer remember what he looks like. One of the peasant women is so curious to find out that when he at last decides to pay the village a visit she sets off for the big house to catch a glimpse of him but all she sees is the master's dog which he has left sitting in the carriage. When asked on her return about the *barin*'s appearance she replies: —

> " — Да який! Зовсім як наш барбос, тільки уші довші."[5]

The 'master and man' theme was well known in Russian popular and folk literature. Typical is the *Skazka o xozjaine i rabotnike* in which the master tells his servant to buy eggs and cook them very lightly. The servant, afraid that they won't turn out right, keeps on tasting them until only three are left. The master, furious, asks how he managed to do this and the servant eats the remainder to demonstrate how it was done. Where this theme occurs in the folk theatre it may have suffered a certain amount of influence from the plays based upon the Italian *commedia dell' arte* popular in the urban democratic theatre of the eighteenth century. There is certainly a very strong similarity between a scene in Abramov's text of *Car' Maksimilian*[6] and a scene in the interlude *Xerlikin i šljaxtič.*[7] In the folk play there is a comic exchange between the Cossack and the Jew over the buying of fish at the market; in the interlude the servant (Harlequin) is sent out to buy fish but trips up and scatters it over the floor. An argument ensues between master and man over the cost of the fish.

One of the earliest references to this theme in the Russian folk theatre dates to the latter half of the eighteenth century and is to be found in the childhood recollections of A.A. Šaxovskoj: —

> "Я еще помню, что в доме бабки моей слуги представляли 'комедь': выходили на средину комнаты, один — будто господином в самом нарядном платье, какое мог достать, другой — его слугой в лохмотьях, и разговор начинался:
> Господин: — Малой подай водки алой!

Слуга: — Да где, сударь, она стоит?
Господин: — В поставце.
Слуга: — Да не чорт ли ее поставил?
Я забыл прочее, но помню, что этот разговор и в таких же виршах с появлением мальчика, одетого горничной девушкой, продолжался, по крайней мере, с полчаса в насмешку над промотавшимся помещиком."[8]

One can also find examples of it in the puppet theatre. In Čiž's shadow theatre of the 1860s in Toropec among the comic scenes there is the familiar dialogue between the *barin* and his bailiff, Vanja.[9] Similarly, one of the popular scenes after the serious part of the Siberian *vertep* was one in which the stupid and vain Polish *Šljaxtič* was made to look foolish by his impudent servants.

An interesting example of the extent to which these satirical dialogues had become an integral part of the repertoire of folk amusements can be seen in the following description told to Opočinin by an old woman from the village of Kuznecov (in the Rybinskij *uezd* of the Jaroslav government). Here the tale was performed in the manner of a *xorovod* which disintegrated abruptly at the end into a chasing game with the boys in hot pursuit of the girls: —

"В середину круга, состоящего из парней и девиц, выходили двое наиболее речистых и бойких молодцов, долженствовавших изображать Алешку малого и Барина голого; они принимали каждый соответствующее своей роли положение и, при общем смехе стоящих в кругу, а так-же и посторонних зрителей, сходившихся со всей деревни, вели такой разговор . . ."[10]

Although a common element runs through all these antifeudal playlets and tales, it is also possible to discern certain differences in attitude from one to another. Among the humorous monologues of the eighteenth century popular theatre there were many mocking the bankrupt Moscow or St. Petersburg dandy who, in spite of his airs and graces, cannot conceal his tattered appearance. This fairly mild poking of fun at the discrepancies between the financial position and the haughty behaviour and condescending manner of members of the impoverished minor aristocracy towards their supposed inferiors can be felt in some of the scenes in the folk repertoire. In several versions the opening scene is set in a wayside tavern (*traktir*) where an officer or gentleman enters and begins by asking for the best room, the best wine (Champagne, Château Lafitte) and the best food. When told the cost, however, he is forced to change his mind: —

"Барин: — Шампанское есть у вас?
Афонька: — Есть, барин, самое лучшее, петербургское.
Барин: — Подай мне стакан холодной воды."[11]

A note of keener approbation, however, enters into those scenes where the results of the *barin*'s lack of funds and lack of interest in the well-being of the estate and its tenants reflect not only upon himself but also upon those who depend on him. Here the satire becomes an unconscious protest against the whole structure of the feudal society. Not only are his lands producing no crops through lack of proper equipment, attention and supervision but the peasants who live on them are dying of starvation: —

"Барин: — ... скажи мне, собрал ли ты с крестьян оброк?
Староста: — Собрал, барин батюшко.
Барин: — Поскольку и с кого именно? (Староста вынимает из сапога палку с зарубками и говорит):
           — Слушай, барин батюшко, сколько с кого именно.
Барин: — Слушаю. Читай.
Староста: — С Хомки грош, с Еремки грош, а с Ворфоломейки одну копейку.
Барин: — Почему с него мало?
Староста: — Да он голый, как бес,
           По 3 дня хлеба не ест,
           А ребятишек-то полна изба."[12]

Scenes of actual hatred and violence may also have occurred in the folk theatre although examples of these are not always properly authenticated. In two games supposedly dating to the 17th century,[13] the vices of two members of the 'privileged classes' are portrayed: the greed of the merchants and the corruption and callousness of the *voevoda* (provincial governor) who accepts bribes from but refuses the petitions of the poor peasants, who, not unnaturally, take revenge in their own way: —

"Из ряда скоморохов выскакивало двое других, садились воеводе на плечи и начинали его тузить, приговаривая:
— Ой, боярин, ой, воевода! Любо тебе было поминки брать да людей безвинных обижать! ... Ну-ка, брат, вези нас на расправу с самим собой."

Although P.N. Berkov includes this among his collection of folk plays from the seventeenth to twentieth centuries it is not at all certain whether it was in fact a folk play at all. This version is taken from an anonymous article,

"Skomoroxi na Rusi" (*Illjustrirovannaja gazeta*, 1868, No. 3 for 18th Jan., p. 38), where it was quoted without reference to the author's source.[14] Two other references to the play known to me personally come in an article on the folk theatre by P.O. Morozov,[15] and in Golovačev and Laščilin's *Narodnyj teatr na Donu*, both of which could well have been taken from the same dubious article as Berkov's version.

Another decidedly agressive play is *Samobojnye knuty*,[16] in which the landowner is outwitted by a cunning Cossack who sells 'automatic whips'. He warns the *barin* that they only beat those "who live by deception and lies". When the *barin* sets out to thrash his farm labourers he finds that the whip beats not them but himself and the scene ends with the threatening cries of the peasants: —

> " — Бейте его, кнуты, не робейте. На весь век барину память вложите! Вот так! Вот так его!"

According to Golovačev and Laščilin this play was written down as late as 1937 from a Cossack woman in Stalingrad *oblast'*, whose father and husband had taken part in this and other plays during the second half of the nineteenth century. It is, of course, possible that such a play did exist among the Don Cossacks but because of its narrow sphere of influence and comparatively late appearance it can hardly be said to belong to the main core of the Russian folk theatre. Moreover, the authenticity of some of the plays in the Golovačev and Laščilin anthology is suspect.

Although many of these scenes, particularly the dialogue between land-owner and bailiff appeared independently it is probable that a number of them at one time formed the separate scenes of a single drama, which later became split up. In a number of versions, the dialogue between master and servant, the recital of all the ills which have befallen the village during his absence (the house burnt down, the death of his favourite horse, the death of his mother, etc.), the dispute between *barin* and tavernkeeper over the cost of food and drink and other episodes are linked together quite naturally during the master's stay at the local inn.[17]

The humour of all these scenes depends to a large extent upon a number of techniques in the linguistic structure of the dialogues as well as the carica-tured, grotesque appearance and behaviour of the main character, and these will be discussed in a separate chapter.[18]

2. *How the French took Moscow*

Sten'ka Razin was not the only historical character to figure in the Russian folk theatre. Another play known to have been popular among the soldiers, although certainly not as widespread as either *Lodka* or *Barin* centres round the Emperor Napoleon and the campaign of 1812. *Kak francuz Moskvu bral* was presumably compiled shortly after the 1812 campaign, or at least at a time when the events of the campaign were still fresh enough in the minds of people to give rise to such an expression of patriotic fervour.

This play is a satirical description of Napoleon's attempt to capture Moscow and the nature of the opposition he encountered. Its material is drawn partly from popular anecdotes of the time, half fact, half invention, about the stupidity and cowardice of the French and the bravery and patriotism of the Russians, partly from the satirical folk pictures and cartoons such as those depicting the ignominious flight of the French from Vasilisa, the female village elder, or the lamentable state of the kitchens at the French general headquarters during the occupation of Moscow, and partly from a somewhat naive and muddled interpretation of the historical facts all strung together in the manner and style of the folk theatre in general and interspersed with stock characters and situations from the comic repertoire.

The play opens with a discussion between Napoleon and his adjutant about the course of the campaign, in which the size of the Russian army, the number of divisions captured and Alexander's Manifesto are all mentioned. There follow two scenes based upon patriotic anecdotes of the time.[19] In the first we hear of the sacrifice of Countess A.A. Orlova-Česmenskaja (here called *Osoba grafa Orlova – doč Ičmenskogo*) who volunteered all her jewels towards the war effort, and of the Russian prisoner who, imitating the actions of Scaevola, cut off his right hand so that he could not be made to fight for Napoleon. This action was commemorated both in anecdotes and folk pictures.[20] The second scene deals with the capture, temptation and execution of a certain General Potemkin (sic!). Napoleon offers him an honourable position in the French army and when he refuses has him taken away to prison and later executed. K.N. Deržavin[21] suggests that the anachronistic appearance of Catherine's famous general in the 1812 campaign may be due to a confusion of family names. The plot of this scene is reminiscent of the deeds of the Smolensk partisan P.I. Engel'gardt. Potemkin's sister married into the Engel'gardt family and the younger generation of this line were considered as the 'nephews of Potemkin'. Engel'gardt was something of a national hero and his deeds may have inspired the play. However, it is also a fact that in the historical songs and other examples of folk literature based upon historical events and characters confusion of names and dates is always prevalent, popular heroes being moved from one period to another.

The main part of the plot ends with two scenes depicting Napoleon's defeat. He discusses with Colincourt the fate of the thousands of wounded French soldiers who must somehow be returned to France. Colincourt suggests that they should simply be poisoned to save the expense of transporting them home or building a hospital to accommodate them. Colincourt

150

appears alongside Napoleon as a subject of Russian satire in the folk pictures of the period.

The play ends with Napoleon and his army in full flight before the furious pitchforks of a band of ferocious peasant women partisans (an obvious reference to *starostixa* Vasilisa, immortalised in numerous folk pictures, many of which can still be seen in the collection of the Kutuzov cottage museum in Moscow).

Various other scenes, small playlets and games deriving their content from historical or social sources are known to have formed a part of the folk theatre repertoire, appearing sporadically for brief periods of time and in restricted localities. But on the whole, there are too few extant texts and too little available material on these to warrant more than a fleeting reference. There is, for example, the series of scenes based upon the adventures of the popular hero, the Cossack Čiguša (*Kazak Čiguša i monax, Kazak Čiguša i okrutnoj Ataman*, etc.) which are given in Golovačev and Laščilin's anthology *Narodnyj teatr na Donu*, and *Velikij grex vodku pit'*, a comic scene popular in the Urals.[22] In both this scene and *Kazak Čiguša i monax* the clergy are singled out for satirical treatment. In the first, the Father Superior of a monastery and his two monks, both bearded and venerable in appearance, try to take a swig from a bottle of vodka while the others are not watching, instead of concentrating their attention on the holy book which each holds. In the second, the Cossack unmasks a monk who is found near his monastery carrying a large sack, supposedly full of cabbages but in fact containing a couple of girls for the monk's pleasure. Čiguša, bold, impudent and invariably master of the situation, is clearly a descendant, albeit totally divorced from his historical origins, of the popular *vertep* character, the *zaporožec*. Such scenes are, however, only of marginal interest to the student of the folk theatre.

Up to this point the folk theatre has been discussed mainly with regard to its evolution within or away from ritual drama. The three plays, *Lodka, Barin* and *Kak francuz Moskvu bral* on the contrary, reveal a stage of development at which the creators of the folk drama were able to work independently from ritual although perhaps not entirely forgetting ritual antecedents. The life of the village, the social structure, social conditions, history and politics, literature and music — all these considerations totally unconnected with the suppressed and almost forgotten pagan motivation of the drama in the mediaeval and pre-mediaeval village society, yet vital to the interests of the modern peasantry, began to be reflected in their dramatic entertainments. In the variants of *Barin* one sees the theatre used as a means of reflecting political and social realities, in particular the facts of life in a poor village with an absentee landlord, and, what is perhaps more important, as a means to comment on and judge them. The crops are bad, there are no tools, no horses to plough the fields, too little flour produced, the hens do not lay well and the unlucky are even likely to die of starvation. The picture is presented not realistically but satirically both in the way in which the facts are selected and the way in which they and the *barin* himself are presented to the public. Although at first sight *Barin*, even in the more organised variants, appears to be little more than a series of comic dialogues loosely strung together by threads of thematic similarity, its construction is in fact a little more ingenious, depending for its effect not only upon the verbal skill of the servant or bailiff, but upon a series of paradoxical situations. There is, for instance, the contrast between the way in which the words of the servant are heard and interpreted by the audience and the master respectively; the paradox of the cunning of the servant and the stupidity of the master, the paradox of the relative social positions of the two main characters and the psychological relationship in which they actually stand to one another. However, from a dramatic and aesthetic point of view *Lodka* is much more complex. Social notes are apparent here too, particularly in the scenes of the descent of the robber band upon the house of the rich landowner or merchant. In the *Drama o Ermake*, where the plots of *Lodka* and *Barin* have become confused, Afon'ka warns his master that Ermak will soon come and avenge the ills of the peasants: —

"– Скоро он вас – хлоп! Вот вам и холоп."23

But social comment is only a subordinate factor. *Lodka* is essentially a drama for entertainment. It provides elements of adventure, danger, romance, the exotic, divorced from everyday realities, yet at the same time expressing through the popularity of the *ataman* hero, the strong, ruthless leader of an anarchical movement against the forces of order and authority and to a certain extent of the oppressed against the oppressors, the same sort of hopes and ideals which induced the peasants to support leaders like Pugačev in the eighteenth century uprisings. *Lodka* has action, a variety of characters and situations, alternating moods, violence, anger, laughter, pathos. It is above all a work which is basically the product of fantasy, in which historical characters mingle with characters from popular fiction and with stock characters of the folk theatre. There is no attempt either here or in *Kak francuz Moskvu bral* at historical accuracy. Razin and Pugačev, Potemkin and Napoleon, meet as contemporaries and nobody is astonished. The folk theatre is not concerned with historical or objective reality. It exists according to its own conventions and peculiar logic. These conventions impose themselves upon the synthesis of themes, ideas, characters, songs and jokes drawn from many fields which form the nucleus of each drama. It is these conventions which allow the historical figure Napoleon to take on the features of one of the stock characters of the folk theatre, the 'tyrannical *car'* ', typified by *Car'* Maksimilian and Herod in the *vertep*. The conflict between the Emperor and Potemkin develops along parallel lines to that between Maksimilian and his son Adol'f. Napoleon tries to bribe the Russian general with rewards and promises of honours. On Potemkin's refusal he is flung into prison with almost exactly the same command as is Adol'f by his father: —

"— Отвесть Потемкина в темную темницу — не утолит ли он свое лютое сердце и не победит ли он своей гордости."[24]

The comic gravedigger, a stock figure in the folk theatre, is summoned to remove the body of Potemkin just as he removes that of Adol'f and the dead knights in *Car' Maksimilian* or a fallen brigand in *Lodka.* The same inner logic which, as we have seen, allows king Herod of the *vertep* to become identified with *Car'* Maksimilian also allows the bailiff from *Barin* to become one of the robbers of the brigand band, and Afon'ka, the servant, to threaten his unjust master with retribution from Ermak.

It is clear that all the plays mentioned in this and the preceding chapter represent a considerable departure away from the exigencies of ritual towards a more widely understandable concept of dramatic entertainment yet at the same time they are all a part of a unique dramatic tradition with its own conventions and mysteries. The specific stylistic and dramatic features of these plays together with the acting techniques of those who performed in them will be examined in a separate chapter.

NOTES

1. Kuz'mina, pp. 26-27.
2. Maksimov, pp. 302-303.
3. Ončukov, *Severnye narodnye dramy*, pp. 127-129.
4. I.S. Turgenev, *Zapiski oxotnika* (Kiev, 1955), p. 130.
5. A.N. Afanas'ev, *Narodnye russkie skazki*, Vol. III (Academia, Leningrad, 1940), p. 311.
6. I.S. Abramov, *Car' Maksimilian* (St. Petersburg, 1904). Offprint from *Izvestija otdelenija russkogo jazyka i slovesnosti*, Vol. 9, Book 3 (St. Petersburg, 1904), pp. 28-29.
7. P.N. Tixanov, *Odinnadcat' intermedij XVIII v.* (St. Petersburg, 1915), pp. 5-7.
8. Quoted in Kuz'mina, *Russkij demokratičeskij teatr*, p. 67.
9. *Supra*, p. 120.
10. E.N. Opočinin, *Teatral'naja starina* (Moscow, 1902), pp. 283-284.
11. "*Šajka razbojnikov*", Berkov, *Russkij fol'klor*, p. 358.
12. *Ibid.*, pp. 363-364.
13. Berkov, *Russkaja narodnaja drama*, pp. 43-44.
14. *Ibid.*, p. 317.
15. Morozov, "Narodnaja drama", p. 14.
16. Golovačev and Laščilin, pp. 101-102.
17. See e.g. Česalin, "Novaja zapis' *Lodki*", and "*Šajka razbojnikov*", Variant 1, Birjukov, *Dorevoljucionnyj fol'klor*.
18. *Infra*, pp. 232-236.
19. Berkov, *Russkaja narodnaja drama*, p. 335.
20. See, for instance, pictures like the one depicting a 'Russian Scaevola': —
"Он только что отрубил себе топором руку; отрубленная кисть руки,

заклейменная вензелем Наполеона "N", лежит на столе, за которым сидят французские воины."Rovinskij, Book 4, p. 445.

21. *Bolgarskij teatr* (Leningrad, 1950) quoted in Berkov, *Russkaja narodnaja drama*, p. 28.
22. Birjukov, *Dorevoljucionnyj fol'klor*, pp. 57-59.
23. Moxirev, "Vjatsko-poljanskij variant", p. 260.
24. P.N. Berkov, *Russkaja narodnaja drama*, p. 167.

CHAPTER VII

CAR' MAKSIMILIAN

1. *An outline*

A variety of embryonic and unsophisticated forms of the Russian folk theatre have been examined so far; remnants of pagan rituals, dramatised songs, the puppet plays and a number of others. The wide variety of dramatic experience gained in these excercises and preserved for centuries in the minds and hearts of the people, in spite of persistent and often ferocious persecution by church and state, reached its culminating point in the relatively sophisticated folk play *Car' Maksimilian.*[1]

Car' Maksimilian is not a single unified drama but, rather, an amorphous collection of scenes, only tenuously linked together, the number and content of which varies considerably from one text to another. As the majority of these texts are not readily available, a brief survey of the main characters and scenes which appear might be useful at this stage.

The central theme of the play is to be found in all variants and consists of the religious conflict between a pagan *Car'* Maksimilian and his Christian son Adol'f. The latter, three times summoned to adore the pagan gods, three times refuses. He is fettered by a blacksmith, sent to prison on bread and water or banished to the wilderness to reconsider his disobedience and finally he is executed by Brambeus (Burmail, Brambivul, Branbeul), the court executioner, a knight who has been kept in prison for thirty three years (thirty five, thirty six) and is released specifically for this deed. In this fundamental conflict the two opposing elements of regal power perverted to dictatorship, and Christian humility leading to martyrdom, are clearly depicted. In some variants,[2] the *Car'* 's attitude towards his son is reinforced by the demands of his second wife, a pagan goddess or princess. The marriage of the father, like the funeral of the son, is sometimes celebrated with a mock ceremony,[3] reminiscent of the parody church services discussed in Chapter II.[4]

Adol'f and his supposedly subversive activities against the crown are in a number of variants betrayed to the *Car'*[5] (by the prince's new stepmother, by a certain King Nikej, by an anonymous slanderer). Adol'f is not, however, completely without friends for at least in a few versions his cause is pleaded by a foreign ambassador (*krymskij posol, rimskij posol*), or by a knight who turns up to defend him by force of arms.

Closely connected with the central plot are several comic interludes which recur at different times throughout the play. The most important figure here, appearing in virtually all the extant texts, is the gravedigger Markuška who is summoned to remove the bodies of Adol'f and Brambeus, who commits suicide after the execution of the prince, as well as those of the knights killed in the second half of the play. Along with Markuška appear several other comic characters, his friend, also a gravedigger, his old woman, a tailor, a devil, a doctor and a variety of humorous antics take place, such as the measuring of the body for the coffin,[6] or the sewing of a hat or sheepskin coat for Markuška as a reward for his work.[7] The most important of the characters thus drawn into the play is, however, the doctor who is called to cure Markuška of his aches and pains or to tend the wounds of the fallen knights. He is sometimes accompanied by his assistant, Paška, whose drunkenness further adds to the hilarity. The scene which follows the doctor's appearance takes the form of a mock examination of the patient with ridiculous remedies offered for imaginary illnesses.

These comic scenes together with the martyrdom of Adol'f form the first half of the performance. The second part of *Maksimilian* consists basically of a series of duels (*rycarskoe šturmovanie*) between the *Car'*'s champion Anika and a variety of enemies who come to overcome Maksimilian and capture his capital city Antongrad. These include such characters as the Black Arab (in at least 11 variants), the Zmejulan (at least 9 variants) and, most frequently King Mamaj with his nephew (in 13 variants). These last two demand tribute from Maksimilian and send him 'challenging letters' (*groznye pis'ma*). Anika, however, is consistently victorious and a 'triumph' is ordered in his honour.

A similar scene to the above in construction, yet differently motivated is that between Venus (Venera) and Mars (Mars, Marec). They too fight and Venus, defeated, is left to the mercy of her enemy until her brother appears to defend her. The content of this scene is very confused. On occasions Venus is saved, on others her brother is killed, in others again Mars himself is defeated by Anika.

Car' Maksimilian usually ends on a highly moral note with the boastful knight Anika struck down in his turn by Death with her scythe. Anika at first challenges her boldly, then, horrified at the inevitability of destruction, begs for just a little longer to live — three years, three months, three days, or even three hours — but all in vain.

The problems facing scholars studying this loose-knit collection of scenes are many and varied. There is, for example, the problem of deciding when it was first written and performed. The play was not recorded until the 19th century and without more detailed documentary evidence it is impossible to date it with any real accuracy although many historians of folk literature and the theatre have agreed in naming the early or mid-eighteenth century as its probable period of genesis. The earliest extant variants of *Car' Maksimilian* can be traced to the first quarter of the 19th century but there are references, albeit rather vague ones, to performances before this. For instance, after 1743 when the Tobol'sk Archbishopric school became a seminary, we are told, the pupils performed plays at Christmastide including *Maksimilian* and *Car'Irod*.[8] On extremely tenuous evidence Vsevolodskij-Gerngross quotes 1810 as one of the earliest mentions of the existence of *Car' Maksimilian*. It occurs in the play *Mitjuxa valdajskij* by the Decembrist writer P.N. Semenov, when one of the characters, recounting his knowledge of the theatre, speaks of a play "about some *Car'* or other", which was popular at that time among the ordinary people.[9] Another vague hint as to the play's existence in the 1830s can be found in Leskov's story *Grabež* (first published 1887) set in this period, when the narrator exclaims: —

> "Нет маменька, как вам угодно, но я дяденьку без родст-
> венной услуги не оставлю. Неужели я буду неблагодарный
> как Альфред, которого ряженые солдаты по домам
> представляют."

In 1863[10] an unknown writer published an article in *Iskra* in which he gave the first eyewitness account of the play. According to him it was originally called *Car' David i ego nepokornyj syn Adol'f* and was performed at Christmas by young soldiers. He tells us it was more popular than *Georg, Milord anglijskij* (!) and that an Englishman of his acquaintance had praised it as "a good farce".

The revival of interest in folklore towards the end of the 19th century led to the first appearances of the play in print, in versions collected by amateur observers as well as professional folklorists all over the country and published by various ethnographical journals; a large number of such texts were printed during the 1880s, 1890s and the first decade of the 20th century. However, performances of *Car' Maksimilian* began to die out from the beginning of this century. The advent of mass entertainment, the breakup of rural seclusion and the upheavals of war, revolution and civil war hastened this process and eventually closed the door irrevocably on all such phenomena. Only sporadic performances were noted in the twenties, in outlying districts. In 1937, for instance, a Polish version, *Maskarada*, was recorded in the village of Lachewka (in the district of "Łachw, province of Łuninsk"). Among the last witnessed performances of *Car' Maksimilian* was that filmed in Gor'kij *oblast'*, in the early 1960s by a group of ethnography students from Moscow. The actors in this case were workers from a collective farm who were playing from memory the parts familiar to them from the days of their youth in the 1920s. I was fortunate enough to see this film, shown at the Ethnographical Institute of the Academy of Sciences in Moscow in 1963.

The continuous popularity of *Car' Maksimilian* among the people for over one hundred years, is as unquestionable as it is extraordinary. *Car' Maksimilian* penetrated to all sections of the 'folk', being played by artisans, factory workers, sailors, peasants and especially by soldiers. Versions of it have been found scattered over the length and breadth of European Russia from the Xerson government in the extreme south of the Ukraine to the Onega and Archangel governments in the far north, from the Orenburg district on the frontier of south-east European Russia to Minsk government in western White Russia.

This dissemination of the known variants of the play over such a wide area, coupled with the fact that only a handful of variants in any one region were ever published while many other regions remained totally unexplored, makes any definite pronouncements about its place of origin purely hypothetical. The existence of many versions in the central belt round Moscow (the Rjazan' and Jaroslav governments, for example) led to the idea that the play grew up among the industrial (predominantly textile) workers in this area. Ončukov, on the other hand, stresses the importance of the sawmills in the northern maritime regions of Russia round Archangel in particular, as a repository and dispersal point for the folk theatre.[12]

One fact which seems to be quite clear, however, is that the basic text of the play must have originated in Great Russia as opposed to White Russia or the Ukraine, although a number of features, both in the content and in the language, reflect the different areas in which it settled and became part of the local life. In the Ukrainian and White Russian texts one finds characters which traditionally belong to the popular literature of these regions, the Jew, the Cossack, the Ukrainian Hetman, etc.[13] Here too occurs the strongest influence from the *vertep* and the allied play of *King Herod*. Several versions from the Xerson government, for instance, present *Herod* and *Maksimilian* combined into one under the title *The Throne (Tron)*.[14] Similarly, regional influences can be found in one of the variants collected by Ončukov in the north of Russia. Here, there are two old men, the gravediggers Patrakej and Mokej, who have served with the Baltic fleet; their conversation about ships and sailing is full of nautical terminology: —

> "Второй старик: — у нас был 'Сильвестр' на семнадцать верст. У нас на марсах можно было жить, на люке был питейный дом, а на гроте, там харчевня. На крюселе там была лавочка артельна."[15]

One might imagine that the language of *Car' Maksimilian* would help to decide the region of origin but here again unfortunately, there are problems, since many of the texts now extant do not truly reflect the language of their original version. The nineteenth century copies of the play were often collected by untrained observers, unaware of the importance of exact reportage. Most of the texts were therefore copied down or communicated by a narrator in standard literary Russian with most regional features removed from the text for the sake of clarity. Before publication, the texts were often 'bowdlerised', odd spellings were altered, obscure passages omitted or 'corrected', artificial divisions into acts and scenes introduced and so on. However, it is generally agreed, on the basis of texts not so deformed, that the language of origin was Russian. The stability of Russian as the language of *Car' Maksimilian* is borne out particularly by the fact that even in those places where the population did not normally speak Russian the language of the text remains basically unchanged. Abramov, for example, says of his variant (found near Voronež) which, incidentally he has left in its original form: —

> "Нужно заметить что население местечка Воронежа говорит на <u>малорусском</u> языке, но названная мною 'кумедия' всегда разыгривается на языке <u>великорусском</u>, впрочем не совсем чистом."

The text contains Ukrainianisms like бачите, уся, забув, наробил, etc., and the gypsy's comic monologue at the end is a good example of what Abramov meant by describing the language as "Great Russian, although not quite pure": —

> "Умею читать, писать, рисовать и преотлично коныков воровать . . . хуркуля, муркуля на крученой ковбасе. Як бы у вас в печи сало не цвирчало, то-б до вас Иван-цыган не зайшов."[16]

Similarly, a variant in an anthology of White Russian folklore[17] is not written in White Russian proper but rather in Great Russian heavily influenced by a mixture of west Russian and Ukrainian phonetic and dialectal forms.

There is often an interesting difference between the serious and comic scenes of the play. If we look at texts like Kallaš's first variant or Abramov's variant, both from Černigov government, we see that while the regional comic scenes contain many Ukrainian words and expressions the serious part of the plot is in Great Russian, although a few Ukrainianisms can be found here too. Indeed, it is generally true of the folk plays, in particular *Car' Maksimilian*, that while serious characters try to keep as close to the literary language as possible, comic characters are free, even encouraged, to get as much local colour into their speech as they can.

In *Car' Maksimilian* the reader is presented with a confusing jumble of elements traceable to a wide variety of different sources. Many of the variants lack one or more scenes common to other variants; the order in which scenes

160

appear is variable; some variants contain scenes which appear nowhere else, others offer hints of scenes long forgotten and nowhere recorded. Yet, in spite of its apparently haphazard organisation *Car' Maksimilian* still gives the impression of an organic whole because of the unifying effect of the oral tradition in which it existed and developed over so many years.

2. *The main characters and scenes of Car' Maksimilian*

For purposes of analysis *Car' Maksimilian* may be divided into three main sections: — a) the martyrdom of Adol'f, b) the duel scenes, c) the interludes.

a) The martyrdom of Adol'f

This intriguing scene which forms the nucleus of the play has in the past attracted a great deal of attention from both scholars of literature and folklorists. Its obvious literary flavour has encouraged many attempts to discover its origins, or at least possible antecedents, in various types of literature, lives of the saints and plays from the repertoire of either the academic theatre or the urban democratic theatre being among the most popular.

The main exponent of the idea that *Car' Maksimilian* could be based on a hagiographical tale, in particular the *Life of St. Nikita*, was Vladimir Kallaš[18] who suggested that the original brief framework of the religious tale, once adapted into dramatic form and folklorised, gradually accumulated a variety of extraneous elements which eventually formed the complex text of *Car' Maksimilian* as it was known in the 19th century. His theory is based upon certain similarities in the plot of the two works and on the appearance in both of the pagan *Car'* Maksimilian / Maksimiian, persecutor of Christians. However, in order to uncover the basic thematic similarities between the *Life of St. Nikita* and *Car' Maksimilian* it is necessary to strip the former of a considerable part of its contents. The religious plot of the folk play consists only of the *Car'* 's refusal to accept his son's faith and the latter's imprisonment and execution, whereas in the hagiography St. Nikita is subjected to a whole series of tortures and temptations; the people rise up against the *Car'*, the soldiers, wizards and finally Maksimilian himself are saved by a miracle and converted.[19]

Moreover, hagiographies tend to follow a sterotyped pattern and the events which Kallaš sees as significant can be found in other tales, for example in the *Life of St. Egor'*. He too had a pagan father, was persecuted and flung into prison. His life as retold in the *duxovnye stixi* (sacred verses of partly folk and partly literary origin) is in fact remarkably close to that of Adol'f. The *Life of Nikita*, in any case, was neither particularly well known nor particularly popular and why it should have been chosen to form the basis of a folk play remains a mystery.

Another popular theory is that *Car' Maksimilian* is a folklorised version of some unknown religious drama of the academic repertoire dating to the early 18th century. While V.D. Kuz'mina,[20] for instance, is content to consider the basis for the play as simply "a nonextant early 18th century drama, the dramatised version of some tale about the execution by a pagan *car'* of his disobedient Christian son", other scholars have made more specific claims. Both Berkov[21] and Vsevolodskij-Gerngross[22] connect *Car' Maksimilian* with one play in particular; Dimitrij of Rostov's *Venec slavnopodobnyj velikomučeniku Dimitriju* (1704). Both agree that there are close similarities between the two plots. Vsevolodskij-Gerngross lists the following: (1) the name of the persecutor, Maksimilian, (2) the fundamental conflict between father and son, (3) military action against the *car'*, (4) Dimitrij's imprisonment, (5) the intervention of a third party on his behalf (in the *Venec* . . . this is Nestor, in *Car' Maksimilian* the executioner Brambeus), (6) the execution of both Nestor and Dimitrij.

This explanation of the origin of *Car' Maksimilian* suffers from the same basic defects as that of Kallaš; it does not take into account the fundamental sameness of stories and plays based upon the lives of the early Christian martyrs. In fact, the differences between these literary works and the folk plays are as obvious as the similarities.

Following the lead given by Morozov,[23] who was the first to suggest the idea, scholars like Vsevolodskij-Gerngross, Berkov, Sobolevskij, Volkov, Krupjanskaja and Akimova among others have seen in such elements as the courtly setting of the play, the foreign names, the mythological characters Venus and Mars, the tragic exile of the hero to the wilderness, the duel scenes and so on, signs of influence from another quarter, that is from plays based upon the *rycarskie povesti* (knightly tales) such as *Akt o Petre zlatyx ključej* or *Komedija ob Indrike i Melende*, which were popular in the repertoire of the later academic theatre and the urban democratic theatre throughout the 18th century. Certainly there do seem to be stylistic and structural similarities between *Car' Maksimilian* and plays of this type.

Dramatically speaking, one of the most developed passages in the first half of *Car' Maksimilian* concerns the bringing in of the royal regalia with which the *Car'* assumes the power, duties and privileges of the monarch: —

> "Появляется торжественная процессия: впереди два пажа на подносах несут золоченую корону, скипетр и державу, за ними, по два в ряд, несколько воинов с обнаженными шашками; пажи, подавая царю Максимилиану корону, становятся на колени, . . . пажи поют — Мы к царю идем, Злат венец несем — Царь Максимилиан надевает корону и берет в руки скрипетр и державу."[24]

In the courtly plays, too, kings (most of the characters in these plays were drawn from the upper levels of society, kings, princes, knights) were seen in all their royal majesty; seated on their throne, dressed in regal purple, carrying the sceptre and mace, they interviewed their knights and commanded their servants. Coronations were a regular occurrence; there are at least four in *Kaleandr i Neonilda*[25] alone. Periandr, Poliartes, Alkoles, Tigrina are all crowned with a similar display of pomp as in *Car' Maksimilian*. In another drama of the Petrine period *Istorija o care Davide i care Solomone* the stage directions to the coronation of Adonij indicate a scene very similar to that in *Car' Maksimilian*: —

> "Когда проговорит Виафар речь, то взять 4-м сенатором парфиру и наложить на плечи Аданию; а корону взять 2-м сенатором и 2-м воинам и наложить на главу, а скрипетр взят единому от первых сенаторов и положить на блюда и поднесть . . ."[26]

Equally close in both language and structure are the duel scenes which are to be found scattered through the texts of the courtly plays. The knightly protagonists boast of their strength and prowess, challenge each other to fight boldly and defiantly in much the same terms as the challengers who came to destroy Antongrad in *Car' Maksimilian*. One can compare the Swedish king's challenge to the Danish king in *Indrik i Melenda* with the Black Arab's speech from *Car' Maksimilian*: —

> "Король шведский: — Встани с престола, мне покорися,
> Своим королевством под мой скрипетр смирися!
> Аще не восхощешь, велю тя смерти предати,
> И мои вои зде будут побеждати."[27]

> "Араб: — Сходи, царь, с трона,
> Сходи немедленно с трона!
> А не то я тебя сшибу,
> В твое царство войду
> И тебя злою смертю казнить буду."[28]

The heroes join battle with a similar impudent invitation to fight. Kaleandr in *Kaleandr i Neonilda* exclaims: —

> "Изволь со мной ныне в том смело сражатца
> На преострых шпагах зде рапироватца."[29]

A knight in *Car' Maksimilian* retorts in similar vein: —

"Выходи на чистое поле:
Побиться, порубиться
На острых мечах потешиться."[30]

Typical of the style of the courtly plays were the monologues of introduction and self-praise delivered by each new prince or knight as he joined the action — King Atigrin in *Kaleandr i Neonilda* boasts of his conquest and the lands he has in his power: —

"Аз есмь Атигрин цесарь трапезонскии,
Владею и царствы силны амозонскии.
Всю Азию, Африку в команде имею,
Содержителем света назватися смею."[31]

Such monologues, although generally much shorter and simpler are also to be found in *Car' Maksimilian*. The *Car'* introduces himself as follows: —

"Прошел я и покорил я Австрию, Азию, Америку, Европу. Был я у шведского короля, отбил у него все столичные города . . ."[32]

Although there are many other small points of style and language which seem to link the two types of play it is not really possible to speak of direct influence from any specific direction. One must bear in mind that in the first half of the 18th century, before the advent of the neoclassical theatre, secular popular literature in general and drama in particular were in their infancy in Russia. The inexperienced authors of the new literary trends and the translators of the new literature for entertainment coming in from western Europe had no indigenous literary tradition to learn from. Not only did they rely heavily on foreign models but they also drew inspiration from their native folk literature which had for centuries provided the people with the entertainment which their written literature lacked.

Car' Maksimilian, typical of this transitional phase, is essentially a hybrid, reflecting features of both folk and written literary traditions, and was clearly compiled at a time when plays like *Kaleandr i Neonilda* or *Indrik i Melenda* were popular on the Russian stages not only among the aristocracy but among a wide cross section of the population.

b) The duel scenes

(i) The battle with Mamaj
The great and significant battle of Kulikovo Field (1380) between the Tartar *Xan* Mamaj with his Golden Horde and the Russian Prince Dmitrij Iva-

novič naturally fired the patriotic feelings of the Russians and it passed not only into history but into legend. First related in the Kulikovskij cycle of the Chronicles, the story was retold thereafter in many different versions. Most of these date to the 15th-17th centuries but some are known to have appeared as late as the 18th and 19th centuries. Folklorised, the battle became the subject of innumerable tales, *byliny* and historical songs and was pictorially represented in the folk pictures.

The battle between Mamaj with his nephew and the *car'*'s champion Anika is, of course, merely a distant echo of the original story. Mamaj issues a challenge to *Car'* Maksimilian through his nephew, by means of a threatening letter. This formula is reminiscent of certain historical songs popular in the 17th century such as *Pišet, pišet sultan tureckij carju belomu* or *Ne v lužjax to voda polnaja razlivaetsja.*[33] In these songs the threats of the Turkish, French or Swedish king, as the case may be, to the Russian *Car'* and the *Car'*'s replies closely parallel those of Mamaj and Maksimilian respectively. Compare the Russian *car'*'s reply to the boasts of the French king: —

"А мы столики поставим ему — пушки медные, а мы скатерти ему постелем — вольные пули, на закусочку поставим — каленых картеч, угощать его будут — канонерушки"[34] —

with Maksimilian's reply to Mamaj: —

" Дам я твоему дяденьке, королю Мамаю, дань. Только как ему понравится? Первая встреча — бомбы, картечи, стрелы гранены, ядра калены . . ."[35]

This convention also occurs in the *bylina Mamaevo poboišče* where Vasilij, Mamaj's son-in-law, is told to write: —

"ярлыки скорописные . . . с угрозами великими."[36]

(ii) Anika and Death

This scene occurs in almost all variants of *Car' Maksimilian.* In it the royal champion Anika in the midst of his boasting after victory is visited by the white-robed figure of Death who, in spite of all his pleading for mercy, strikes him down with her scythe, allowing him at most a few minutes in which to bid farewell to the world or to sing a favourite song for the last time.

Tales of the inevitable enemy Death, of the eternal combat between Death and Life, enjoyed widespread popularity in mediaeval Europe. For a time the theme was one of the most prominent in popular literature, inspiring many paintings, etchings and poems. It had its influence too upon the popular theatre, occurring, for example, in the English miracle and morality plays, as in the *Slaughter of the Innocents* when Death comes to Herod, or in *Everyman* where there is a close similarity to the mediaeval tales of the battle between Life and Death. The theatrical historian E.K. Chambers mentions a certain play, both history and morality, based on the *danse macabre* which was acted before Philip the Good at Bruges in 1449[37] and in 1510 a painter named Pietro Cosimo organised a macabre Triumph of Death, a pageant which paraded through the streets of Florence: "Upon the top of the chariot sat a figure with a scythe in his hand, representing Death, having under his feet many graves, from which appeared, half-way out, the bare bones of carcasses."[38]

The sixteenth century saw the appearance and growth of tales upon the theme of the contest of Life and Death in Russia — *Prenie Života so Smert'ju* or *Skazanie o nekoem čeloveke bogobojaznike* — which, originally translated from the German, gradually adapted themselves in the new milieu and evolved peculiarly Russian features. It is in these later versions that there are unmistakable similarities to the dramatic scene *Anika-voin i Smert'*. In the tales Life (*Život*) is represented as: —

> "Некий человек, воин удалой, езжа по полю по чистому и по роздолию широкому."[39]

He has not found anyone to fight with him for a long time and proclaims his valour and his great deeds: —

> "Многое время никого же себе имея противника и размышляя в себе: — Яко несть мне подобна на земли и прежде мене не бысть такова, яко же аз . . ."[40]

Death comes to him but he does not recognise her, calls her

> "Злообразная баба."[41]

She is carrying all sorts of instruments and weapons of torture,

> ". . . мечи, ножи, пилы, рожны, серпы, сечива, косы, бритвы, уды, теслы . . .",[42]

but Life refuses to be intimidated: —

> "Рече же ей живот: — Аз есми силен и храбр, и на ратех многия полки побиваю . . . а ты како ко мне едина пришла еси."[43]

When at last he realises that Death stands before him he falls to his knees and begs for mercy: —

> "— Дай же мне сроку, госпоже моя, на три дни, дабы аз просил у господа бога милости" . . .[44]

But Death merely replies: —

> "— Несть тебе строку не токмо на три дни, но и на три часы не будет,"[45]

whereupon she strikes him down with her scythe and the other implements.

This compares very closely with the text of the folk play, for like Life Anika, after his many battles, seeks a further challenger: —

> "— Хожу, стражду, по чистому полю,
> По широкому раздолью,
> Ищу себе встречного и поперечного,
> С кем бы я мог побиться, порубиться."[46]

Death comes up to him and he addresses her rudely: —

> "— Что ты за баба
> Что ты за пьяница?"

Finally Anika, like Life, is forced to plead for three years, months, days, etc., of respite: —

> "— Дай ты мне хоть три года пожить,
> Свои грехи замолить."[47]

Although in most versions of *Car' Maksimilian* Death's only weapon is her scythe there is one version in which there is a hint of the array of the mediaeval text. In Kostin's version Death has knives and files as well as the scythe.[48]

Anika has been the subject of many folk legends: he is supposed to have been a brigand, robber of monasteries and the subduer of many kings and knights, living to a great old age (220, 390 years). In some places he was equated with an infamous robber, executed in the reign of Peter I, the Brigand of Vologda. Anika appears too as the hero of folk tales, songs and spiritual verses (*duxovnye stixi*). In the folk ballad *Žil-byl Anika - voin* he sets off to capture Jerusalem, but Death in spite of offers of money and riches will not let him commit this sacrilegious act.[49]

The further popularity of Anika among the people is attested by his appearance on folk pictures, of which Rovinskij describes several in his major collection. The description of one of these, in which Anika, sword in hand, is mounted on his horse, closely corresponds to the *Car' Maksimilian* version and to the texts of the mediaeval tales.[50]

It has been suggested that the Russian folk hero may originally have sprung from a Byzantine tale about Digenis the Warrior (warrior in Greek being $\alpha \nu \iota \chi \eta \bar\iota o \varsigma$) and his famous exploits. But the tale as it appears in its mediaeval Russian version *Devgenievo dejanie*[51] seems to have little in common with Anika and his struggle with Death.

Scenes bearing some resemblance to those discussed above were not unknown in early Ukrainian and Russian dramatic literature. Among the Ukrainian interludes of the 18th century was an interlude of this type, *Intermedija na tri persony; smert', voin, xlopec.*[52] In moralising Russian academic plays too the abrupt appearance of Death in person before a sinner was a common element. Thus in *Carstvo natury ljudskoj* (1698) Death appears with a speech much resembling those of the mediaeval tales. Similarly, Death acts very much as a *deus ex machina* in the later academic plays from translated literature, as, for example, in *Kaleandr i Neonilda.*

There is one somewhat different version of this scene in *Car' Maksimilian* which really takes the form of parody. In Kallaš's 2nd variant[53] instead of Anika we find Fedot and Death. The scene follows essentially the same pattern except that Fedot is a comical character in whose mouth the brave words of Anika take on a humorous tone. This sort of aping of serious scenes was typical of the interludes of the academic theatre. The interlude, for example, might present a realistic peasant character drawn from everyday scenes familiar to the audience to correspond to an allegorical 'tiller of the soil', in the serious part of the drama.[54]

There would seem to be little doubt that the scene between Anika and Death in *Car' Maksimilian* was based upon a combination of the mediaeval *Contest between Life and Death* with the tales about the folk hero Anika. Its inclusion in the play may be due partly to a knowledge of the traditions of the academic theatre and perhaps even more so to the analogous scene in the *vertep* where Herod is justly felled by a mocking Death for all his wickedness. The influence of the *vertep* can be seen most clearly in the few versions of *Car' Maksimilian* in which it is the *Car'* himself who is killed by Death rather than Anika. In one of Vinogradov's texts,[55] the *Car'*, terror stricken, commands his warriors to defend him but Death strikes down their swords with a wave of her hand. In the same way Herod's warriors are powerless to defend their king.

(iii) The Black Arab

Blacking the face with soot was one of the most popular ways of disguising in the Russian Christmastide mummings. It is probable that the Black Arab of the folk play, who is similarly daubed, springs from the same source. Many peoples considered that the colour black and in particular the blackness derived from the soot and ashes of the fire was extremely powerful in warding off evil spirits. Figures with blackened faces were common in ritual games and processions all over Europe. In the sword dances of England, the Basque country, Spain, Portugal and others these characters became known as Moors (because of their black faces) and the battles of the sword dancers were explained as clashes between them and the Christians. It was assumed that these 'Moors' had in fact given their name to the dances — the Morris dance in England and the Moriscos of Spain and Portugal. However, many scholars[56] now believe that this was merely a rationalising of an already existing custom and that the blackened faces themselves gave rise to the title Moors rather than vice-versa. It is interesting to remember too that May-day (when the sword dances were often performed in England) was traditionally the day of chimneysweeps. It is probable then that the Black Arab from *Car' Maksimilian* belongs to a very ancient European ritual tradition.

(iv) The Zmejulan

The serpent (*zmej*) was one of the traditional enemies of the Russian knights in the epic tales or *byliny* (see e.g. *Aleša i zmej Gorynič* or *Dobrynja i zmej*). The Zmejulan of *Car' Maksimilian* is doubly serpent-like since the last part of his name *ulan* also means 'snake' in Persian. In the folk play, however, the character appears in human form, as one of the foreign knights who threaten Maksimilian and his kingdom. The terms *zmej* and *ulan* were both applied derogatively to the Tartars and other heathen peoples from the east who overran Russia in the Middle Ages and subjected her to several hundred years of foreign domination. These replaced the serpents as the traditional enemies of the *bogatyri* (knights) in the epic tales.

The snake was not only the symbol for the pagan enemy but for evil in general and the powers of darkness. It is as such that they appear on the whole in the fairy tales and epic poetry, possessed of extraordinary magical gifts and forbidden knowledge, inhabiting the frontiers of the known world and beyond.

(v) Mars and Venus

During the pre-Christian period, burlesques on the lives of the gods were a feature of popular dramatic literature and this continued into the Christian era. St. Cyprian, for instance, complained of the wanton Venus, and the adulterer Mars, being shown on stage.

The renewed interest in classical literature and ancient mythology brought to Europe by the Renaissance resulted in the reappearance of the gods as literary characters. Along with personified vices and virtues and abstract qualities they became implicated in the plots of the academic plays and even the neo-classical plays, discussing and influencing the fate of the heroes.

The lives of Mars and Venus seem to have been particularly popular as a dramatic subject and a number of plays on this theme have been recorded in seventeenth and eigtheenth century England, for example J. Weaver's "Mars and Venus" (1717) and P.A. Motteaux's "The Loves of Mars and Venus", performed in 1696 and 1697.

A similar phenomenon can be noted in Russian academic plays where gods and goddesses and qualities like Charity, Honour, Faith, etc., are often portrayed. Venus appears alongside Virtue, Religion and the Angels in *Aleksej čelovek Božij*. Mars is to be found in the historical school play *Drama o Ezekii*.[57] Both Mars and Venus together with the other gods on Olympus take an active part in the dénouement of *Kaleandr i Neonilda*.

c) The interludes

In Russia, interludes were originally short scenes of a humorous nature played in the intervals between the serious acts of the academic plays. They could be of two kinds: — firstly, they might in some way imitate the serious content of the preceding act, or they might be entirely independent of the rest of the play. The content of these interludes was drawn from popular anecdotes, from the comic tales of wandering mediaeval story tellers where characters and scenes from daily life were often depicted with satirical wit. Taken out of context these interludes were carried about the countryside and performed by poor seminarists trying to earn themselves a little extra money.

Comic interlude scenes were also found in the *vertep*, where they were no doubt inherited straight from the religious plays of Western Europe but, as has been seen, with the comic parts removed from their natural setting within the body of the play to form a separate part of the performance.

With time the interlude lost its connection with the academic theatre and became almost an independent genre, a name for any one-act play or scenes of comic or topical nature. Such playlets became extremely popular in the urban democratic theatre for instance, where they constantly attracted new characters and situations. When the Italian *commedia dell'arte* became popular in Russia in the eighteenth century, characters from it too were incorporated into the interlude repertoire.[58]

(i) The Jew (the tailor), the Cossack, the Devil

Since none of these three characters appears frequently in the Russian folk plays, but are on the other hand often to be found in the Ukrainian *vertep* and south Russian popular literature, it is reasonable to assume that they have entered plays like *Car' Maksimilian* and *Lodka* as a result of southern influence. The variants in which they occur are often, in fact, from the southern regions, as for example Abramov's variant of *Car' Maksimilian* which is from the northern Ukraine, or Kallaš's first variant from the boundary government of Černigov; in both of these the Jew and the Cossack play a part in the comic interludes. One of the songs the Jew is made to sing in the Abramov variant: —

> "Танцует жид ходором перед паном Федором. И задком и передком перед паном Федорком." —[59]

is a variant of one well known in the *vertep*. It occurs, for instance, in Vinogradov's *Velikorusskij vertep* (p. 375) and in an eighteenth century Russo-Polish variant described by I. Franko.[60]

The tailor appears only in a very few variants of *Car' Maksimilian*, and *Lodka* and that south Russian amalgam of the *vertep* with *Maksimilian* known as *Tron*. He is usually a Jew, an indication of Jewish interest in the cloth trade in Russia. There is a scene in the play *Ataman*[61] where a Jew is approached and asked about his profession: —

> "Занимаюсь красным,"

he answers. *Krasnyj tovar* was an old term for textile manufacturing and the *ataman* jokingly suggests that he should sew *kaftans* for the whole robber band. In Gruzinskij's variant of *Car' Maksimilian* (p. 165) the tailor is called upon briefly to sew funeral garments for Adol'f and in Vinogradov's second variant (pp. 85-86) he has to make a coat (*tulup*) for the old gravedigger as a reward for his services. In such scenes it is the Jew's professional, rather than ethnic or religious peculiarities which are depicted. However, in several other texts the attitude towards him appears in quite a different light.

In both Abramov's and Kallaš's first variant of *Maksimilian* there occur again the mockery and hostility towards the Jewish character, religion, dress and customs typical of the Polish and Ukrainian *vertep*. The first play ends with several comic scenes in which the Jew is made to dance and sing for the general amusement of the audience. In both there are the familiar inferences about the Jewish 'national characteristics' of cowardice and avarice: —

> " — Правда, Янкель, что у тебя много денег?
> Жид. — Ай, вей, васе царское и императорское велицество! Яки у зида гроси, хиба только одни воси!"[62]

In Abramov's variant the Jew joins forces with that other antipathetic character, the gypsy, in attempting to rob the unconscious body of the Cossack, but as they start to draw off his long boots the Cossack, as bold and offensive as ever, leaps to his feet and sends them flying. The Jew is addressed in a tone and manner which express in forceful terms the sense of superiority and scorn of the masters for the suppressed and alien minority. The Cossack and other characters in Abramov's variant address him most of the time as "Жидовская морда," and both variants are full of latent violence.

In one White Russian text, however, the Jew plays an entirely different role. Here, he is an ubiquitous character who bobs up at the most unexpected and inappropriate moments, mimics the other players, twists their words and gets in everyone's way (e.g. when he offers to help the gravedigger remove Mamaj's corpse he merely manages to trip him up).[63] He performs a similar function to the 'devil' in Mjakutin's variant. The 'devil' too keeps interfering with the plot. As well as playing tricks with the gravedigger's horse he pushes himself between the old man and his wife as they try to kiss and puts his own hand forward along with hers when she is offered some snuff which makes the gravedigger retort indignantly: —

"Вот она, тут и была с двумя руками."[64]

The devil in the Russian and Ukrainian folk theatre was not necessarily a sinister character, although in the *vertep* his main task was to assist Death in dragging Herod off to Hell. In the role of an ubiquitous and interfering shadow, however, he performs a function similar to that of his ancestor, the devil of the mediaeval miracle plays and later of the academic theatre. His role is an ambiguous one. He is a jolly, comic character amusing the audience with his tricks, yet these tricks are often macabre. He is, too, a reminder and a warning to those whose way of life is not as blameless as it might be!

(ii) The gravedigger

Among the most frequent and popular comic scenes in *Car' Maksimilian* are those involving the old gravedigger, known variously as Mark, Marko, Markuška. He is always reluctant to answer the summons to clear the bodies off the stage and once there manages to find many excuses for doing no work. He is usually highly disregardful of the *Car'* 's rank, bargains for wages with him, disobeys him, mimics him, sits on his throne and, in spite of Maksimilian's threats, seems to enjoy the same degree of immunity as the mediaeval court jesters. Sometimes he is accompanied by his old woman; they bicker at each other, take snuff, fool about, try to measure the corpse for a coffin and generally manhandle it to such an extent that in one variant the supposedly dead Adol'f causes great consternation by leaping up and biting the old man's finger.

The most distinctive things about the gravedigger's appearance are his hump-back, his sheepskin coat turned inside out and his generally tattered look. The following description is typical: —

"С длинной клочковатой бородой, в полушубке овчиной наружу, сгорбленный, с палкой в руке."[65]

In the Russian folk theatre he has many 'brothers'; the hump-backed ritual bear, the old hunchback Semik, the tattered old beggars of the Christmastide mummings.[66] His old woman too may be seen again in the grotesque figures of the *kikimora*, the witch and Semičixa.[67] The old *ded* and *baba* who sometimes took part in the secular half of the *vertep* also have much in common with these characters. In one text of the *vertep* with human as opposed to puppet actors an old peasant converses as impudently with Napoleon (!) as Marko does with *Car'* Maksimilian and, like him too, misunderstands, either deliberately or through deafness, all the questions put to him. Not only his character and actions but also his appearance resemble those of Marko. He is described as "a *hump-backed* peasant dressed in rags."[68]

Similar figures can of course be found in the ritual or folk drama of other countries, for example, the hunchback fool of the English *St. George* plays who has a number of titles, Red Jack, Happy Jack, Big Head, Beelzebub. The hump-backed clown *Dossemus* was one of the stock masks of the Atellan theatre of ancient Greece and the figure seems to have retained its popularity through the ages. Names like Morychos, Momar, Marikas, etc. were frequently given to the comic figures of the ancient mimes, and it has been suggested that these should be connected etymologically with *moros*, the common generic name for a mimic fool.[69] One wonders if there could be any similarity between these names and that of the Russian gravedigger, the mimic fool of the Russian folk theatre.[70] The gravedigger's female companion may also be descended from one of the stock characters of the ancient theatre. Allardyce Nicoll describes the haglike female counterparts of the ancient *moros* and suggests that "the mime, until its latest days, loved this witch-like old woman, a descendant of whom in the spirit is to be discovered in the Mome Helwis of mediaeval times."[71]

(iii) The doctor

Another of the basic comic scenes in *Car' Maksimilian* involves the doctor and sometimes his assistant. Two separate episodes are to be distinguished here, the first in which the doctor tries to cure the old gravedigger's aches and pains and the second in which he is called upon to revive the fallen knights. The doctor introduces himself in much the same way as the *Car'* and the warriors except that his speech is in a humorous tone: —

"Вот я доктор-лекарь, из-под каменного моста аптекарь."

He reels off a list of his accomplishments, of the miraculous cures he has worked: —

"— Не даром про меня прошла слава, что я вылечил не мало: десятков пять-шесть в сырой земле есть. Ко мне ходят на ногах, а уходят на дровнях."[72]

In the following extract he details his somewhat peculiar methods of treatment: —

"— Умею лечить,
Умею тащить,
Умею летать,
Умею с белым светом разлучать!
Живые места вырезаю
И на место их мертвые вставляю,
Кровь мечу,
Баб лечу,
Глаза выкалываю,
Титьки подкалываю,
Всякое дело умею."[73]

In the first episode, the gravedigger pretends to be ill in order to get out of burying Adol'f and Brambeus. The doctor begins by asking him where the pain is. The old man mentions various parts of the body — head, eyes, nose, stomach, back, legs, teeth — and the doctor offers suitably inept cures: —

"— Взять твой нос,
Оторвать и выкинуть на мороз
И будет здоров твой нос!"[74]

or: —

"— В это пузо
Надо набить тридцать три арбуза —
Вот и заживет твое пузо!"[75]

Eventually, the old man is cured, by fright if not by the doctor's suggestions. A different method of treatment is found in Berkov's variant where the doctor tries to make his patient repeat certain spells after him: —

"Доктор. — Ну, говори за мной, старик,
Зубы мои зубы,
Отвалитесь, нос и губы."
. . . .
— Ну говори за мной.
Зубы мои и десны,
Болите зиму и весну."[76]

Additional humour is brought to the scene by the doctor's 'examination' of the patient. A good example of this is to be found in one of Ončukov's texts. The old man cannot tell exactly where the pain is and keeps on saying, "Higher! Lower!" until the doctor loses patience with him and gives him a slap with his sabre.[77] This scene as might be imagined was primarily one of rude, rough humour.

In the second episode, although the basic intent is still comedy a faintly sinister note creeps in. In a number of texts (see Kallaš, Variant 1, Volkov, Vinogradov, Variant 3), an actual resurrection from the dead takes place. These scenes are of particular interest since they connect the Russian play not only with the beginnings of ritual drama in Russia itself[78] but also with a widespread tradition in European folklore, in particular with the English folk play *St. George*.[79]

The first of the comic doctor episodes in *Car' Maksimilian* probably owes a lot to the comic dialogues of the urban democratic theatre, where the language and approach was very similar. For example in one such dialogue a gypsy quack doctor advises an old man with a headache after shaving his head: —

> "Затылок огнем пожарить," "об угол ударитца," "в темя ударить обухом,"

while in another a French doctor boasts: —

> " — Ко мне приведут на ногах, а от меня повезут на дровнях."[80]

The second episode, however, the resurrection scene, finds its parallel in European folklore. A death and resurrection scene with the participation of a doctor occurred in the spring dramatic rituals of many countries. According to Frazer, "in some parts of Swabia on Shrove Tuesday Dr. Iron-Beard professes to bleed a sick man who thereupon falls as dead to the ground; but the doctor at last restores him to life by blowing air into him through a tube."[81] In some of the English sword dances a doctor is summoned to resuscitate a character who has been accidentally killed. In the Basque mascarades there is the same scene again. There, the doctor tells boastfully of his travels, of the distant countries in which he learnt his work. "Après avoir fait le tour de la Prusse et de LA RUSSIE, de l'Angleterre et de la Turquie je suis revenu chez moi."[82] The Russian doctor describes his travels likewise: —

> "Был я в Италии, был я и далее . . .".

The closest and most interesting analogy to the Russian play can be found in the English folk play *St. George* and a comparison between this and *Car' Maksimilian* will be given in the following chapter.

The extreme diversity of sources upon which the various scenes and characters of *Car' Maksimilian* are based is a strong indication that it should not be regarded as an adaptation from any particular tale or play as some scholars have suggested, but that it is in fact a compilation of items some of literary, some of folk origin, which, to begin with, may not even have been connected.

In uniting these diverse scenes into a single dramatic spectacle the creators of the folk play have been indebted to the traditions of both written and oral literature.

NOTES

1. For the sake of convenience all texts of the play *Car' Maksimilian* in this and succeeding chapters are referred to by an abbreviated title. Full details of all the plays may be found in the bibliography pp. 251-252.
2. See e.g. Abramov; Gruzinskij; Kostin; Ončukov, Variant 1.
3. Vinogradov, Variant 3.
4. *Supra*, pp. 74-77.
5. See e.g. Berkov, *Russkij fol'klor*; Vinogradov, Variant 5; Mjakutin.
6. Vinogradov, Variant 3, p. 239; Gruzinskij, p. 165.
7. See, e.g., Vinogradov's Variant 2, p. 81, and Kostin, p. 111.
8. Protopop A. Sulockij, "Seminarskij teatr v starinu v Tobol'ske", *Čtenija v imperatorskom obščestve istorii i drevnostej rossijskix pri Moskovskom universitete*, Book 2, Part 5 (April-June) (Moscow, 1870), p. 157.
9. Vsevolodskij-Gerngross, *Russkaja ustnaja narodnaja drama*, p. 100.
10. P., "*Car' Maksimilian*", *Iskra* No. 6 (St. Petersburg, 1863), pp. 82-85.
11. Jozef Gołabek, "*Cár Maksymilian*: Widowisko ludowe na Rusi," Polska akademia umiejętności, *Prace komisji etnograficznej*, No. 17 (Kraków, 1938), p. 20.
12. N.E. Ončukov, "Narodnaja drama na severe," *Izvestija otdelenija russkogo jazyka i slovesnosti imperatorskoj akademii nauk*, Vol. 14 (St. Petersburg, 1910), p. 219.
13. See, e.g. the Gruzinskij, Abramov and Volkov variants.
14. *Supra*, pp. 103 and 105.
15. Ončukov, Variant 1, p. 29.
16. Abramov, p. 32.
17. E.R. Romanov (Ed.), *Belorusskij sbornik*, Vol. 1, Issue 5 (Kiev, 1891), pp. 273-283.
18. V.V. Kallaš, "K istorii narodnogo teatra: *Car' Maksimilian*" (Moscow, 1899), p. 3. Offprint from *Etnografičeskoe obozrenie* Book 39 (Moscow, 1898).
19. N.S. Tixonravov, "*Nikitino mučen'e*", *Pamjatniki otrečennoj russkoj literatury*, Vol. 2 (Moscow, 1863), p. 15.
20. Kuz'mina, *Russkij demokratičeskij teatr*, p. 71.
21. P.N. Berkov, "Verojatnyj istočnik narodnoj p'esy *O care Maksimiliane i ego nepokornom syne Adol'fe*," *Trudy otdela drevne-russkoj literatury A N SSSR*, Vol. 13 (Moscow-Leningrad, 1957), pp. 308-311.
22. Vsevolodskij-Gerngross, *Russkaja ustnaja narodnaja drama*, p. 102.
23. Morozov, *Istorija russkogo teatra*, pp. 284-286.
24. Vinogradov, Variant 3, p. 202.
25. V.N. Peretc (Ed.), *Pamjatniki russkoj dramy epoxi Petra Velikogo* (St. Petersburg, 1903), pp. 1-387.
26. *Ibid.*, p. 464.
27. Berkov, *Russkaja narodnaja drama*, p. 284.
28. Vinogradov, Variant 3, p. 207.
29. Peretc, *Pamjatniki russkoj dramy*, p. 349.
30. Vinogradov, Variant 1, p. 33.
31. Peretc, *Pamjatniki russkoj dramy*, p. 3.
32. Kostin, p. 103.

33. Lopatin, pp. 148 and 154.
34. *Ibid.*, p. 148.
35. Ončukov, Variant 1, p. 38.
36. V.Ja. Propp and B.N. Putilov (Ed.), *Byliny*, Vol. 1 (Moscow, 1958), p. 175.
37. Sir Edmund K. Chambers, *The mediaeval stage*, Vol. 2 (Oxford, 1903), p. 153.
38. Sir John Hawkins, *History of Music* (Vol. 3) (London, 1776), p. 448.
39. R.P. Dmitrieva (Ed.), *Povesti o spore žizni i smerti* (Moscow – Leningrad, 1964), p. 179.
40. *Ibid.*, p. 175.
41. *Ibid.*, p. 176.
42. *Ibid.*, p. 172.
43. *Ibid., loc. cit.*
44. *Ibid.*, p. 177.
45. *Ibid., loc. cit.*
46. Ončukov, Variant 1, p. 46.
47. Vinogradov, Variant 2, p. 93.
48. Kostin, p. 115.
49. A.M. Astaxova (Ed.), *Narodnye ballady* (Moscow – Leningrad, 1963), p. 224.
50. Rovinskij, Book 4, p. 553.
51. V.D. Kuz'mina (Ed.), *Devgenievo dejstvo* (Moscow, 1962).
52. Beleckij, p. 89.
53. Kallaš, Variant 2, pp. 17-18.
54. Beleckij, pp. 86-87.
55. Vinogradov, Variant 5, pp. 198-199.
56. See e.g. Chambers, *The mediaeval stage*, Vol. I, p. 199.
57. Peretc, *Pamjatniki russkoj dramy*, pp. 400-401 etc.
58. See e.g. the eleven interludes describing the adventures of Harlequin in P.N. Tixanov, *Odinnadtsat' intermedij XVIII veka* (St. Petersburg, 1915).
59. Abramov, p. 28.
60. Franko, Vol. 72, p. 23.
61. Drizen, p. 272.
62. Kallaš, Variant 1, p. 11.
63. Romanov, p. 280.
64. Mjakutin, p. 286.
65. Kallaš, Variant 1, p. 10.
66. See e.g. *Supra* pp. 14 and 23.
67. See e.g. *Supra* pp. 6-7.
68. Malinka, "Zivoj vertep", p. 39.
69. Allardyce Nicoll, *Masks, mimes and miracles* (London, 1931), p. 28.
70. Perhaps, however, Marko owes his name to a more prosaic although no less intriguing source. In Rovinskij's *Russkie narodnye kartinki*, in a list of saints from the Kievan *Pečerskaja Lavra*, there is a reference to a certain "*Prepodobnyj Marko grobokopatel'* "; Rovinskij, Book 4, p. 763.
71. Nicoll, p. 28.
72. Kallaš, Variant 2, p. 16.
73. Vinogradov, Variant 3, p. 154.
74. Vinogradov, Variant 2, p. 88.
75. Vinogradov, Variant 1, p. 48.
76. Berkov, *Russkij fol'klor*, pp. 352-353.
77. Ončukov, Variant 1, p. 28.
78. *Supra*, pp. 9 and 30-31.
79. *Infra*, p. 181.
80. Kuz'mina, *op. cit.*, p. 117.
81. Sir James G. Frazer, *The golden bough* (Abridged ed., London, 1923), p. 307.
82. Violet Alford, "The Basque masquerade", *Folklore*, No. 39 (London, 1928), p. 80.

CHAPTER VIII

"CAR' MAKSIMILIAN" AND THE "ST. GEORGE" PLAYS OF ENGLAND

In spite of its obvious connections with written literature of one sort and another *Car' Maksimilian* must be regarded as an integral part of an oral rather than a literary tradition. Like the other plays in the repertoire the text of *Car' Maksimilian* was rarely written down but was transmitted orally from one generation to the next. This task was performed by one of the most experienced actors of the troupe, often the person playing the part of Maksimilian himself. The folk plays reveal the same balance between improvisation on the one hand and, on the other, the rigid adherence of its creators to the norms of traditional style inherited from their forefathers, which is typical of most works of oral literature.

Abramov, in the introduction to his text of *Car' Maksimilian* underlines the characteristic deference to tradition of the folk actor. He tells us that most of the actors and especially those playing serious roles were required to have their words by heart and that improvisation was not permitted. Only in the case of some of the comic characters, Markuška the gravedigger, the gypsy and others, was a relaxation of this rule possible. These characters were allowed to interpolate their own jokes and remarks on topical events.[1]

This attention to exact repetition may be considered one of the reasons for some of the more confused passages of the text of *Car' Maksimilian* and other folk plays where words have been reproduced parrot-fashion by an actor who did not fully hear or understand them. Rather than alter the accepted text the meaningless phrases have been repeated and further distorted until garbled passages like the following version of a popular ballad are arrived at: —

> "— Я в темницу удаляюсь
> С распрекрасных здешних мест.
> Сколько горестей терпел я . . .
> А в разлуке тяжесть есть.
> Зоставляю, друг любезный,
> Зоставляю для того,
> Что дороже есть милее
> И прекраснее всего."[2]

The irregular verse form in which *Car' Maksimilian* is written also indicates that the roots of the play are to be found in a popular or folk tradition rather than in any of the more serious genres of literary endeavour.

Anyone reading a text of *Car' Maksimilian* would gradually become aware that it was written neither in pure prose nor in pure verse. He would notice, for instance, that passages of apparent prose had suddenly taken on a definite rhythm of their own and a definite rhyme pattern. It was because of this irregularity of the metrical structure of the play, because of its obvious lack of a specific metre and apparent lack of syllabic organisation that scholars for many years considered it to be written in a sort of rhythmic or rhyming prose. It is in fact written in *raešnyj stix*, a primitive verse form used in the 18th century, the most likely period of the genesis of the folk play, almost exclusively in popular and folk literature, particularly of a comic or satirical nature. Although a few of the plays in the later repertoire of the academic theatre employed a sort of rhythmic prose or a mixture of prose and verse the vast majority were written in syllabic verse and if even the 'serious' parts of *Car' Maksimilian* had been adapted from a hagiographical play one would expect at least traces of the syllabic verse structure to have remained.

Raešnyj stix was so called because of its extensive use in the humorous monologues of the fairground comics and puppeteers (*raešnyj ded*) of the 18th century. It is, however, an offshoot of a much older poetic device. From about the 15th century in Old-Russian prose writings of a kind where legal precision or strict accuracy were not prerequisites some writers were attempting to achieve a more pleasing effect by organising the balance and rhythmic flow of the lines. It became common to place verbal constructions at the end of the clause or sentence and this automatically gave rise to a primitive morphological type of rhyme. The gradual awakening of writers to the stylistic possibilities of this custom, perhaps under the influence too of Byzantine rhymed prose, led to conscious refinements and to a more symmetrical arrangement of the words between the rhyming endings. By the seventeenth century the better examples of this style were being recognised by writers such as Simeon Polockij as poetic rather than prose forms. These early attempts at versification, ousted in serious writing by the appearance of syllabic verse in the latter half of the 17th century also bear some resemblance to the verse structure of certain types of Russian folk literature. In the *byliny* too, the occasional rhymes arise from syntactic parallels and the rhythmic flow of the line comes from the three or four major stresses rather than the number of syllables or the metre.

The most constant thing about *raešnyj stix* is its rhyme pattern which consists mainly of rhyming couplets, but sometimes extending into 3, 4 or even more lines, all with a single rhyme scheme, for example: —

"А вот и я, развеселый потешник,
Известный столичный раешник,
Со своею потешною панорамою:
Картинки верчу — поворачиваю,
Публику обморачиваю,
Себе пятачки заколачиваю![3]

The couplets, however, may be freely interspersed with nonrhyming lines. A certain amount of internal rhyme can also be found and alliteration is quite frequent.

There is no metre and the divergence between the number of syllables in each line shows that the verse structure does not depend upon syllabic equality. But it is not true to say that there is no attempt at syllabic organisation at all, for within the couplet the variation in the number of syllables per line is rarely greater than 1/2 whereas the difference from couplet to couplet can be as much as 5/18 or 3/19.

Apart from the rhyme, the other most constant feature is the stress pattern. If only the major stresses are counted (as in the *byliny*) it will be found that there are usually 2 per line, with a common variant of 3 and occasional exceptions. The line thus falls into 2 (or 3) parts each containing a major stress.

The looseness of this structure gave its users considerable scope for improvising, using their wit and natural talent for rhyme and word selection to obtain the greatest effect.

In general *Car' Maksimilian* is full of words, phrases and constructions habitually used in folk literature in the singing of songs and the telling of tales and epic verses. Constant epithets which helped to crystallise an image in the minds of the audience are to be found in the folk plays as well as in other branches of folk literature. Tautological constructions and retardation by repetition of various kinds, a device constantly used in the *byliny* are also common in the folk play.

In the search for *Car' Maksimilian*'s origins in some long-forgotten piece of written literature the play's position with regard to the folk theatre of Europe as a whole has been largely ignored. Nevertheless, an examination of west European dramatic folk literature reveals some interesting parallels. There are striking similarities between parts of *Car' Maksimilian* and the English folk play *St. George.*

Like *Maksimilian*, *St. George* was a Christmas play performed as a regular part of village entertainment over the festive season by enthusiastic groups of amateur players or mummers who toured the big houses of the neighbourhood. Performances in both Russia and England were prefaced by the polite request of the actors for permission to act their play and rounded off by their requests for remuneration in the form of small sums of money or food and drink.

The action of the English play begins when the hero, St. George (King George, King William, King Alfred, etc.) steps forward, introduces himself to the audience, praises his own valour and challenges any man to stand against him: —

> Here comes I, King George, the valiant man,
> With naked sword and spear in hand,
> I fought the fiery dragon and brought him to slaughter,
> And by these means I won the King of Egypt's daughter.
> And what mortal man dare to stand
> Before me with sword in hand
> I'll slay him and cut him as small as flies,
> And send him to Jamaica to make mince pies.[4]

The rest of the play then develops along very similar lines to the plot of *Car' Maksimilian* after Adol'f has been executed and removed from the stage. A series of kings and knights from distant lands (the Turkish knight, the Prussian King, the Black Prince of Paradise, etc.) enter and challenge the champion just as they do Anika, each in turn boasting of his prowess. They are all vanquished by St. George.

When all the enemies have been conquered a doctor is called in to cure the slain and wounded. This character may be seen as one of the major links not only between *Car' Maksimilian* and *St. George* but between the Russian play and a ritual dramatic cycle known throughout Europe. Both in dress and speech the English Dr. Brown (Dr. Martin Dennis, Dr. Lamb, Dr. Ball) closely resembles his Russian counterpart.[5] E.K. Chambers describes him thus: —

> "The Doctor's 'piked' hat of Cornwall has usually become a top hat, but his appearance remains professional, with black clothes, spectacles and a black bag."[6]

In Berkshire variants he was similarly attired and carried a black bag, a box of pills or bottles of 'reviving' mixture, a pair of pliers or sometimes a bladder on the end of a stick with which he would knock anyone who came too close.[7] Both doctors reel off a list of unlikely diseases they can cure and describe their dubious skills. The English doctor boasts: —

> "I can cure the itch, the stitch, the palsy and the gout,
> all the pains within and all the pains without.
> Bring me an old woman four score years and ten,
> if she has not a tooth in her head, I'll bring her round young again."[8]

In *Car' Maksimilian* the Russian *lekar'* makes similar claims: –

"Болятки вынимаю,
Чирьи вставляю,
Старых на молодых переделываю."[9]

A comic scene follows the English doctor's entrance during which he attempts to revive his mortally wounded patients by the use of some special medicine or treatment. In a Berkshire variant, for example, he sprinkles two of the dead combatants with some magical potion, muttering at the same time: —

"A drop on thy heart, a drop on thy skull,
Arise, arise oh Turkish knight,
And go to thy Turkey land to fight."[10]

A revival of the dead occurs frequently also in *Car' Maksimilian* as well as in the robber play *Lodka* and *Car' Irod*. In the Volkov variant of *Maksimilian* there occurs the unusual circumstance of the *car'* himself being killed by Mamaj. An *English* doctor is called in to cure him: —

"Доктор: Подай живительных духов!"
(His assistant brings the potion.)
"Доктор (points at Maximilian): Спрысни, сбрызни,
на мороз поставь и будет здрав!"

As the doctor's assistant scatters the drops on him Maksimilian revives, exclaiming: —

"Ох, как я уснул!"[11]

Even the actual physical appearance of the actors and their methods of presenting the play resemble those of *Maksimilian*. In many instances there are the same quasi-military uniforms liberally covered with decorations, pasteboard crowns, wooden swords and primitive make-up, although of course unique features can also be found, such as the tall, conical caps often worn by the English players and the ribbons and streamers which were fastened to every available space on both hats and clothing. In 1951 the English Folk Song and Dance Society made a film of the Symondsbury mumming play. In it the costumes of all the 'serious' characters were in the traditional military style with red, white or blue uniforms, the trousers having military stripes down the side of the leg. The warriors wore imitation helmets decorated with paper streamers. Their jackets were decorated with rosettes and medals and they had a broad ribbon across their shoulders and chest. St. George, for instance, was in a white uniform with a red ribbon across the shoulder. His jacket was covered with medals and had epaulettes cut from black and red paper. He wore a tall hat, conical in shape and covered with red paper streamers. A red sash round his waist, a sword and long black boots completed his outfit. The similarity between this description and the costumes of *Car' Maksimilian* is not difficult to see.[12]

The acting methods too, and the grouping of the characters on stage in a straight line or a semi-circle, from which each steps forward to declaim his part, the foot-stamping and sword-waving — all these remind one strongly of *Car' Maksimilian*.[13]

Playlets, games and dances involving either duelling scenes or a resurrection (or both together) and characters similar to those occurring in *Car' Maksimilian* or *St. George* are of course common to the whole of European folklore. In England itself, quite separate from the *St. George* play, but similar to it in several respects, there are the traditional sword-dances or Morris dances. Elements common to *St. George* and *Maksimilian* are to be found in several of the celebrated Basque dances, *Danse du chef mort*, *Danse du coffre*, *Danse des epées*, *Danse du verre*, etc. According to E.K. Chambers the sword-dance can be dated at least to the times of Tacitus. It was later adopted into the repertoire of the mediaeval minstrels of which our first records refer to 1350.[14] Scenes involving a ritual death with or without an actual battle and a subsequent resurrection by the doctor are also to be found in the spring agricultural rites of several European countries.

A.J.B. Wace's accounts of mumming plays in the southern Balkans reveal the same familiar pattern. The scenes which he describes were performed in a number of different villages with local variations and by different ethnic groups including Bulgarians, Vlachs, Albanians and gypsies. An account sent by an eyewitness of scenes played by nomadic villagers from Semarina, the largest of the Vlach villages in the Pindus, is particularly interesting since in it there occur not only the duel, the death, the doctor and the cure but also the fool who like the Russian gravedigger gets in everyone's way and creates comic situations around the corpse: —

> "You would see on one side a ring dance of brides and bride-grooms dancing to the hoarse notes of the pipe and the heavy beat of the drum. The old woman with her baby in her arms sat in the middle and rocked the child to sleep. The Punches (Karag' ozŭ) would do all sorts of ridiculous tricks to raise a laugh and annoy the brides. The robber chief (or bridegrooms) would often get angry when they saw this and rushed to beat them; often they pretended to kill them and they would fall down dead. Then came the doctor's turn. He would come in with a paper of ashes, some garlic and an onion or two, and would begin his work. First he felt the pulse, then he listened at the soles of the feet to see if the heart was beating. He would rub the eyes with garlic or an

onion. All the time the old woman was weeping at the dead man's head. Then another Punch would come, who, after looking at what the doctor was doing, and seeing that he was doing nothing would get to work himself. He would drag the dead man by the feet along the ground a little, hit him with a stick on the chest and indulge in other horseplay not infrequently obscene, at his expense. Then the dead man would jump to his feet again alive.[15]

The origins of all these plays and scenes have been the subject of much controversy. Some scholars hold that the sword-dances and duels are a relic of ancient military practices, a sort of war cult, while others find in them an analogy to the spring rites where summer struggles with winter and the dying year is inevitably revived by the forces of spring. When comparing *Car' Maksimilian* with *St. George* and the sword-dances or the ritual dramas of other countries one cannot speak in terms of derivation of the one from the other nor even of common origins, but it seems unquestionable that the Russian folk play *Car' Maksimilian* must be considered as belonging to a dramatic and ritual tradition common to most of Europe.

NOTES

1. Abramov, p. 2.
2. *Ibid.*, p. 12.
3. Alekseev-Jakovlev, p. 55.
4. Stuart Pigott, "Mummers' plays", *Folklore*, No. 40 (London, 1929), p. 263.
5. For a description of the Russian doctor see *Infra*, p. 204.
6. Sir Edmund K. Chambers, *The English folk-play* (Oxford, 1933), p. 86.
7. Stuart Pigott, "Berkshire mummers plays", *Folklore*, No. 39 (London, 1928), p. 272.
8. "Mummers' play", *Notes and Queries*, No. 146 (London, 1924), p. 437.
9. Vinogradov, Variant 2, p. 87.
10. Pigott, "Mummers' plays", pp. 267-268.
11. Volkov, p. 335.
12. For description of the Russian actors see *Infra*, pp. 197-201
13. *Infra*, pp. 213-214, 216, 217-218.
14. Chambers, *The mediaeval stage*, Vol. 1, pp. 190-191.
15. A.J.B. Wace, "Mumming plays in the southern Balkans", *Annual of the British school at Athens*, No. 19 (session 1912-1913) (London, 1913), p. 255.

PART FOUR

THE FOLK ACTOR AND HIS ART

CHAPTER IX

THE FOLK ACTOR

Although the history and content of the Russian folk theatre have been discussed at some length in this study, little has been said of the people — actors, producers, costume makers and their large following of helpers, without whose constant enthusiasm and active participation the plays themselves would long ago have disappeared and been forgotten.

Little is known of Russia's earliest semiprofessional entertainers, the *skomoroxi*, counterparts of the strolling players and *jongleurs* of mediaeval western Europe and the skilled nucleus around which a popular dramatic tradition was beginning to emerge centuries before the arrival of the literary theatre in Russia at the end of the seventeenth century.

The activities of the *skomoroxi* are reasonably well documented from the eleventh century. They were perhaps best known for their skill with the *gusli*, a stringed instrument held upon the lap. We know that Prince Svjatopolk kept such musicians at his court at the beginning of the eleventh century. One of the ancient Chroniclers describes him as: —

"Любяй вино пити с гусльми и с младыми светники."[1]

Again in the eleventh century Theodosius, abbot of the Kievan Monastery of the Caves from 1051 until his death in 1074, a man renowned for his adherence to the ascetic way of life and his abhorrence of all earthly pleasures, upbraided Prince Jaroslav for watching and encouraging the antics of the *skomoroxi*. Coming into his apartments one day he found: —

"Многих играющих перед ним: овых гусльные гласы испускающих, иных органьные писки гласящих, иных же мусикииские, и тако всех веселящихся, яко же обычай есть пред князем."[2]

The imaginary epic hero Dobrynja Nikitič was famed for his *gusli* playing and those *byliny* which tell of his masquerading as a *skomorox* paint a vivid picture of the artistry of such musicians whose presence gladdened the hearts of prince and warriors at the court of Vladimir: —

"А ведь начал струнушки ён натягивать,
А по гусёлышкам да похаживать:
А ведь припевочок завел Добрынюшка от Киева,
А ведь доводит Добрыня до Чернигова;
А ведь и вси на пиру позатихнули, —
А ведь такой игры ввек не слыхано,
А век не слыхано и не видано."[3]

The term *skomorox* covers a wide variety of artistic accomplishments. Earning a precarious living by his skills the *skomorox* had to be a jack-of-all-trades able to provide a choice of entertainments as the need arose. But the majority of them no doubt specialised in one or two fields. Apart from the *gusli* players, who sang to their own accompaniment about the wonders of the distant lands they had visited and of the exploits of heroes, there were others who were acrobats and tight-rope walkers, jugglers and conjurors. The Church considered these entertainers to be in league with the devil and many of the ordinary people accredited them with supernatural powers. Conjuring and magical tricks were also used, although for different purposes, by the *kudesniki* and *volxvy* (wizards of Old Russia), such as those who, as we are told in the Chronicles, by their cunning and sleight of hand caused the death of many innocent people in the Rostov *oblast'* in the year 1071.[4] It is not surprising therefore that the Church viewed these particular activities of the *skomoroxi* with such suspicion. Exhibitions of dancing, not always of a respectable kind, was another of the entertainments offered by the *skomoroxi*.

The *skomorox* entertained both high and low and catered for all tastes. At the royal court and the houses of princes he played the *gusli*, sang songs and told tales; in the village market places and on the streets his humour was cruder and broader, his antics unrestrained, his songs often bawdy, and his dancing obscene. He was a perennial favourite at village festivities, taking an active role in all the available types of entertainment, training and leading bears and playing the music for their clumsy dances, showing puppets and, at Christmas and Shrovetide, leading the games, dressed in the traditional animal mask. It was for their prominent role in these remnants of pagan ritual, which seemed to awaken ancient instincts, luring people away from decorous behaviour and Christian devotion to heathen practices and orgies of often flagrantly immoral revelry, that the Church authorities mainly persecuted them. Nestor, for instance, writes thus: —

". . . но сими дьявол льстит и другими нравы всячьскими лестьми, пребавляя ны от Бога, трубами и скомрахи, гусльми и русалья. Видим бо игрища утолчена и людей много множьство, яко упихати начнут друг друга, позоры деюще от беса замышленного дела."[5]

These games and maskings were referred to as *besovskie igrišča* or *pozory* and all the entertainments with which the *skomoroxi* were connected were in general described as "of the devil" (*besovskoe*).

The earliest mentions of the *skomoroxi* are accompanied by accusations and condemnations from the Church. During the fifteenth, sixteenth and seventeenth centuries these were followed by direct prohibition against participating in their amusements and against encouraging or inviting the presence of the strolling players. Severe punishments were threatened for those who disobeyed. The most destructive and conclusive of these prohibitions was *Car'* Aleksej Mixailovič's order (*ukaz*) of 1648 which forbade people to take part in a wide variety of entertainments including not only the more obvious maskings and games, leading of bears and goats, dancing and singing, frequenting the *skomoroxi* and all the non-Christian activities connected with Christmas and Shrove, but also such apparently innocuous pastimes as swinging, chess, telling stories, hand clapping and boxing. All musical instruments were to be handed over to the authorities, broken and burned. Those caught persistently contravening the act were liable to be sent into exile.

As a result of such persecution, by the middle of the seventeenth century, the *skomoroxi* had almost disappeared from the scene, being replaced in the favours of the princes, at least, by musicians imported from abroad.

One of the major guardians of the folk theatre among the people of Russia was of course the peasantry, originators and perpetuators of seasonal masking, ritual drama, *xorovody* and other early dramatic forms. The knowledge gained in these pursuits was used to expand the dramatic repertoire of the countryside leading to such developments as the addition of new themes to the *xorovody*, the incorporation of new characters into the seasonal games and eventually to the growth of a lively dramatic instinct among the peasantry, eager not only to preserve the aesthetic heritage of the past but also to create afresh and assimilate new ideas from a wide variety of sources.

Most popular in the peasant repertoire of this later phase were the plays *Barin* and *Lodka*, both of which reflect in varying degrees specific aspects of the way of life, the attitudes and fate of the prerevolutionary Russian peasant.

Although the peasantry was the creator and, for centuries, virtually the sole bearer of embryonic dramatic forms in Russia, such factors as the beginning of a literary theatrical tradition with Simeon Polockij and the academic theatre in Moscow in the latter half of the seventeenth century, the expansion of urban civilisation in the eighteenth century, the growth of secular literature and a corresponding increase in the reading public all had a profound effect not only upon the content of the folk theatre but upon the composition of both audience and actors. Among the immediate results of these changes were the development of an urban folk literature and the interchange of methods, ideas and repertoire between the old theatrical traditions of the country and the new ideas of the towns. On the one hand, for example, the repertoire of the academic theatre was brought to the peasants by wandering students performing dramatic scenes to earn a little extra cash during the vacations, while on the other hand students brought up in the country took their early theatrical tastes to the seminaries where folk plays were often performed in leisure hours. A similar process is to be seen among the soldier actors[6] whose repertoire reflects both the peasant background from which many were recruited and the urban democratic theatre with which many of them had the opportunity to familiarise themselves in the towns. This hybrid repertoire was then reintroduced to the peasant population by soldiers billeted in country villages or by retired soldiers eager to perpetuate the amusements of their army days. Thus the cycle of mutual influence was completed.

The significance of the emergence of the urban democratic theatre[7] in the second half of the eighteenth century is twofold. Firstly, it indicated the existence of a lively interest in amateur theatricals on the part of the urban proletariat and artisan classes, and secondly, it provided the first opportunity for such people to become acquainted with the repertoire of the literary stage. The audiences and actors of these theatres, the artisans, factory workers, clerks, students, domestic servants, small shopkeepers and the like were essentially also those of the urban folk theatre.

Apart from the peasantry and the urban proletariat there was a third and extremely important centre for the folk theatre — the army. Speaking of the folk theatre in Russia after watching a performance of the little known play *Kedril Obžora*, by his fellow prisoners while in exile in Siberia, Dostoevskij said that folk plays would be found: —

"... у солдат, фабричных, в фабричных городах, и даже по некоторым бедным городкам у мещан. Сохранились тоже они по деревням и по губернским городам между дворнями больших помещичьих домов."[8]

One has only to glance at the list of actors attached to the many variants of *Car' Maksimilian* or at the accounts of eyewitnesses to see how well Dostoevskij's judgement fits this folk play in particular. Kallaš's first version is accompanied by a note to the effect that the troupe of actors performing the play were all apprentice or working lads aged between 12 and 20 years.[9] In a variant from Kovla the reader is again informed that the actors were lads from artisan families.[10]

The role of the military in the Russian folk theatre, however, far exceeds that of the urban artisans. Various sources indicate that one of the most popular amusements of the soldiers during the eighteenth and nineteenth centuries was the staging of plays. The Tver' *Vojskovye vedomosti* for 1869 (No. 4) informs us that: —

"Говоря собственно о солдате нужно заметить, что он всегда любит 'строить комедии' и даже издревле имеет свой лубочный репертуар.'Царь Ирод, Царь Максимилиан и его непокорный сын Адольф' известны каждому жившему в штаб-квартире какого-нибудь полка."[11]

Indeed, many variants of the folk plays, in particular *Car' Maksimilian*, appear to owe their existence or their first appearance in a particular village or town in some way to the army (or, in some cases, the navy). One of Vinogradov's texts[12] came indirectly through the grandfather of its then present owner, when he returned from his naval service. Another text also collected by Vinogradov[13] was copied in 1904 from a noncommisioned officer of the 139th Moršansk infantry regiment where the play was regularly performed. The two texts of *Maksimilian* and *Šajka razbojnikov* published by Berkov in the journal *Russkij fol'klor* are part of the Arens MS collection of *naval* plays and songs. Several of the men who were able to give Ončukov information about *Car' Maksimilian* and other folk plays during his expedition in north Russia said that they or some other soldier had learned it while on military service and brought the text back to their villages.

A version of *Maksimilian* was brought to the settlement (*posad*) of Nenoks by Prokopij Sergeevič Skrebcov after his return from military service in Kronstadt in 1877. Similarly, a version of *Šajka razbojnikov* was brought to the village of Nižmozero by a young peasant after military service in the Far East.[14] There can be little doubt that the immense area over which such plays spread by the end of the nineteenth century was largely due to the nomadic existence of the Russian soldier and his love of acting.

Upon retirement it seems that old soldiers still used to enjoy taking part in amateur productions and by teaching the lads of the places where they settled all they knew about the plays continued to further the knowledge and enjoyment of the folk theatre among the people.

The fact that *Car' Maksimilian* was the favourite play of the military repertoire has left its mark in more ways than one upon it. The abundance of battle scenes and the important role of the field-marshal are typical of many plays of the eighteenth century, yet in many variants of the folk play they tend to dominate the whole action. Additional, quite superfluous characters often appear to have a military connection, for example the drunken *fel'dšer* who on occasions accompanies the doctor, or the Cossack and the Hussar who swell the list of warriors in some versions.[15] Although the text of *Maksimilian* cannot exactly be said to have a military bias there are to be found among the constituent elements many traces of military influence or knowledge of military terminology. These can be seen for instance in the exchanges between the *car'* or the field-marshal on the one hand and Adol'f or the pages or warriors on the other. Of such a kind is the speech between the field-marshal, Adol'f and the rest of the cast in Kostin's variant: —

"Адольф: — Здорово, братцы!

Все: — Здравия желаем, ваше императорское высочество!

Царь: — Здорово дети!

Все: — Здравия желаем, ваше императорское величество!

Царь: — Хорошо, дети!

Все: — Ради стараться, в.и.в."[16]

Odd references to the military (or naval) way of life are scattered through the many variants of the play. These are particularly numerous in one of Ončukov's texts where the connections with the Baltic fleet and the military experience of the actors (and presumably the original audience) are quite clear. The conversation between the two old sailors is particularly striking. Here there is a lot of naval jargon, a description of the ships upon which they have served and reminiscences of the Crimean campaign.

As will be seen later,[17] much of the action, movement and gesture in the play is based upon military customs and techniques so that many variants of *Maksimilian* are pervaded with a predominantly martial atmosphere.

The troupes of enthusiastic amateur actors, whether peasants, soldiers, sailors or factory workers, would begin preparations for their annual performances well in advance, gathering together anything up to two months before Christmas for rehearsals. These would take place in their spare time, the performers hiding away in barns and outhouses so as to keep the preparations secret. It was sometimes possible for those in the towns to hold rehearsals at their place of work during the meal break. In fact, if their boss or foreman was sufficiently interested, an empty room might be put at their disposal. The whole troupe consisted not only of the actors but also of a number of assistants who helped to get the costumes ready while the actors were learning or practising their parts. During the actual performances these helpers often used to take a hand with musical accompaniments, choir participation and sound effects. It was not customary for women to take part in any of the plays and therefore female roles were played by youths, as can be seen from the remarks to many of the texts. In the Abramov variant of *Car' Maksimilian* there is, for example, a young girl (*devica*): —

"Переодетый мальчик с красивыми чертами лица"; [18]

in *Ataman*[19] we are told that the part of Marija was usually taken by a male actor; in one of the variants of *Car' Irod*, Rachel is described as: —

"хлопец одетый в женское платье с тряпочной куклой в руках".[20]

Apparently this custom eventually had a detrimental effect upon acting standards. The young men themselves were unwilling to undertake female parts since this often made them a laughing-stock among their friends and a target for offensive remarks. As a result, rather than allow the performances to disintegrate, the female roles were given to anyone willing to take them on. These actors were often quite unsuited to the task and inevitably lowered the standard of the acting.

Usually the actors were young men and youths rather than older men and most of the extant descriptions, texts and recollections of the plays seem to underline this fact. For instance in Abramov's experience: —

" 'водить царя' один из наиболее любимых святочных развлечений воронежских 'паробков' ";[21]

the young actors in Kallaš's first text were aged between twelve and twenty; in the two variants of *Car' Irod* noted down by V.A. Moškov in the winter of 1896/97 in the Volynsk government the players were respectively youths of eighteen to twenty and boys of thirteen to fourteen.[22] The 'carrying of the star'[23] and the singing of Christmas carols to go with it was left for even younger children. However, older men did on occasions take part especially in those roles which required experience and an air of authority or a particularly 'aged' appearance, such as *Car'* Maksimilian, *Car'* Irod, the excutioner, the *ataman* and of course the 'old men' who appeared in various guises.

Once a large enough group had been collected the producer came to the fore and began to direct the course of the rehearsals. He was often the traditional bearer of the title-role in *Car' Maksimilian* or he might be the person owning the only copy of the text or the one to whom it had been transmitted through the oral tradition, or he might simply be an older actor with long years of experience in folk plays. Laščilin has a word of praise for these producers: they were "experienced men, wonderful connoisseurs of folk song and tale, masters and creators of folk poetry, who taught the members of the collective their art, their methods, their ability to arouse the feelings of the audience. But their task did not stop there. Being talented people they were able to show each actor how to create and perform each individual role and character."[24]

The producer's task was indeed a responsible one for he had to know all the parts by heart and be able to act as prompter if required. One of the well known producers of *Car' Maksimilian* in the nineties of the last century, Panov, a factory worker from Jaroslavl', included in his duties the distribution of parts, acting the *car'*, writing out the text for each actor, showing them how to act, how to stand, which words to stress and so forth.[25] R.M. Volkov[26] also indicates that in texts which included songs it was the task of the producer to teach them too. Performances of *Car' Maksimilian* in Novgorod-

Seversk were thus led for a considerable period by the conductor of the local church choir.

Eventually the leader would get down to the business of dividing the roles. This was not done haphazardly. The most important role in *Car' Maksimilian* was of course that of the *Car'* himself who was often played by the producer. But in some districts the speaking parts for both *Car'* Maksimilian and Adol'f were handed down in oral tradition from father to son, each generation having the right to play irrespective of talent. The hereditary holders of this privilege had the right also to alter the text, to combine scenes, add or omit according to their inclinations; in other words, to exercise a licence not normally permitted by the strict rules of folk tradition. As far as the other actors are concerned it seems that it was sometimes difficult to find enough suitable people because of the considerable demands made upon the men's time and energy. Actors were required not only to be able to learn and declaim their part but also, in many cases, to have a good singing voice. According to Abramov[27] the best actors were considered those who could sing well, had a loud voice and: —

"... умеет молодщевато выступать перед публикой."

Laščilin, in his notes to the text of *Ataman Čurkin*,[28] also states that from among the various candidates those with good singing voices were usually preferred because this text contained many songs.

The field-marshal had an exacting task, filling as he did one of the longest and most responsible parts in *Car' Maksimilian*, and therefore particular care had to be taken in choosing a suitable candidate: —

"Скороходом обыкновенно бывает какой-либо шустрый, бойкий на словах и на деле парень, который, как говорится, за словом в карман не полезет."[29]

There were of course also physical restrictions and qualifications. The royal pages, for instance, were played by young boys, female parts by boys, particularly those with attractive faces. Age, height and physique were all determining factors. Adol'f the martyr was usually played by a youth of slender and delicate build to underline his innocence and helplessness. *Car'* Maksimilian also had an individual appearance and the following descriptions all indicate a similar physical type: —

"высокого роста, с бородой, лицом грозный, речь громкая, резкая"; [30]
"высокий, толстый мужчина лет 40, с бородой, грозного вида."[31]
"высокий, красивый, статный парень."[32]

Descriptions of Brambeus, the executioner, show that he was usually portrayed by a very tall, strongly-built man: —

"высокого роста, могучаго телосложения . . ."[33]

The parts of the various knights and warriors were usually played, understandably, by tall men, for example: —

"Черный Араб — самый высокий парень."[34]

In Vinogradov's 1st variant of *Car' Maksimilian* the Arab, Zmejulan and Mars are all tall.

Among the better-organised and established groups it was not unusual to hire a room and charge a small admission fee, the proceeds of which were then split among the actors as a reward for their enthusiasm and hard work. However, it was much more common for the bands of mummers to be entertained at the expense of their hosts in the kitchens of the local landowners or merchants or in the cottages of the wealthier peasants: —

"Им за это платили, поили вином, брагой, вообще у кого что было."[35]

The generosity of appreciative audiences was such that many of the actors scarcely had time to sober up from one day to the next.

NOTES

1. Adrianova-Peretc (Ed.), *Povest' vremennyx let*, Vol. 1, p. 95.
2. *Pečerskij Paterik*, 1806, quoted by Famincyn, p. 10.
3. B.N. Putilov (Ed.), *Byliny* (Sovetskij pisatel', Leningrad, 1957), p. 405.
4. Adrianova-Peretc, *Povest' vremennyx let*, Vol. 1, p. 117.
5. *Polnoe sobranie russkix letopisej*, I, 6, 73, quoted by Famincyn, p. 79.
6. *Infra*, pp. 327-331.
7. For further details about this semi-amateur, semi-professional theatrical development see Kuz'mina, *Russkij demokratičeskij teatr*.
8. F.M. Dostoevskij, "Zapiski iz mertvogo doma," *Sobranie sočinenij v 10 tomax*, Vol. 3 (Moscow, 1956), p. 546.
9. Kallaš, Variant 1, p. 6.
10. I.B., "*Car' Maksimilian* v Kovle", *Kievskaja starina*, Vol. 19 (December) (Kiev, 1887), p. 798.
11. See Volkov's introduction to "Narodnaja drama *Car' Maksimil'jan*", p. 49.
12. Vinogradov, Variant 5.
13. Vinogradov, Variant 4.
14. Ončukov, "Narodnaja drama na severe," pp. 215-217.
15. See e.g. Kostin, p. 106.
16. Kostin, p. 103.
17. *Infra*, pp. 217-219.

196

18. p. 5.
19. Drizen, *Materialy k istorii russkogo teatra*, p. 281.
20. Eremin, "Drama-igra *Car' Irod*", p. 233.
21. Abramov, p. 2.
22. Eremin, "Drama-igra *Car' Irod*", p. 233.
23. In some parts of Russia, but particularly in White Russia and the Ukraine an ornamental star made by the children themselves and illuminated inside with a candle was carried round the village to an accompaniment of carol singing.
24. B.S. Laščilin, "Vozroždenie narodnogo teatra na Donu," *Kratkie soobščenija instituta etnografii AN SSSR*, No. 11 (Moscow, 1950), p. 31.
25. E.V. Pomeranceva (Ed.), *Pesni i skazki Jaroslavskoj oblasti* (Jaroslavl', 1958), p. 152.
26. See Volkov's introduction to "Narodnaja drama *Car' Maksimil'jan*," p. 4.
27. Abramov, p. 2.
28. Golovačev and Laščilin, p. 173.
29. I.B., "*Car' Maksimilian* v Kovle", pp. 798-799.
30. Vinogradov, Variant 5, p. 180.
31. Vinogradov, Variant 1, p. 17.
32. Abramov, p. 5. The *Car'* in this text was, however, played by a youth and not an older man as was more usual.
33. *Ibid.*
34. *Ibid.*
35. Moxirev, "Vjatsko-poljanskij variant", p. 251.

CHAPTER X

COSTUME IN THE FOLK PLAYS

The types of costume and make-up used both in the dramatic rituals[1] and in scenes such as *Paxomuška*[2] where the connection with ritual is very strong have already been touched upon. Within the repertoire of the nonritual theatre, although the traditions of the rituals are by no means entirely forgotten, the general approach to the subject is somewhat different.

As one examines the various types of costume which appear in each of the main plays of the repertoire several distinct patterns begin to emerge, one of the most striking of which is the military air which dominates plays like *Car' Maksimilian, Kak francuz Moskvu bral* and *Mavrux*, all of which belonged to the repertoire of the soldier theatre.[3]

For performances of these plays it was not unusual for the soldier or, for that matter, civilian actors to borrow any military uniforms they could find; to these they would later add the various specific features of dress which distinguished one character from another. Abramov, for instance, tells of costumes for his variant of *Car' Maksimilian* hired from retired army men living in the district: —

> "Наряды играющих представляют порядочную смесь, начиная с формы какого-нибудь майора времен очаковских и покоренья Крыма и оканчивая пестрым одеянием отставного драгуна."[4]

A troupe described by Kallaš also wore borrowed uniforms. The field-marshal was dressed thus: —

> "На нем солдатский или офицерский мундир, сообразно с тем, какой удалось достать артистам . . ."[5]

But suitable uniforms were not always easy to obtain and, as with the other costumes, the folk actors were content for the most part to make their own. A wide variety of materials, anything that came to hand, was used in the construction of the costumes for the folk plays; odd pieces of wood for swords; cardboard: —

"Каска делается из кардона",[6] "на мундире погоны или висячие эполеты подлины или сделанные из картона, цветной бумаги и шумихи";[7] эсаул берет картонную трубку";[8]

scraps of coloured materials; oddments of sheepskin or fur for beards and moustaches, strands of flax for hair; straw was used for making epaulettes amongst other things ("на плечах соломенные эполеты");[9] gold and silver tinsel produced decorative effects: —

"Скипетр — палка обклеенная сусальным золотом с сусальной звездой на верхушке и держава — шар обклеенный сусальным золотом";[10]

coloured paper was also a popular material: —

"Он подпоясан широким кушаком, оклееным золоченой бумагой, через левое плечо повешана цветная бумажная орденская лента, а через правое — шашка на портупее обклееной золотой бумагой."[11]

Once the basic military uniform essential to *Car' Maksimilian* and other plays of the soldier repertoire had been borrowed or improvised a variety of decorations and elaboration, ribbons, belts, sashes, medals, crosses and epaulettes, were added in order to distinguish ranks and characters. By studying eyewitness accounts, old photographs and the remarks to the various extant texts one can build up a general picture of the appearance of the main characters. Maksimilian himself wore a military uniform approximating to that of a general, decorated with straw epaulettes, trousers with a broad stripe down the side, knee-boots and, inevitably, a broad military sash of blue or, less frequently, red or green material worn across the left shoulder. Like all the knights he carried a sword. His royal rank was marked by the abundance of medals, crosses, rosettes and stars with which the breast of his jacket was decorated and by his tinsel crown. Compare the following descriptions: —

(1) "Одевает одежду сиртук военной с висящими погонами, на штанах генеральские ломпасы, через плечо голубая лента, потом есть и корона из железа и визолочена, еще имеет шашку, потом еще есть ордена, делают своеручно с золотой бумаги."[12]

(2) "Посреди них находится сам царь Максимилиан, одетый в военный сюртук с висящими погонами, представляющими из себя кисточки. На штанах канты. На груди перекинута через плечо голубая лента и ордена из разных видов

жестянок. На голове надета корона из картона и вызоло-
ченная в золотого цвета краску."[13]

In one of Kallaš's texts there is a description of how the crown was made: —

"Впоследствии ему приносят корону такого вида: обруч,
охватывающий голову; к нему приделаны вверху две
полосы накрест, правильно изогнутые. Наверху или на лбу
короны иногда находится звезда."[14]

Towards the beginning of this variant Maksimilian is invested with the royal
regalia, the sceptre and orb, a description of which can also be seen on page 7
of the text. The royal attributes were symbolic of regal power and authority
and the portrayal of the King in the folk theatre was not complete without
them. In the variants of *Maksimilian* where the *Car'* was forced to take on his
challengers in person the crown and regalia were often laid upon the throne
as a sign that the rights of the monarch were in question and the victor invested himself with the regalia of the vanquished to show that a change of
leadership had been effected.

Very rarely was any attempt made to dress Maksimilian in a manner more
suited to his role in the play as a pagan persecutor. A small move in this
direction may be seen in a reference to be found in the notes to Vinogradov's
5th variant. Here Maksimilian is supposedly dressed in the "garb of the
ancient *Car'*'s", but in the actual description of the costume the only unusual
note is the one archaic piece of clothing, the *kamzol*.[15] A flowing cloak
however, often gave added authenticity to the *Car'* 's regal appearance.

The other king who figured in *Car' Maksimilian*, Mamaj of the Golden
Horde, differed from his antagonist basically in the style of his crown and
regalia, although his general appearance also tended to be more exotic with
an oriental flavour as in Kallaš's first variant: —

"В противоположном углу сидит король Мамай, одетый как
Максимилиан, но в зубчатой короне (обруч, отделанный
вверху зубчиками) с полумесяцем на ней . . . .
Мамай держит в руках скипетр и державу с полумесяцем
наверху."[16]

The royal prince Adol'f also wore military dress, but rather that of an officer
than of a general, complete with sword or sabre. He differed from his father
mainly in the lack of a crown (although not always) instead of which he was
provided with a military hat or helmet made from gilded cardboard. His costume was not so elaborate and he wore fewer decorations. An essential
feature of his dress, the heavy chains which were a part of his punishment,
were added later in the play.

The field-marshal's costume was basically similar to that of his master and the royal prince except that his medals were fewer in number and he wore a red sash rather than the blue one associated with the *Car'*.

It is interesting to compare the costume of the royal personages as presented in *Car' Maksimilian* and *Car' Irod* respectively, for whereas in the former play historical costume is very rare, in the religious drama there is a definite hesitation between the traditions of the *vertep* which gave the original impulse to its creation and the traditions of the soldier theatre which had a very strong influence upon it. Thus *Car'* Irod in one variant may be dressed much like Maksimilian: —

> "В солдатском мундире, поверх которого накинута красная мантия, он подпоясан широким кушаком, оклееным золоченой бумагой, через левое плечо повешена цветная бумажная орденская лента, а через правое — шашка на портупее обклееной золотой бумагой, на голове картонная корона, обклееная золоченой бумагой, на руках белые перчатки."[17]

In another variant the three Wise Men who pay homage to the infant Christ are clothed quite differently and resemble their predecessors of the *vertep*: —

> "Они в белых, чистых сорочках, 'гарно' вышитых, подпоясанные широкими цветными поясами; две широких ленты обхватывают накрест грудь, как орарь дьякона; на груди иконы с изображением рождественского вертепа; на голове картонные шестизубчатые короны, оклееные золотой бумагой, украшенные серебряными звездами и крестами . . ."[18]

The Emperor Napoleon, on the other hand, who appears from time to time in the Russian folk plays was not depicted in either of the ways mentioned above. As a real historical character of what was to the folk actor the not too distant past, his actual appearance was widely known even if only through the caricature portraits of folk pictures and cartoons contemporary to the 1812 campaign. In the plays he therefore retains the costume with which we usually connect his pictorial image: —

> ". . . в белых штанах, ботфортах, мундире и треуголке."[19]

All the warriors taking part in the duel scenes in the second half of *Car' Maksimilian* wore military uniform. The chief of these, Anika, retains the epaulettes, sash, etc. of the royal characters but is, like the knightly enemies he defeats, without military decorations. He usually carried both a sword and a spear. Among the other knights who took part in the duels the Hussar and the Black Arab tend to be the most striking, the former by a certain amount of extravagance in the colour and style of his costume,[20] and the latter by the fact that he is all in black: —

> "Сиртук военной чорный и обшивается белыми ленточками как рукава, грудьи и полы, каска шьется с материи черной вроде пирога . . ."[21]

Herod's bodyguard in *Car' Irod* and the officers who bear the coffin in *Mavrux* were also all dressed in 'ordinary' military uniforms.

The predominantly military note in the costumes of these characters is an indication that the plays in which they appear had become a part of a specifically military theatrical tradition within the wider range of the folk theatre itself, a tradition where high rank and royalty is identified, no matter to what period it belongs, with the full dress uniforms of the *Car'* or Prince acting in their military capacity and warriors or knights are associated with the style of dress familiar and contemporary to the soldier actors themselves. This is particularly significant when we consider that these conventions persisted even when the plays were being performed neither in the garrison nor by a military troupe.

In the popular folk play *Lodka* which was not essentially a part of the military theatrical repertoire the traditional costume of the actors in the serious part of the drama is quite different. All the robbers, including the *ataman* and the *esaul*, were almost invariably dressed in scarlet shirts with broad belts or sashes behind which they stuck their weapons in true brigand fashion: —

> "Есаул одет был в красную длинную рубашку, запоясанную черным кушаком; в сапогах. Брюки широкие, синие, напущенные на желтые сапоги — ичиги. На голове — чалма."[22]

In another version he is dressed similarly: —

> "Атаман . . . в красной рубашке, на голове шапка, сабля деревянная, на груди две медали, усы и борода . . ."[23]

The robbers carried many weapons to create a more ferocious and realistic effect. The *ataman* in *Mašen'ka* has a formidable array: —

> "На шее револьвер висит на шнуре, за поясом заткнут пистолет и кинжал, с боку висит шпага . . ."[24]

The *esaul* from *Drama o Ermake* has a similar collection: —

> "На нем — воинские доспехи, меч, лук, стрелы, в руках плетка, щит, шапка; за поясом — пистолет."[25]

The military influence is not, however, totally absent from *Lodka*, for the play was extremely popular in some areas settled by Cossack regiments such as the Don region and the Urals. In these Cossack texts there is a tendency to make use of aspects of Cossack military dress. For example the robbers in Golovačev and Laščilin's *Ataman Burja* were originally dressed in Cossack *čekmeni* (a Cossack version of the *kaftan*) trimmed with silver lace although in 1912 these were replaced by more modern clothing: —

> ". . . мундиры с погонами, шароварами с лампасами и казачьими папахами."[26]

In another text, the *ataman* is dressed thus: —

> "В красной рубахе, в пиджаке с полковничьими эполетами с кистями уральской казачьей дивизии, шапка с красным верхом, в виде треугольника, перекинутым на бок, с серебряной кистью на конце верха."[27]

But on the whole the semi-romantic, semi-historical popular image of the early robber heroes was not fixed to any specific military tradition.

The dress of the *ataman* and *esaul* was distinguished from the rest of the band by being more elaborate and often richly ornamented with braid and silver or gold lace, like the *ataman* in Sipovskij's *Lodka*: —

> "В красной рубашке, черной поддевке, черной шляпе, . . . поддевка и шляпа богато украшены золотой бумагой."[28]

The characters and costumes discussed above form two quite separate although internally coordinated groups, in the one the warriors and the royal characters, in the other the robbers and their leaders. Within the groups only small variations are made to distinguish one member from another, but characters not belonging to the basic group are dressed quite differently.

Characters outside the group fall into two main categories: —

(a) those who belong specifically to the 'plot' of each play (such as the captured girl or the rich landowner in *Lodka*);

(b) stock, peripatetic characters whose role is not fixed in any one play and who belong jointly to all or most of the genres of the folk theatre (such as the gravedigger and his old woman, the Jew, the parodied ecclesiastical characters and the doctor).

Many of the incidental characters in the first category do not receive any kind of special costume but appear in more or less everyday clothing. Such is the girl captured by the robbers in some variants of *Lodka*: —

"Переодетый парень, в юбке и платье, кисея на лице."[29]

Similarly, Rachel in *Car' Irod* is dressed as an ordinary Russian or Ukrainian peasant woman as in the *vertep* prototype: —

"Хлопец, одетый в женское платье с тряпочной куклой в руках."[30]

Even the goddess Venus who appears frequently as one of *Car'* Maksimilian's challengers is not exotically dressed as one might have expected. Played, like the other female characters, by a boy in female clothing, she wears peasant dress, sometimes holiday finery or a costume slightly more elaborate than ordinary everyday garb. In the film variant of *Car' Maksimilian* which I saw in 1963 she had on a long white dress with a tweed jacket over it and a scarf on her head. An eyewitness account dating to the middle of the 19th century conveys a vivid impression of the grotesque effects sometimes produced by this convention. In this performance of *Car' Maksimilian* the role of the enchantress (*volšebnica*) was played by a soldier: —

"с толстым, темным и лоснящимся лицом."

He wore a shortish, tattered, woman's dress which revealed his fat legs. On his head was an old hat decorated with paper flowers. When defeated by the *Car'* he fell to his knees before him and asked for mercy in a hoarse squeaky voice.[31]

The old woman who sometimes accompanied Markuška, the gravedigger, was also dressed in peasant style, e.g.: —

"В пестрядинном сарафане и во всем старушечьем уборе, как по-крестьянски ходит, на голове кичка."[32]

There are, however, other characters whose role in the play is to fulfil some particular *professional* function. These are immediately recognisable from their appearance which underlines their respective callings. The court executioner and the smith who chains Adol'f are obvious examples of this type of costume. The dress of Brambeus is very distinctive. In it red is the predominant colour; a red shirt, red trousers or a red hood or cap (*kolpak*). In one variant his arms are painted red.[33] Sometimes he also wears a black mask. Traces of the military theme from the warriors can be detected now and again in his dress. High boots may be worn, or a military cap. Like them he carries a sword, usually in addition to some other weapon such as a spear. Note, for example, the following description: —

> "Брамбеус — в черной маске, с черным шлемом на голове, с черными перьями на шлеме, в засученных руках, выкрашенных в красную краску, обнаженная сабля, одет он в красную рубашку."[34]

The smith is always identified by his hammer, long apron and various other signs of his trade: —

> "Одет по-мужицки, в рубахе, в лаптях, без шашки, при фартуке, весь в уголье";[35] "кузнец при фартуке, с клещами в одной руке, с молотком в другой."[36]

This method of identifying characters is similar to that used in the academic theatre, still flourishing in Russia in the first half of the 18th century, which was largely based upon a tradition of symbols. According to the principles of the Jesuit theoretician of this school, Francisco Lang, each character had to have his proper costume, each being distinguished from the other by some symbol which indicated his rank, profession, etc. Thus, soldiers were differentiated by their swords and spears, workmen by their hammer and other tools, peasants by their agricultural implements.[37]

Symbolic representation of character is by no means limited to the serious parts of the folk drama but can also be found in the humorous scenes. Characters like the doctor, the *barin* and, to a certain extent, the rich landowner of *Lodka*, all received this sort of treatment. The actual clothing of the doctor varies from one text to another. Some of the costumes, for instance, were intended to look particularly German since this character was frequently supposed to have come from Germany, e.g.: —

> "Одет на немецкий лад: шляпа, узкий белый китель узкие штаны, на ногах чулки и башмаки, в руках ящик, трубка и молоток . . ."[38]

But the essential ingredients of the costume were to be found in the various properties connected with the doctor, in particular his spectacles, his medicine bag and a variety of medical instruments, clyster pipe, hammer, bottles and phials of medicine. Typical is the following: —

> "в коротком пиджачке, брюки на выпуск, на голове котелок; длинный нос и длинные изо льна волосы; в одной руке тросточка, в другой пузырек с лекарством."[39]

Although the *barin* was presented in more or less everyday clothes he was always made clearly recognisable by several features, the most common of which was his general stoutness and in particular his fat stomach. Among the other attributes which are constantly associated with the *barin* are a walking stick, a straw hat, umbrella or a pipe. A typical description can be seen in the variant of *Barin* published in Berkov's anthology: —

> "В красной рубахе и пиджаке; на плечах соломенные эполеты; на голове соломенная шляпа с вырезанными фигурками из бумаги; в руках трость, украшенная фигурками из бумаги. У барина большое брюхо и пиджак не застегнут на пуговицы."[40]

The scenes in which the *barin* is a central figure are of course satirical in content and this affects the physical appearance of the characters as well as the dialogue. The fatness of the master and the ragged appearance of the servant are deliberately exaggerated as in the *Komedija ob Aleške malom i barine golom*: —

> "Алешка Малый облачался в изорванный донельзя пониток, снимал сапоги, и босой с растрепанными волосами, изображал барского наемного слугу . . ."[41]

A similar effect was obtained in the parody funeral and wedding scenes which occurred frequently in *Car' Maksimilian*. As in the similar scenes in *Paxomuška*,[42] the priest was dressed approximately as in real life, complete with various attributes of his calling, holy books, cross, censer, and so on, but the strange manner in which these were made created a comically grotesque effect rather than a realistic one.

The costume of Markuška the gravedigger and of Death and the Devil respectively, fall again into separate categories. Markuška's dress is basically that of an old Russian peasant: —

> "В кафтане, волосы и борода длинные, с толстой палкой в руках, в лаптях и в ончуках, шапка мужицкая и все — помужицки."[43]

But his true nature is revealed by certain constantly recurring features, namely the sheepskin coat which he wears inside out and his humped back connecting him with the ritual fool of Russian and other European agricultural ceremonies: —

> "Старик Марко гробокопатель, в полушубке на верх шерстью, на спине горб, в старенькой шляпе, в руках рожок

> табак нюхать, и палка, сам в мазке";[44] "дедушка –
> гробокопатель – с длинной клочковатой бородой, в
> полушубке овчиной наружу, сгорбленный, с палкой в
> руке."[45]

Devils appear rarely in the folk theatre outside the *vertep*. When they do they
are represented as black, hairy creatures with horns: –

> "Одет во все обтянутое черное, на руках черные перчатки,
> лицо вымазано сажей, на голове шапка с черным мехом,
> вывороченным наружу."[46]

Although their occasional appearance in plays like *Mašen'ka, Car' Maksimilian*
and *Lodka* is probably the result of borrowing from the *vertep* there is in
their appearance an element too of ritual origins, to be seen particularly in
the copious use of soot for the blacking of faces and hands and the wearing
of fur or sheepskin turned inside out.

Death in all the folk plays closely resembles the figure in the *vertep*. As in
the puppet theatre, the figure is invariably feminine, is dressed from head to
foot in white (a sheet or nightgown) and carries a scythe.

In certain cases primitive forms of make-up were used in order to further
enhance the appearance of the actors, to emphasise character and type, to
heighten an already grotesque effect. We know for instance that where long
hair or a beard were considered an embellishment to a character these could
easily be made from strands of flax or tow. Such treatment was often given
to the 'ecclesiastical' characters whose long hair was a necessary part of their
appearance, or characters who are intended to look old like the gravedigger
or even, on occasions, the bailiff in *Barin*. The Jew usually has a beard and
even *Car'* Maksimilian, for whom a beard was essentially a sign of age and
dignity, sported one on occasions, e.g.: –

> "К нижней губе привязан лоскут черной овчины, заменявший
> бороду и усы."[47]

Clearly, some actors were prepared to go to considerable lengths in order to
produce the desired effect, as a description of the making of a wig for the
doctor shows. The doctor in this case was to be shown as bald! First of all a
piece of leather of the requisite size was found, soaked and then stretched
over a heavy, rounded weight to give it the shape of a head. Hair of a bright,
gingery colour snipped from a dog (!) was then attached to the leather and
the wig was complete.[48]

Eyebrows were darkened and whiskers drawn in with burnt cork. The
Black Arab in addition to his black costume frequently had his face blackened

with soot. Cheek colour could be heightened by using the dye from red paper.

All these points, primitive as they may seem to us, are a further illustration of the care taken by the folk actors to produce an effective, satisfying and, to a certain extent, realistic appearance, in spite of their lack of money and the limited materials available.

On the whole in the plays of the folk theatre proper, although ritual elements are not entirely absent, the overall effect and intention bears little resemblance to that of the ritual. In the rituals, the actors whether animate or inanimate, were significant not so much as individuals, but as the bearers of an idea, a symbol, and therefore they were presented in such a way that only, or at least mainly, those features essential in the given circumstances were included. In nonritual folk plays the action is itself the important feature along with the portrayal of the characters and the development and interplay of their relationships. Each character and his role within the play has to be made explicit. However, it is quite clear that even within the scope of such plays characterisation although advanced by comparison with the ritual, does not progress beyond a rudimentary level. In the absence of both a highly developed plot and deep characterisation, one of the simplest methods of presenting characters and their function is by means of costume, which must necessarily be both striking and immediately recognisable. An easily identifiable costume helps to focus the attention of the audience during the amorphous collection of characters and repetitive actions typical of such plays as *Lodka* or *Car' Maksimilian*. It is for precisely the same reason that the characters usually announce their name, title and position during their opening monologue.

One of the most striking features of the costume in the folk theatre is the diversity of types and methods of costuming to be found not only between different plays but even within the framework of a single text, such as the mixture of military influences, symbolism, attempts at historical accuracy and remnants of ritual masking to be found all together in *Car' Maksimilian*. Indeed, few of the characters in the folk plays belong to the same dramatic or literary tradition but are drawn from a wide range of different sources, from the ritual *ded* to the historical Napoleon, from well-known ethnographical types to fictional heroes from popular literature. All of these retain the dress of the group or type to which they belong and there is little or no attempt to rationalise the diversity.

This disparate collection of characters and costumes is held together by the strong conventions of the folk theatre which both actors and audience understood and accepted.

The folk theatre is in fact a strange mixture of realism, even naturalism, with convention. It is pure convention, for instance, that the *Car'*, prince and knights should be dressed in pseudo-military uniforms which reflect neither the period to which the action properly belongs nor even, in the case of actors from peasant or urban proletariat communities (and only approximately in the case of military actors) the dress of familiar, contemporary society. Yet within the convention every attention is paid to detail and accuracy. If by the convention Maksimilian was to resemble a Russian general then it was the task of the producers to make him as resplendent a general as possible and much effort and ingenuity was spent on the creation of his uniform and decorations.

It must be remembered that the aims of the producers of folk plays were not those of their modern counterparts. As far as its characters and their presentation were concerned the folk theatre was not specifically interested in logic, realism or attention to purely historical accuracy but rather in recognition and identification.

Subtlety in general is not one of the characteristics of the folk theatre and this is strongly felt in the depiction of the characters. Distinctions are sharply drawn — highborn or rich versus poor or peasant, good versus bad, comic versus serious or tragic. Each character must be known at a glance for what he represents and the desire to avoid mistaken identity often leads to exaggeration.

The necessity for immediate recognisability of the characters and for the strict adherence to the convention of dress and behaviour to which each belonged was in part a result of the retention of audience participation which had been an integral feature of the ritual drama. One of the major differences between the literary and the folk theatre is to be found in the reactions of their respective audiences. Even in the nineteenth century the folk audience felt an obligation not merely to watch but to *participate* in the drama. The audience identified itself with the plot and characters, condemned Maksimilian, pitied Adol'f, laughed with Afon'ka at the *barin*. It was one of the pleasures of the show to be able to recognise old friends or old enemies whose appearance followed an unchanging pattern, and to enter with them once more the strange world of the drama where reality and fantasy met.

The folk theatre on the one hand set its characters apart from the audience by the use of various conventions, distortions and exaggerations. But at the same time the basis of the costumes was usually familiar.

Through the use of costume and other means the Russian folk actors contrived to achieve a strange balance between historical and contemporary events, creating an environment and a time scale which was neither completely real nor totally fictional.

NOTES

1. *Supra* pp. 4-7, 33-34.
2. *Supra* pp. 69-70, 71.
3. *Supra* pp. 74-75, 148-150, 190-192.

4. Abramov, p. 2.
5. Kałłaš, Variant 1, p. 6.
6. Abramov, p. 6.
7. Kallaš, Variant 1, p. 6.
8. "*Lodka*", Berkov, *Russkaja narodnaja drama*, p. 145.
9. "*Mavrux*", Ončukov, *Severnye narodnye dramy*, p. 134.
10. Kallaš, Variant 1, p. 7.
11. Eremin, "Drama-igra *Car' Irod*", p. 233.
12. Abramov, pp. 5-6.
13. Akimova, p. 29.
14. Kallaš, Variant 1, p. 7.
15. P. 181.
16. Kallaš, Variant 1, p. 10.
17. Eremin, "Drama-igra *Car' Irod*", p. 233.
18. A. Smirnickij, "K voprosu o vyroždenii vertepnoj dramy", *Izvestija Odesskogo bibliografičeskogo obščestva pri imperatorskom novorossijskom universitete*, Vol. 2, Issue 5 (Odessa, 1913), p. 195.
19. Malinka, "Živoj vertep", p. 38.
20. See e.g. Vinogradov, Variant 3, p. 130.
21. Abramov, p. 6.
22. Moxirev, "Vjatsko-poljanskij variant", p. 251.
23. "*Šajka razbojnikov*", Ončukov, *Severnye narodnye dramy*, p. 99.
24. Dobrovol'skij, "*Mašen'ka*", p. 117.
25. Moxirev, "Vjatsko-poljanskij variant", p. 251.
26. Golovačev and Laščilin, p. 170.
27. "*Šajka razbojnikov*", Variant 2, Birjukov, *Dorevoljucionnyj fol'klor*, p. 47.
28. Reprinted in Berkov, *Russkaja narodnaja drama*, p. 143.
29. "*Šajka razbojnikov*", Ončukov, *Severnye narodnye dramy*, p. 99.
30. Eremin, "Drama-igra *Car' Irod*", p. 233.
31. P., "*Car' Maksimilian*", p. 83.
32. Vinogradov, Variant 5, p. 181.
33. Kallaš, Variant 1, p. 9.
34. *Ibid.*
35. Vinogradov, Variant 5, p. 181.
36. Vinogradov, Variant 3, p. 136.
37. V.P. Adrianova-Peretc, "Scena i priemy postanovki v russkom škol'nom teatre XVII-XVIII v.", *Starinnyj spektakl' v Rossii: sbornik statej*, ed. by V.P. Adrianova-Peretc and others (Leningrad, 1928), p. 47.
38. "*Šajka razbojnikov*", Variant 2, Birjukov, *Dorevoljucionnyj fol'klor*, pp. 47-48.
39. Vinogradov, Variant 3, p. 134.
40. Berkov, *Russkaja narodnaja drama*, p. 46.
41. Opočinin, p. 284.
42. *Supra* pp. 68-69.
43. Vinogradov, Variant 5, p. 181.
44. Abramov, p. 7.
45. Kallaš, Variant 1, p. 10.
46. "*Šajka razbojnikov*", Variant 2, Birjukov, *Dorevoljucionnyj fol'klor*, p. 48.
47. A.I. S olevskij, Introduction to Vinogradov, "Narodnaja drama *Car' Maksimil'jan*", p. 11.
48. "*Šajka razbojnikov*", Variant 2, Birjukov, *Dorevoljucionnyj fol'klor*, p. 48.

CHAPTER XI

THE ARTISTIC METHODS OF THE FOLK ACTORS

In the previous chapters I have tried to give some idea not only of the sort of people who were accustomed to participate in the amateur performances of folk plays but also of the manner in which they were dressed for the various roles and the way in which these costumes were prepared. The next task is to examine the conditions under which these actors were required to play and the various methods used by them in the declamation of their speeches and the presentation of the characters. This subject has been largely ignored by folklorists and a representative picture can only be built up by careful analysis of the texts themselves. Most of the material in this chapter relates specifically to *Car' Maksimilian*, the texts of which seem to contain more relevant information in the form of brief remarks and footnotes than the other folk plays.

There has been a general tendency among scholars to express surprise at the immense popularity enjoyed by such plays as *Car' Maksimilian* and to regard both the content and the manner of presenting them as naive, monotonous and completely lifeless. Thus, Ivan Sergeevič Aksakov, describing a soldier performance in the 1850s, remarked that the doctor and his assistant were "the only animated characters in the whole performance".[1] A typical assessment of the play came too from Professor A.N. Veselovskij who was puzzled not only as to the origins of this "apparently negligible comedy" but even more as to its popularity throughout the length and breadth of Russia.[2]

This view of the artistic talent of the folk actors requires considerable modification for the apparently primitive acting methods of these people were by no means entirely due, as is usually inferred, to ignorance, stupidity and lack of taste. After all one should not forget that most of the extant texts of the folk plays belong to a period dating from the middle of the nineteenth century and that most of these texts do not come from very remote regions. By this time the traditions of the literary theatre had for long been an established and integral feature of Russian cultural life, not only in the big towns but in the provinces as well. There were many theatres not only to cater for the tastes of the intelligentsia and upper and middle classes but also, from the first quarter of the nineteenth century,[3] a swift development of theatres designed for the entertainment of the masses, in Moscow and Petersburg and in provincial centres. Many of these theatres, functioning principally during major holidays, in particular Shrovetide and Easter, made an important contribution to the stimulation of interest in and enjoyment of the stage among the ordinary people, and, in general, to the history of popular drama. Later, towards the end of the century, there came the foundation of people's theatres with an educational and enlightening function such as the Vasileostrov Theatre for workers (1887).

Performances on the legitimate stage were well within the reach of many people during the course of the nineteenth century and folk actors could not have remained entirely ignorant of them. On the contrary, what does seem surprising is the fact that the methods of the folk theatre managed to remain so aloof from those of the literary theatre and to present, viewed as a whole, a surprising degree of homogeneity which is still in evidence even in the latest records.

Methods of presentation in the folk theatre were considerably influenced by the limitations imposed by the amateur and seasonal nature of the companies' activities; a great deal was left to the audience's imagination. The conditions under which the actor performed did not permit much refinement whether of movement, gesture, speech or general delivery. Obviously, no theatrical building or proper stage was available for them. The nature of the space upon which they were invited to perform could vary not only from year to year but from day to day or performance to performance. The better organised and prosperous troupes might manage to hire a barn, an outhouse or a room specially for the occasion, but most had to be content with the kitchen of one of the large houses in the area, or even a simple peasant *izba*. If no special room could be provided a suitable space had to be cleared in the open air. In the summer, naturally, this was the rule rather than the exception.

The itinerant and purely temporary nature of the troupe had an undoubted effect upon the character of the performance. Cumbersome scenery, backcloths and stage props were out of the question for a small band, travelling from house to house, often to outlying districts and in the depths of a Russian winter, uncertain moreover of the size and appearance of their next stage. Even a curtain would be an unnecessary encumbrance. The only large piece of equipment really needed on stage in any of the folk plays was the *Car'*'s 'throne' and this could, if necessary, be constructed on the spot from several chairs tied together. The throne might then be suitably decorated to convey a more realistic impression as in one description from the play *Tron* where a tall chair was embellished by a heightened back made from pieces of stick covered over with a strip of cloth and decorated with gold paper.[4]

Properties too were kept to the absolute minimum, and apart from some objects like the swords for the knights which were specially made, were confined to things which were small and easily carried or which could be borrowed immediately before the performance, such as a snuffbox for the grave-digger, a walking-stick and box of pills for the doctor, a hammer for the smith, a straw hat for the *barin*, and so on.

As there were no wings the normal methods of exit and entry of players could not be observed. The actors therefore evolved various means of their own for grouping themselves on stage and for arranging their exits and entries. The latter presented little difficulty when performances were taking place in a room where either a corridor or another separate room opening off the first was available. In such cases the actors simply passed from one room to the other, as required.

Other ways of arranging the actors, whether indoors or outdoors, also existed. It was possible, for instance, for the actors to stand among or along-side the audience and to emerge from the crowd when called to the centre of the acting area. However, even taking into consideration the small amount of available evidence on the subject, it seems clear that two main methods of or-ganisation were used. According to the first of these, actors were arranged in two straight lines on either side of the main area of the action. In *Car' Maksi-milian* this would be the royal throne and the seated *Car'* placed in a central position. Each actor would step forward from one or other of the two lines to declaim his speech before the *Car'* and then return to the line when he had finished. Typical of this sort of arrangement is the Abramov variant: —

"Все вынимают сабли из ножен и становятся ПРАВИЛЬНЫМИ РЯДАМИ; ВПЕРЕД выступает царский сын Адольф . . ."[5]

Similarly, in the scenes from *Lodka* which have contaminated Volkov's text of *Maksimilian* we find: —

"МЕЖДУ ДВУМЯ ШЕРЕНГАМИ воинов ходит воин . . ."[6]

In the filmed version of *Maksimilian* from Gor'kij *oblast'* the action also took place between two lines of actors.[7]

According to the second method the actors formed a circle or a semi-circle around the *car'* and his throne, or around the *ataman*, and stepped from the periphery to the centre in order to deliver their lines. Note for instance: —

"Все участники представления выходят на середину избы и ОБРАЗУЮТ КРУГ, В СЕРЕДИНУ КОТОРОГО становятся друг против друга Атаман и Эсаул",[8]

or: —

"Участники представления образуют посреди избы свободный полукруг, на средину которого выходит Посол . . ."[9]

Once the action had begun there was little movement of any specific nature about the stage, probably for two main reasons. In the first place, the primitive nature of the plot made it unnecessary for more than two or three people at most to be present on stage at the same time and their dealings with each other were simple and direct, with the addresses rarely involving more than the two people immediately concerned. Secondly, since the stage was empty of all decoration and equipment, even the most conventional, actions on the part of the actor were restricted to the bare essentials. Those which do remain are usually very stylised and can be found throughout the folk theatre. The actor, delivering his speech from the centre of the 'stage', would often stand stiffly facing the person to whom he was speaking or else in the direction of the audience. Apart from this somewhat static approach to dramatic delivery it was also common for the actors to declaim their part while walking back and forth across, up and down or even round the acting space. In fact, in view of the number of references to such movements to be found in the remarks to the folk plays, it would seem that this was the most popular method of execution. It occurs in the following examples: —

"Надев рыщарское платье, Брамбеус ходит ВЗАД И ВПЕРЕД перед Максимилианом и поет . . .";
"Доктор вынимает из ножен шашку и говорит, расхаживая ВЗАД И ВПЕРЕД . . .";
"Тусарин вынимает шашку и расхаживая ВЗАД И ВПЕРЕД говорит . . ."[10]

or: —

"Адольф удаляется тихим шагом, и ходя ВЗАД — ВПЕРЕД по комнате, поет . . .";
"Встает с трона и, ПРОЙДЯСЬ раза два по комнате, говорит . . .";
"ПРОХОДИТ несколько раз по комнате, а затем говорит . ."[11]

These are only a few of innumerable such examples. Occasionally, there is a more detailed description of dramatic delivery such as that in the Mjakutin text where Maksimilian, as he boasts about his royal power, takes up a stance with his right leg slightly forward and waves his revolver in the air, presumably to add force to his words.[12]

Most of the movements and gestures to be found in the folk plays, except in the comic scenes, are of a very stylised nature. They are repeated again and again and are orientated towards the expression of specific ideas or emotions.

Kneeling, either upon one or both knees, was a constant feature of *Tron, Lodka* and *Car' Maksimilian*, particularly the latter, where Adol'f kneels before his father, the warriors before Anika, Anika before Death and so on. Going down on both knees with outstretched hands is invariably a plea for mercy, used in cases where death or punishment is imminent. Adol'f's speeches to his father are therefore largely pronounced from a kneeling position, e.g.: —

> "Адольф приходит, становится на одно колено и говорит . . ."13

or: —

> "Входит Адольф, сопровождаемый двумя воинами, подходит к трону и становится на колени . . ."14

In *Mašen'ka* and *Lodka* the heroine pleads with the robbers on her knees, in the *Živoj vertep* it is Rachel who kneels in the hope of saving her child. Kneeling on one knee only can also be a mark of respect or acceptance of subordination before the *Car'* or any other superior leader. Thus the Roman ambassador bends one knee before Maksimilian,15 and Anika does likewise in several variants,16 to quote but two examples. Alternatively, falling on one knee may be a token of defeat and is particularly in evidence during the duel scenes between the warriors: —

> "Оба сходятся. После второго удара Аники воин Змиулан становится на одно колено . . ."17

A similar device can be found in the English folk theatre where the defeated warriors retreat to the back of the stage where they wait balanced upon one knee for the end of the performance.

Equally rooted in convention was the scene of Adol'f's execution or Anika's death or the killing in battle of the champions. The execution was carried out not behind the scenes, with an accompanying speech to describe the fate of the victim, as was usual in the academic theatre, but in full view of the audience. The folk actors, however, made no attempt to give the scene an appearance of reality by the use of such subtleties as bladders of blood hidden beneath the clothing. Instead, the execution and the other deaths were presented in symbolic fashion. In some cases a sword would be swung several times over Adol'f's head, whereupon he would fall to the ground and cover his head over with his arms to show that he had been executed. In the Mjakutin variant both Adol'f and Anika are dispatched in this way.[18] Another method can be seen in a version of *Car' Irod*, where Death kills Herod by touching him lightly on the neck with her scythe. Another conventional method of executing or destroying an enemy was for the victor to lift the victim's cap from his head on the point of his sword. This action is very interesting, coming as it does from a purely folk tradition. It can be observed in the Kostin variant of *Maksimilian*: —

"Они сходятся, и Аника побивает Мамая и снимает с него шапку . . ."[19]

Adol'f met his end in like fashion in the film version from the Gor'kij *oblast'*. The device was also known in the Czech folk theatre.

Although some attempts were made by folk actors to convey various emotions by means of vocal inflection and facial expression this was never developed to any great degree. Emphasis and point was, however, often given to speeches, particularly those of a belligerent nature, by the traditional actions of furious sword waving and foot stamping which accompanied them. This can be clearly seen in the following instances: —

"Атаман (ТОПАЕТ НОГОЮ и кричит грозно) : — Эсаул! Эсаул точно также ТОПАЕТ НОГОЮ и кричит в ответ"; [20]

and: —

". . . При этом посол ТОПАЕТ НОГОЮ 1 раз, делает прием саблей и ожидает ответа.
Царь: — Прочь, дерзкий посол.
Посол (также ТОПАЯ НОГОЮ и ВЗМАХИВАЯ САБЛЕЙ, говорит) : — О варвар, убийца! Кровопроливец!"[21]

When a character rushed on stage wildly flourishing a weapon of some sort this was accepted as a sign of extreme displeasure and was usually the preface to a challenge and duel as is the case here: —

"Медленными шагами, как бы гуляя, выходит Богиня. После ее первой речи, как бешеный, размахивая обнаженной шашкой, выскакивает Марец . . .";
"Поклонившись царю Максимильяну, он быстро поворачивается к рьцарю Марцу и, вытащивши шашку, начинает ею размахивать и топать ногами, наступая на Марца . . .";
"Обращается к Змиулану, грозно на него наступая и размахивая над его головой шашкой . . ."[22]

Stamping the feet on its own may be used simply to add a note of authority or to stress an important speech. The actor playing the part of Adol'f in the film version of *Maksimilian* employed it for this purpose during the scene of his 'farewell to the world' before execution, facing one by one the four corners of the globe with his sword raised in military salute and giving an emphatic stamp of the feet at each turn.

The sword, on the whole, played a considerable part in the traditional actions of the plays and this is one of the many indications of the strong military atmosphere which surrounds them. It was customary for characters appearing before the *Car'* to unsheathe the sword and perform a military salute and then, after the address, to return it to the scabbard, as in: —

> "Скороход быстро появляется, шага за три перед царем становится на одно колено, вынимает саблю, салютует и вонзает ее в землю с левой стороны, продолжая держаться за нее рукой . . . встает, вкладывает саблю в ножны и уходит."[23]

or: —

> "С двух сторон появляются два Пажа, быстро подходят к самому трону, делают 'на караул' обнаженными шашками, и говорят поочередно . . . делают 'налево кругом', вкладывают шашки в ножны и идут за короной . . .";

and: —

> "Царь Максимильян обнажает шашку и, делая 'на караул', говорит . . . Вкладывает шашку в ножны и садится."[24]

There are even texts where these gestures, so much an integral part of the action, have, by parody and distortion, become incorporated into the comic scenes as well. The old gravedigger of Vinogradov's 1st variant, for instance, hobbles in coughing and spluttering and saluting with his crutch, makes fun of a device intended to add importance and dignity to the serious members of the cast.[25]

In the English folk plays, actors often tried to place greater emphasis on their speeches by banging heavily upon the ground with their swords. A description in Thomas Hardy's *The Return of the Native* gives a clear impression of this habit. "Eustacia then proceeded in her delivery, slapping the sword against the staff or lance at the minatory phrases, in the orthodox mumming manner, and strutted up and down."[26] Similar actions were performed by their Russian counterparts. In the Romanov text of *Maksimilian*

Anika beats three times upon the floor with his spear as he issues his challenge to the world at large,[27] and in one of the texts collected by Vinogradov the knight known as the *Ispolinskij rycar'* beats the floor with the blunt end of his spear, presumably to attract attention before he begins his address to the *Car'*.[28]

The sword is also predominant in several more important actions, namely, in the protection of the *Car'* from his enemies, in the carrying out of the dead and in the delivery of the royal regalia.

When Maksimilian or Herod is threatened by the approach of a possible enemy his loyal guards form a barrier of crossed swords in front of him. In the Mjakutin variant (p. 262) as the field-marshal rushes on stage the pages in alarm form a barrier over the *Car'*'s head. As he makes his way to the *Car'* he has to break their blades apart with his own. Similar episodes can also be found in other texts.[29]

One of the most spectacular moments in *Car' Maksimilian* consists of the bearing in of the royal regalia, the crown, the sceptre and the orb. One receives the impression from all the variants that this is a scene which was well organised and planned to gain the best effect. The following description is taken from the Vinogradov text republished in Berkov's anthology (pp. 183-4) and it shows signs of careful thought and a sense of dignity appropriate to such an occasion which helps to refute the casual dismissal of the folk actors as primitive and naive: —

> "Растворяются двери избы, два царедворца на золотых подносах несут корону царскую, скипетр, державу, золотую саблю и пр. За ними идет свита, несколько войнов с обнаженными саблями на плечо. Все поют: — Мы к царю, царю идем . . . Воини заходят и поровну становятся вокруг царского трона, держа все время сабли на плечо. Царедворцы подходят к самому трону, становятся на колени перед Максимилианом и протягивают ему подносы с царскими регалиями . . . Царедворцы снимают с него военную фуражку, медали и простую саблю, надевают корону, ордена, дают в руки скипетр и державу, кладут прежние уборы на подносы и уходят, низко кланяясь. Свита все время стоит около трона."

In some cases there is more emphasis on the military aspect of the occasion, the regalia being borne in upon the warrior's swords.[30]

As one proceeds with an examination of the action in *Car' Maksimilian*, and to a lesser extent in the other plays, one becomes increasingly aware that most of the limited movement about the stage is in fact of a predominantly military nature. Apart from the above examples the list can be extended with many more drawn from the traditions and disciplines of a soldier's life. In many variants[31] Adol'f, after his refusal to give in to his father, is removed in disgrace under military escort. It is common, too, for the warriors killed in combat to be borne off the stage upon the crossed swords of their companions-in-arms. In just such a way in one of Berkov's texts the fallen Anika is carried out to the accompaniment of a funeral song.[32] Both Maksimilian and Herod are generally provided with a military bodyguard and Anika is usually offered a military triumph for having saved Antongrad, the royal city.

One should not forget either the numerous warlike battle-scenes which are so much a part of *Maksimilian* and to some extent of *Tron* and *Lodka*. Of the construction of these, on the whole, little can be ascertained except that each duel was usually divided into three encounters typified by a great deal of sword-waving and slashing. A detailed eye-witness account of these duels is given in Smirnickij's variant of *Tron* from the Xerson government: —

> "Происходит сражение. Бойцы, заложив левую руку за спину, становятся в позу, напоминающую первую фехтовальную фразу. Правые ноги почти перпендикулярны левым, голова повернута на полкруга по направлению 'сабли', 'сабля' поднята полусогнутой рукой на высоте глаз; затем они делают движение, напоминающее выпад, два три удара саблями и тот, кто должен быть убит, выпускает из рук 'саблю' и падает к ногам противника, но беспощадно им прикалывается."[33]

If the actions of the actors show a certain lack of subtlety, the same can also be said of their manner of speech. The remark to be found in one text, that "all those taking part in the performance try to speak as loudly as possible and almost shout their lines",[34] may be said to be typical. In addition it should be noted that in general the voices of the actors tended to lack the natural inflections, adopting instead a strangely monotonous intonation, faster than normal speech and with a rising and falling tone reminiscent of a chant. This 'monotony' was, however, not as rigidly adhered to as one is often led to believe and actors did attempt to introduce some variety of tone and expression into their speeches. From the description of the *dramatis personae* in one of Berkov's texts one can see that in this version at least a certain amount of care was taken over the actors' voices. Each character had to sound right. Thus one is told that the *Car'* delivers his speeches in a loud, brusque voice, that Adol'f on the other hand has a quiet voice and Anika a solid, dependable voice; Brambeus's speech is slow and deep and Death speaks in a firm tone, taking care not to rush the words.[35] However, such attention to detail in one of the most sophisticated versions of this play is certainly an exception and attempts to differentiate between the speech of the characters were generally of a much broader nature.

In the same text there are also many examples of individual actors trying to offer a range of emotions through their voice and manner of presentation. The field-marshal delivers a speech, panting and out of breath after rushing to answer the *Car'* 's summons, Maksimilian, angry with his son, speaks to him in a threatening manner, Adol'f's farewell song is sung in a sorrowful tone, Adol'f in chains, weak and scarcely able to move after his spell in prison, speaks to his father in a quiet, pitiful voice.

Although such a degree of variety is unusual in the folk plays nevertheless it is clear that the actors usually made some attempt to differentiate between the personalities, moods and attitudes of the characters they portrayed. Adol'f not only speaks in quiet, subdued tones, he also stays on his knees as a token of weakness and humility, sings melancholy ballads, tries to appear exhausted after his term of imprisonment, holds back when the guard comes to take him away. In contrast, his father shouts, brandishes his sword or sceptre, frowns and tries to look fierce and angry, a figure of power and authority. The same is true to a greater or lesser degree for all the other characters of the folk repertoire. But it is important when assessing the art of the folk actors to remember that the methods they used to achieve their ends were those acceptable to themselves and to the majority of their audiences and that these would not necessarily appeal to or be understood by observers used to the quite different conventions of the literary stage.

It is difficult to decide whether or not the folk plays had to rely purely upon the talents of individual actors, the costumes, the traditional techniques of the acting methods and the entertainment potential contained within the actual text, or whether some further embellishments in the form of light and sound effects were also added. Material on this subject is scarce and the difficulties of arranging anything unusual or original of this kind under primitive conditions probably discouraged much effort in this direction. Nevertheless, there are several indications that some troupes at least made use of special talents discovered among their members! The opening lines of the Arab's first monologue in *Maksimilian* usually contain the words "жаром пылаю", and in several cases there is evidence that these words were interpreted literally. In the Romanov text of *Car' Maksimilian*, the Arab, with his face smeared with soot, comes on stage and produces a startling effect by sending a spray of paraffin from his mouth over a lighted candle, which of course shoots a spout of flame through the room![36]

It seems quite clear that if intelligent eye-witnesses were inclined to think of *Car' Maksimilian* and the other folk plays as being stiff and lifeless, it was not predominantly because the actors were insufficiently talented to make the action seem free and lively, but because they were following a code of conventional acting methods which simply did not lend itself to natural realistic movement or behaviour on stage. The folk plays convey this impression not by accident but by design and in order to understand the folk actors properly it is as necessary to understand the rules according to which they operate as it is for the proper enjoyment of any cultural activity belonging to an age or an environment with which we are unfamiliar.

NOTES

1. In a letter dated 26th December 1855 quoted by Sobolevskij, Introduction to Vinogradov, "Narodnaja drama *Car' Maksimil'jan*", p. 14.
2. Veselovskij, *Starinnyj teatr v Evrope*, p. 399.
3. In the 18th century there was also of course, the urban democratic theatre. For a description of popular and *balagan* theatres see Alekseev-Jakovlev, *Russkie narodnye guljan'ja.*
4. Smirnickij, "K voprosu o vyroždenii vertepnoj dramy", p. 195.
5. Abramov, p. 7.
6. Volkov, p. 324.
7. *Supra*, p. 157.
8. "*Lodka*", Berkov, *Russkaja narodnaja drama*, p. 144.
9. Vinogradov, Variant 3, p. 99.
10. Abramov, pp. 13, 19, 20.
11. Mjakutin, pp. 264, 274, 287.
12. *Ibid.*, p. 261.
13. Ončukov, Variant 2, p. 52.
14. Vinogradov, Variant 1, p. 23.
15. See e.g. Berkov, *Russkij fol'klor*, p. 348.
16. E.g. Ončukov, Variant 2, p. 54.
17. Berkov, *Russkij fol'klor*, p. 342.
18. See pp. 273 and 296.
19. Kostin, p. 115
20. "*Lodka*", Berkov, *Russkaja narodnaja drama*, p. 144.
21. Berkov, *Russkij fol'klor*, p. 348.
22. Vinogradov, Variant 3, pp. 116, 119, 125.
23. Kallaš, Variant 1, p. 7.
24. Vinogradov, Variant 1, pp. 20-21.
25. *Ibid.*, p. 30.
26. Thomas Hardy, *The return of the native* (New York – London, 1912), p. 150.
27. P. 279.
28. Vinogradov, Variant 5, p. 186.
29. See e.g. Berkov, *Russkij fol'klor*, p. 347 and Vinogradov, Variant 5, p. 198.
30. Abramov, p. 10 and Ončukov, Variant 2, p. 51.
31. See e.g. Volkov, p. 329; Vinogradov, Variant 5, p. 186; Mjakutin, p. 268.
32. Berkov, *Russkij fol'klor*, p. 357.
33. Smirnickij, "K voprosu o vyroždenii vertepnoj dramy", pp. 200-201.
34. Vinogradov, Variant 1, p. 18.
35. Vinogradov, Variant 5, p. 180.
36. P. 281.

CHAPTER XII

THE FOLK ACTOR AND HIS AUDIENCE

In the preceding chapters some attempt has been made to explain why the sustained interest of the ordinary people in the folk theatre was not as astonishing as it may at first sight appear. However, one of the main factors contributing to their enjoyment of this form of entertainment has not yet been examined. This lies in the special relationship that existed between the audience and the actors on the stage. The audience of the folk theatre were not passive spectators but active participators. In a variety of ways they helped to create the performances they watched and this in itself was a strong antidote to boredom. The audience was never cut off from the players, either in the physical or the spiritual sense. Personal contact was made right at the beginning with the entrance of the actors when they greeted their host and asked his permission for the play to begin. It was maintained throughout the performance right up to the end when the actors again made a direct approach to the people who had been watching them in order to receive some remuneration from them. Once the show was over they did not retreat into backstage anonymity but mingled once again with the audience from among whose number they had originally emerged, to enjoy with them their share of the festive cheer. The gay songs and dances with which the performance of many folk plays ended were also a part of the communal activity where the entertained and the entertainers all joined in with equal enthusiasm. In this respect the folk theatre may be said to represent a stage halfway between ritual and the literary theatre. In the ritual proper there is no division between actor and audience. It is more a question of larger and smaller roles, for if only a few men are seen to have an obviously active part each person present is to some degree an actor in the drama; by his very presence in the integrated and select group he is committed to total involvement. In the games which developed from ritual and in folk plays where the ritual element is still very strong, such as *Paxomuška*, the division into more and less active groups is already apparent although not particularly strong. Some of the shorter folk plays and scenes, like *Paxomuška* again, the game *Barin* or the central and basic scenes of *Lodka*, could be staged more or less impromptu in the course of an informal gathering. In such cases the actors are only briefly and tenuously detached from their audience and it is probable that both were only tentatively aware of the difference. In more sophisticated examples of the folk repertoire, however, the split between actor and audience is more clearly defined. With plays like *Car' Maksimilian*, for example, requiring long and careful preparation of the speeches, acting techniques and costumes, the actors did make themselves into a distinct and separate body, united among themselves by long rehearsals and cut off from the rest of the community both by the need or desire to preserve secrecy and by their own semi-professional nature.

The development of drama from ritual is in a way the history of its division into two distinct bodies — the players and the audience. Nevertheless, in the Russian folk theatre the split is by no means complete and it is this feature which brings it closer to the ritual on the one hand and which distinguishes it from the literary theatre on the other.

The Russian folk actors were not physically separated from their audience but were often literally surrounded by them and on occasions, during the comic scenes, actually mingled with them. They were usually personally acquainted with those watching, being from the same village community, the same regiment or from the staff of the same factory and the text of the plays was as familiar to those off-stage as it was to those on it. Consequently, the job of prompter was usually quite superfluous, for if any actor ever forgot his lines or became confused there was always someone ready to supply the missing words or to interrupt with corrections or even to enter the acting area with suggestions for improvement. One of the integral features of the majority of the folk plays, the choir, which played an important part in both emphasising and altering the general mood of the action, was often simply composed of members of the audience who were, in any case, always free to join in, particularly with the humorous songs. Although, naturally, all the important roles in the plays were assigned long before performances began it was not unusual for non-speaking parts or those which required little or no action or talent to be filled on the spot by unprepared volunteers.

The basic character of each audience itself was a factor of considerable importance, for the sort of people who composed it, their mood, their tastes, likes and dislikes could determine the very nature of each individual performance. Thus, some of the comic scenes might be omitted in deference to the presence of religious or national minorities in the audience. Others again which could be played before a predominantly male audience might not be included when women were present. The satirical elements to be found in plays like *Lodka* and *Barin* or the parodies on church services scattered throughout the repertoire and completely banned in some regions, had to be kept neutral and inoffensive when the presence of ecclesiastical or civil authorities was known or suspected. Members of the audience or others known to them could be mentioned in the comic scenes and made a laughing stock because of some personal peculiarity, vice or failing. Hostile reactions from those who found themselves in such a position were known to end performances abruptly on an unhappy note for the mockers. The actors therefore had to be keenly attuned to the audience and its reactions. In fact, the folk play, particularly the comic scenes, was largely dependent for its success upon a delicate balance of interaction between audience and actor. Comedy was not static and fixed within the bounds of a particular role but improvised and in a state of development. The comic sounded his audience, roused them to retaliate and they in their turn, by their own quips and witticisms, sparked off new sallies from the actor. Without a receptive audience to use as a sort of verbal trampoline the comic's art was flat and uninteresting. If a particular audience was unforthcoming and refused to react appropriately to the play the troupe might well give only a skeleton performance, leaving a reserve of scenes for a more appreciative one.

In the literary theatre (with the exception of the experimental theatre) the acting body is a homogeneous group with little or no direct links with the audience. The interplay is almost exclusively between the members of the group. In the folk theatre, however, the position is quite the reverse, for the link between each actor and the rest of the company is often, for various reasons, quite tenuous. There is, for example, the lack of connection between the comic and serious scenes and characters, the lack of developed dialogue and the episodic nature of many of the scenes like the duels in *Maksimilian*, where the series of combatants are quite unconnected one with the other. On the other hand, links with the audience are strong. The actors addressed their lines not to some invisible and intangible abstraction but to live people whom they knew and could see. The actor, upon entering the stage greeted his public. Characters bowed to the public before beginning to speak their part, and then introduced themselves. The actor's opening lines were never for the benefit of his fellow actors but for those watching. Thus Maksimilian would address his audience: —

> "Здравствуйте, почтенейшие господа!
> Вот я прибыл из Англии к вам сюда.
> А за кого вы меня признаете? Или же за короля пруського,
> Или же за принца хранцузького? . . ."[1]

The audience could not fail to become emotionally involved as the actor was constantly referring to it for an opinion or to evoke a definite response. When the *Car'*, attacked by Mamaj, exclaims: —

> "Смотрите, господа:
> Залетела ворона у чужия хоромы
> Да й крача",[2]

he is inviting the audience to share his astonishment and annoyance. The executioner, having just killed Adol'f, turns to the audience as if to enlist their sympathy and to show how repentant he is: —

"Эх, друзья,
Так нельзя!
Кого я зарубил,
Или, лучше сказать, загубил —
Можно назвать братом родным."[3]

Although, as has been seen, the 'serious' characters did address the audience, it was through the comic ones that real contact was established. The spectators were certainly intended to tremble with Adol'f and the maiden kidnapped by the robbers and to condemn righteously the wicked deeds of Napoleon, Herod and Maksimilian, but, at the same time, a certain degree of aloofness remained. With the comic characters, however, there was no barrier at all and the audience greeted them as old friends on a common footing. It is relevant here to remember that the popularity of the puppet play *Petruška* lay precisely in the establishment of this unconstrained rapport between the entertainer and the entertained.[4]

In the folk theatre there were no footlights, no artificial barriers and just as the audience was free to enter the acting area so the actors were free to mingle with the audience. In the church parodies spectators placed near the 'priest' stood the risk of being splashed with the unpleasant contents of the censer and being choked with its reeking smoke.[5] The discomfiture and startled laughter of certain members of the audience constituted half the humour of the play. Similarly, the executioner in Ončukov's second variant of *Car' Maksimilian* on being given a glass of 'vodka' invited the audience to share it by splashing the contents over them.[6]

In another variant, the *Car'* orders his soldiers to find an imaginary devil and they carry out his order by creating havoc among the spectators: —

"Идут в толпу и начинают разыскивать беса: залезают в карманы, стаскивают у баб платки, пользуясь случаем, заглядывают под подолы. Начинается визг, ругань, поднимается суматоха, а иногда, если искальщики окажутся слишком дерзкими на руку — и свалка . . ."[7]

A great deal of the humour in the folk theatre was based upon irony of situation. In other words, the audience in league with the comic is, in common with him, aware of the true circumstances of the situation and is therefore able to laugh with him at the expense of a third party. The enjoyment derived from scenes based upon *oslyška* or 'mishearing', in which the gravedigger (and even, on occasions, Adol'f) mocked the *Car'*, or the bailiff mocked the *barin*, or the old peasant Napoleon, was largely a result of this sort of collusion.

The folk audience reacted in a lively and often unpredictable way towards the plays in the repertoire. The actors did not expect, desire or receive a uniform opinion. The main aim was to stimulate and hold interest. The audience was intended to talk back to the actors, to discuss the performances amongst themselves, to comment upon the talents and appearance of the actors. A silent audience meant that the play was a failure. In this respect the folk theatre differs quite considerably from the literary theatre where the actor does not expect to share his stage or his role with the spectators. Ščeglov, writing about the popular theatre, has described with amusement some of the comments overheard in an audience at one of the People's Theatres in Petersburg towards the end of the nineteenth century. These remarks indicate the same sense of personal involvement as among the spectators at the village plays: —

> "— Хромой хорошо играет"; "Старуха похоже сердится!"; "Жениху браво! очень браво."[8]

In the folk theatre the emotional involvement of the audience with the characters and plot of the play was strong but total involvement was prevented by their understanding and acceptance of the dramatic conventions. Faced with the quite different conventions of the literary stage such audiences were often at a loss how to behave. From some of the remarks of Ščeglov and Filippov in their respective works on the People's Theatres it is clear that for many the illusion of reality was total. In one of the plays on village life some members of the audience, according to Ščeglov, identified the scene with either their own or neighbouring villages; in another, some people persisted in referring to one of the characters as Mar'ja Ivanovna and not as Tat'jana Nikolaevna, as she was called in the play, because she was very like someone they knew at home.[9] Filippov tells of simple audiences thrown into confusion when the dramatic illusion to which they had completely succumbed was abruptly broken at the end of the spectacle by the appearance of the actors to take the curtain calls.[10] The more serious consequences of a similar effect are seen in an anecdote of Aleksandr Tairov recollected by P.G. Bogatyrev which tells of a performance of *Othello* during which an enraged member of the audience shot the actor playing Iago, for his treachery.[11]

NOTES

1. Volkov, pp. 326-327.
2. Romanov, p. 281.

228

3. Vinogradov, Variant 3, p. 147.
4. *Supra*, p. 113.
5. *Supra*, pp. 76 and 78.
6. Ončukov, Variant 2, p. 62.
7. Vinogradov, Variant 3, p. 115.
8. Ščeglov, p. 9.
9. *Ibid.*, pp. 10 and 18.
10. V. Filippov, *Zadači narodnogo teatra i ego prošloe v Rossii* (Moscow, 1918), pp. 5-6.
11. Bogatyrev, *Lidové divadlo*, p. 13.

CHAPTER XIII

COMEDY IN THE FOLK THEATRE

The folk theatre, in one form or another, brought much pleasure to wide sections of the Russian people for several hundreds of years. One of the causes of its great popularity was undoubtedly the fact that it was a theatre of comedy in which humour and laughter were predominant, a theatre in which the people could find relaxation and shake off the cares of their difficult life.

The moods portrayed by the folk actors, making the best of limited knowledge and means of expression, were as clear-cut and bold as their voices and gestures. Subtle gradations of character and emotion were foreign to them; anger, tears, laughter were predominant. Although within the framework of each play, particularly the more developed ones such as *Car' Maksimilian* and *Lodka*, alternating moods were not only possible but encouraged for the sake of greater dramatic effect, it was unusual to find a combination of different aspects of serious and comic expression either in one particular character or within one and the same scene. The humorous action was played out on the whole by a set of stock comic 'types' who did not themselves participate in the serious parts of the plays. Serious characters like *Car'* Maksimilian, Adol'f, the *ataman*, are in their turn, rarely, if ever, the bearers of comedy whether in word or action. Comic and serious characters do meet on common ground but only in specific circumstances (as in the funeral scenes in *Car' Maksimilian*), where each retains his own essential function.

In view of the centralised nature of the comedy in the folk plays it is not surprising that comedy of character should be one of its main features. Most obvious among the bearers of comedy is of course the ubiquitous *šut* or fool, the old gravedigger or *ded* who turns up in most of the plays of the folk theatre repertoire. Not only his appearance but also his words and actions and his whole manner and bearing were such as to evoke storms of laughter from his audience: —

"Он глуховатый и глуповатый, подслеповатый и говорит, чмокая беззубным ртом, отчаянно шепелявя."[1]

In every way he attempts to underline this image of grotesque decrepitude and senility. His particular brand of humour was of the coarsest and most vulgar kind and his jokes and comic remarks were studded with obscenities. A typical picture of the sort of amusement provided by the antics of the old clown can be found in Vinogradov's 1st variant of *Car' Maksimilian*. He enters to 'bury' the corpse of Adol'f: —

> "он идет, сгорбившись и опираясь на палку; кряхтит, охает и издает неприличные звуки при помощи спрятанного под мышками пузыря; подойдя к трону, он вытягивается и отдает честь костылем . . ."[2]

As he leaves after the job is done and throughout his several appearances in the play he conducts himself in like fashion, e.g.: —

> "Старик, покряхтывая, почесываясь и издавая звуки, уходит."[3]

In this respect the gravedigger is not in any way unusual, but observes the pattern followed in varying degrees by fools from the times of the ancient classical theatre through the mediaeval jester to Shakespeare's day and beyond. The obscenities of the comic in the Anglo-German theatre, which was popular for a time in Russia in the eighteenth century, resemble those of the *ded* and the language and humour of many of the popular interludes and comedies of the eighteenth century were on much the same level.

A particularly good characterisation of the old man, or rather the *two* old men (for in this text the task of removing the dead bodies is divided between Mokej and his friend Patrakej), occurs in one of the texts of *Maksimilian* in Ončukov's northern anthology. Here the reader will find not only the usual pretence of deafness and stupidity which characterises the play between the old man and the *Car'* or the doctor in other versions but also the development of a relationship between the two comic characters themselves as they compare memories of war service, consider what action to take over the *Car'* 's commands, help each other to answer the doctor's questions, compare finds as they loot Adol'f's body and so on.

Although the old gravedigger was in many ways repulsive and although the laughter he provoked was largely at his own expense he still remained basically a character sympathetic to the audience. His disrespectful mockery of *Car'* Maksimilian, the villain, for instance, was especially endearing. Of quite another type was the Jew who was both a comic figure and the butt for national and religious prejudices. His odd appearance, old-fashioned traditional Jewish garments, his accent, his religious observances were all the subject of mockery and cruel laughter. Not all humour in the folk theatre was of such an innocent nature as that produced by the old gravedigger but could be the result of ignorance and intolerance as well.

Although humour was usually centred upon one or two characters re-appearing at appropriate intervals there are some instances in the folk theatre repertoire where one comedian is constantly present on stage, mimicking the serious characters and generally interfering in the action rather like the Vice of the European mediaeval drama. Such a role is played by the devil in the Mjakutin variant of *Car' Maksimilian* and by the Jew in Romanov's White Russian variant. In the former, for example, the devil keeps getting in the *Car'* 's way as he goes to sit on the throne, pretends to be a horse and throws the old gravedigger off his back, interrupts during the measuring of Adol'f's body and generally creates confusion. In the latter text the Jew mimics and distorts the words of serious characters like Maksimilian himself, as in: —

> "Царь: — Скороход-маршал,
>   Явись пред троном своего монарха!
> Жид (перебивая) : — Сковородник з маслом,
>   Иди к монаху!"4

He also comments sarcastically upon both words and deeds of the *Car'* and the knights. Acting as a mocking shadow he introduces a frivolous note to the usually serious scenes of Adol'f's trial and execution and the duels between the champions.

However, although there was ample opportunity for improvisation and the exploitation of individual wit and talent, the framework of the scenes in which the comic characters usually appeared remained fairly constant. Among such scenes were the measuring of corpses for a coffin, which could lead to a number of odd and humorous 'incidents'; in one such scene the 'corpse' un-expectedly retaliates to the ungentle treatment of the gravedigger: —

> "Маркушка: . . . Еще надо вперед смерять, ведик-ли гроб-от делать (меряет палкой тело, причем тычет мертвому в разные места и приговаривает.) : —
> — Раз, два —
>   По дрова;
>   Раз, два, три —
>   Нос утри;
>   Три, четыре —
>   Прискочили;
>   Раз, два, три, четыре, пять —
> Пора спать! (щелкает мертвого по лбу палкой, тот вскакивает и убегает, причем дает Маркушке по уху здоровую оплеуху . . .) "5

Another is the scene in which Petruška or the Cossack buys from the gypsy and attempts to ride a decrepit old nag which is either so weak that it collapses under his weight or deliberately throws him off at a command from its previous owner. Then there is the scene in which the doctor 'sounds' the patient which gives a chance for much poking and prodding and unexpected tricks, not always of an entirely innocent nature, from both the actors involved. The portrayal of drunkenness, including such features as the clumsy gait, the muddled speech and the tendency of the drunkard to burst into song, was also popular. The chief culprit in this matter was usually the doctor's assistant (the *fel'dšer*).[6]

It is necessary also to include among the predictable humorous scenes of any folk play in the repertoire the brawls and unjustifiable attacks in which many characters became involved. The old gravedigger quarrels with his old woman and their differences are resolved by an exchange of blows; Maximilian constantly threatens his field-marshal and the *ataman* his *esaul* with a thrashing for insubordination. The Jew and the gypsy rarely escape without a kick or a cuff at least. Both Petruška and the Cossack were ready to fly into a rage at the least provocation and anyone who crossed them was liable to be set upon.

For some measure of success in such examples of crude slapstick comedy little more than high spirits and energy was required. However, for some of the other methods of comedy in folk plays a certain amount of real talent was necessary. For instance, apart from the use of appearance, behaviour and ridiculous situations, many linguistic methods were used for humorous purposes. Among the most common of these was the device known as *oslyška* (mishearing), which may be the result of 'deafness' or a deliberate or unconscious misunderstanding. The humour of the situation results from a character's repetition of a given passage in which he substitutes for an original word or phrase homonyms which sound roughly the same but which completely alter the meaning of the utterance. This device can be found in all the folk plays and between many of the characters including 'serious' ones such as Adol'f mocking his father or the *esaul* his *ataman*, but it is mainly exploited by comic characters such as the old gravedigger or the servant or bailiff in the play *Barin*. Two main divisions may be seen within the device. In the first place the humorous distorted statement may proceed directly from the original straightforward one. For example, we find in Ončukov's 1st variant of *Car' Maksimilian* the following dialogue between the two gravediggers who have been summoned to bury Adol'f's body, and the field-marshal: —

"Скороход: — Васька старик, к царю.
Первый старик: — К какому косарю?
Скороход: — Да не к косарю, к царю.
Первый старик: — Скажи что дома нету. Сегодня праздник.
   Мы загуляли.

Скороход: — Василий Иванович, к царю за наградой.

Первый старик: — Ага-га, как пришло туго, дак и Василий Иванович. А за каким виноградом?

Скороход: — Да, не за виноградом, а за наградой!

Первый старик (к второму старику): — Мокей!

Второй старик: — А что, Патракей?

Первый старик: — Пойдем к царю.

Второй старик: — Зачем?

Первый старик: — За наградой.

Второй старик: — За каким виноградом? Теперь зима, виноград не растет."[7]

In Vinogradov's 2nd variant of *Car' Maksimilian* the old man's 'deafness' is so bad that the *Car'* has to repeat his command to remove the bodies five times: —

"Ц.М.: — ... Убери, брат, пожалуйста.

Старик: — Обрать? — Можно.

Ц.М.: — Я тебе говорю: убрать!

Старик: — Обираю, батюшка, обираю . . . Вот, нашол махорки осьмушку, да нюхальнова на понюшку.

Ц.М.: — Я тебе говорю: зарывай!

Старик: — Заси.ать? . . . Ну сичас и заси.ать буду.

Ц.М.: — Я тебе говорю: закапывай!

Старик: — Да я и то закакиваю, чего кричишь-то.

Ц.М.: — Я тебе говорю, старый чорт, зарой!

Старик: — Зарыть, — так бы давно и баял."[8]

This situation can be developed in a variety of different ways in order to increase the comic effect. In some cases, for instance, the gravedigger reveals that he is not as deaf as he at first pretends: —

"Скороход: — Старик, к царю!

Старик: — Я дрова колю.

Скороход: — Старик, пожалуй на бал!

Старик: — Какой там чорт с печи упал!

Скороход: — Старик, пожалуй на водку!

Старик: — Я и сам пойду."[9]

On the other hand there are examples of this device where the original statement itself has a humorous or satirical tone. This statement, which is not properly heard by the person to whom it is addressed, is then repeated in a more acceptable and decorous form which still, however, sounds like the

234

original. This type is found usually, although not exclusively, in the dialogue between the *barin* and his servant or bailiff. Note the following: —

> "Афонька: — Твои хоромы, Барин, сгорели . . .
> . . . .
> Барин: — А ты огонь заливал?
> Афонька: — В окошко солому совал.
> Барин: — Что-о-о?
> Афонька: — Водой заливал, барин.
> . . . .
> Барин: — Скажи, Афонька, толст ли я?
> Афонька: — Как супороса свинья.
> Барин: — Как-как?
> Афонька: — Как все господа.
> . . . .
> Барин: — Афонька, скажи-ка мне, красен ли я?
> Афонька: — Красен, как гусиный нос на морозе.
> Барин: — Как-как?
> Афонька: — Как маков цвет в огороде . . ."[10]

In fact it is in these dialogues between servant and master in particular, that a whole range of humorous linguistic devices appear, not all of which occur elsewhere in the folk theatre. Paradox and climax, for example, are found frequently. In the first of these the comic effect is produced by the answer to a question taking a totally different form from that which the person asking it (and presumably the audience) has been led to expect by preceding statements or events. Laughter is created here by the unexpected: —

> "Барин: — . . . Поди-ко, наши крестьяне на многих лошадях
> и на пашню выезжают?
> Староста: — Порато на многих.
> Барин: — А как на многих?
> Староста: — Всей деревней на одной сохе и то на козе."

or: —

> "Барин: — . . . А что же они из лесу делают?
> Староста: — Домы строят.
> Барин: — Поди-ка большие?
> Староста: — Порато большие, боерин-батюшко.
> Барин: — А как большие?
> Староста: — А собачки бежат, в окошечко глядят."[11]

ог: —

> "Барин: — Нет ли у вас особой комнаты для моих вещей, которых у меня сроду не бывало.
> Хозяин: — Есть самые лучшие, петербургские, в которых собаки спят."[12]

The use of climax for comical effect usually occurs in accounts of incidents or misfortunes suffered by the *barin*'s relatives, animals or property during his absence. The servant or bailiff begins by telling him of the least important of these and finishes up with the most tragic and disastrous. Thus, in many variants the first event is the discovery of the *barin*'s broken penknife. This in turn, it transpires, had been used to skin the *barin*'s favourite horse which itself had died while drawing the heavy carriage containing the corpse of the *barin*'s mother. She had been killed when she jumped off a balcony of the *barin*'s house as it and his stud farm with it were being burnt to the ground. In this way the real tragedies are reduced to the level of trivialities since all the *barin*'s anger and dismay have been wasted on the less important ones, while the audience's laughter increases with each new revelation.

Other humorous linguistic devices do occur in the folk plays but less frequently than those mentioned above. Quite popular is a deliberate, literal interpretation of a speaker's words and particularly of a metaphorical expression. In one variant of *Lodka* there are several such instances in a dialogue between an officer trying to find out who is the village elder and an old man who prevaricates, either deliberately or through his own stupidity: —

> "Офицер: — А кто же у вас был за старшаго?
> Староста: — За старшаго был наш дедушка, ему сот два года, все миряне почитали, да и нас то почитают по вашей милости.
> . . . .
> Офицер: — Кто у вас был за набольшого?
> . . . .
> Староста: — За набольшого был у нас Ванюха, Андрюхин сын, более его у нас во всем селе нет."[13]

An occasional pun creeps into the text of the folk plays and there is also a phenomenon common in the English mumming plays, christened "topsy-turvy humour" by the celebrated English folklorist J.R. Tiddy. In this device the two halves of a sentence are twisted so that each becomes paired with something quite ridiculous, as in: —

"Лекарь: — Что делаешь?
Степка: — Куриц дою, коров на яйца сажаю."[14]

Although it occurs rarely in the folk plays this type of joke was well known in other types of Russian folk literature. It occurs in humorous fairy tales and *nebylicy* as in: —

"Еще овца в гнезде яйцо садит,
Еще курица под осеком траву секет . . ."[15]

Foreign accents and speech defects were also a source of amusement in the folk theatre. Petruška poked fun at the inability of the German to speak Russian and the Jew's odd accent provided yet another reason for ridiculing him.

Although we nowadays may find little that is really amusing in these plays, nevertheless it cannot be denied that in the comic scenes a free rein was given to the development of individual wit, talent and imagination and that simple audiences derived much pleasure from watching them.

NOTES

1. Smirnickij, "K voprosu o vyroždenii vertepnoj dramy", p. 199.
2. Vinogradov, Variant 1, p. 30.
3. *Ibid.*, p. 31.
4. Romanov, p. 274.
5. Vinogradov, Variant 3, p. 153.
6. See e.g. Kallaš, Variant 1, p. 12.
7. Pp. 20-21.
8. Pp. 83-84.
9. Gruzinskij, p. 164.
10. Moxirev, "Vjatsko-poljanskij variant", pp. 260-261.
11. "*Mnimyj barin*", Berkov, *Russkaja narodnaja drama*, p. 56.
12. "*Šajka razbojnikov*", Berkov, *Russkij fol'klor*, p. 358.
13. Česalin, "Novaja zapis' *Lodki*", p. 109.
14. Kallaš, Variant 2, p. 16.
15. V.Ja. Propp and B.N. Putilov (Ed.), *Byliny*, Vol. 2 (Moscow, 1958), p. 455.

In this study of the Russian folk theatre an attempt has been made to bring order and a sense of pattern into one of the most diffuse branches of Russian oral literature. As has been shown, the rituals, puppet theatre, *Car' Maksimilian* and the other plays and games of the repertoire all have their own individual features, stylistic, thematic, historical and social. The impulses which led to their creation, the factors which influenced their evolution, their function within the community are often widely divergent. Yet they should not be regarded as isolated phenomena but rather as different facets of a single dramatic tradition with its own conventions and idiosyncrasies quite separate from those of the literary stage.

In the past the attitude of folklorists and historians of the theatre towards the folk plays has often been orientated by nondramatic considerations. The rituals, for example, have been studied largely for what they reveal of the mythology and superstitions of the peasantry. Nonritual drama, particularly plays of satirical content, was often approached from a sociological point of view, studied as documentary evidence of past political, social and historical attitudes. While not entirely neglecting such nondramatic aspects of the folk theatre I have tried to concentrate on what it has to offer in terms of purely theatrical spectacle, to present a unified picture of drama in evolution from its simplest beginnings in ritual to the relatively complex examples of the folk actor's art such as *Lodka* and *Car' Maksimilian*.

The Russian folk theatre whatever its limitations and however little its customary mixture of superstition and ignorance, rough and tumble, bawdy humour, sentimentality and simplistic moral judgements may appeal to the modern reader, reveals one thing very clearly — a lively and resilient instinct for drama among the Russian folk. Centuries before the appearance of the academic theatre in Moscow in the 1660's, long before the performance on the 17th October 1672 of *Artakserksovo dejstvo*, the 'first play' of the Russian theatre, caused a sensation at the court of Aleksej Mixailovič, the Russian peasant had already learned to create and, more important, to enjoy theatre in his own way; acceptance of the peasant's open and unaffected enjoyment of what appealed to his simple tastes and unspoilt imagination is really the keynote to an understanding of the folk theatre. It is precisely this mood of carefree abandonment to the pleasures of the moment that Alexandre Benoit has captured in the following description of the great Shrove fairs in St. Petersburg as he remembered them from his childhood and youth in the 1870's and 1880's. Here is all the noise, colour and vitality, the atmosphere of festivity and excitement which formed the essential background for so much of the folk theatre: —

> Все еще стоял стон от мычащих оркестрионов, все еще гудела и бубнила огромная площадь — так громко, что даже до Гостинного двора и до Дворцовой площади долетали

238

отголоски этой чудесной какофонии. Все еще чад от
каруселей, качелей и гор дурманил головы, все еще
клубились облака пара от уличных самоваров и от барака, в
котором под рожей немецкого Кладерадатша пеклись
"берлинские пышки". Все еще у малышей болели животы от
пряников, стручков и орехов; все еще у старших болели
помятые в сутолоке бока. Все еще лгали раешники про
королеву Викторию, которая "вот за угол завернула, не
видать стало", все еще вертелись страшные перекидные
качели, гнусавил по прежнему Петрушка в лапах у "ученова-
моченова Барашка", дед ерзал по парапету и нес очень не-
пристойную околесину, а рядом с ним плясали красавицы в
конфедератках и жуткая "Коза" с длинной шеей . . .

И благодаря этому гомону и угару, можно было глотать и
патриотическую чепуху в театрах. Самый спектакль все
более и более начинал походить на просветительную
литературу или даже на настоящие театры. Зато оставалось
по прежнему простудное томление при ожидании очереди,
оставался запах свеже напиленных досок, оставалась
грызущая боль в отмерзающих пальцах ног, оставалась
радость поглядывания в случайно приотворившуюся дверь,
радость от свиста, означавшего перемену картин, или
восторг от звяканья гонга, неминуемо предшествовавшего
всякому появлению ужасного. А потом очень хорош был
момент, когда уже сидя в безопасности на чистых местах,
оглядываясь, видел за собой рушившиеся лавины
пролетарской публики, заполнявшие густым потоком
скамьи третьих мест, топтавшие все на своем пути. Какие
визги, какие вздохи, какой зычный смех! Или вдруг
загнусавит взятая с собой гармоника, или вдруг переброся-
тся крепким словцом приятели, во время штурма попавшие
на противоположные концы верхней трибуны. Естественно
вполне, что после таких эмоций и стряпня г. Малафеева
могла казаться вполне приемлемой. Уже не ее смотришь, а
просто отдаешься балаганной масленичной стихии. Просто
весело, и смешно, и забавно, потому что так необычно, так
непохоже на всегдашнюю нашу хмурость . . ."[1]

The folk theatre should be regarded not merely as a subject for scholarly
research. It was a vital ingredient of communal celebrations and a mirror of
personal joys and sorrows, it was bound up with the daily existence of the
simple people, with the beginning and ending of life, with hopes for happiness
and prosperity both for the community at large and for the family at home.

1. A. Benoit, Introduction to Lejfert, *Balagany*, pp. 14-16.

BIBLIOGRAPHY*

PRIMARY SOURCES

Russian and other Slavonic materials

Abramov, I.S.
  1904 *"Car' Maksimilian*: Svjatočnaja kumedija" (St. Petersburg). Offprint from *Izvestija otdelenija russkogo jazyka i slovesnosti*, Vol. 9, Book 3 (St. Petersburg, 1904), 266-298.
Adrianova-Peretc, V.P. (Ed.)
  1950 *Povest' vremennyx let*, Part 1 (Moscow-Leningrad).
Afanas'ev, A.N.
  1865 *Poetičeskie vozzrenija slavjan na prirodu*, Vol. 1 (Moscow).
  1868 Vol. 2 (Moscow).
  1869 Vol. 3 (Moscow).
  1936-1940 *Narodnye russkie skazki*, Vols. 1-3 (Academia, Leningrad).
Agreneva-Slavjanskaja, O.X.
  1887 *Opisanie russkoj krest'janskoj svad'by s tekstami i pesnjami*, Parts 1-3 (Moscow).
Akimova, T.M.
  1948 "Narodnaja drama v novyx zapisjax: *Car' Maksimilian*", *Učenye zapiski Saratovskogo gosudarstvennogo universiteta*, Vol. 20, philological issue (Saratov), 29-38.
Alferov, A. and Gruzinskij, A. (Ed.)
  1912 "Narodnye dramy", *Dopetrovskaja literatura i narodnaja poezija* (6th edition, Moscow), 349-383.
Andreev, N.P.
  1938 "Poxoronnye obrjady i pričitanija", *Russkij fol'klor: Xrestomatija* ed. by N.P. Andreev (Moscow-Leningrad), 115-126.
  1938 "Svadebnyj obrjad i pesni", *Russkij fol'klor: Xrestomatija* ed. by N.P. Andreev (Moscow-Leningrad), 79-114.
Anon.
  1891 "Svadebnyj obrjad v Ugor'skoj Rusi", *Živaja starina*, Issue 3 (St. Petersburg), 137-223.
  1891 Issue 4 (St. Petersburg), 131-138.
Astaxova, A.M. (Ed.)
  1963 *Narodnye ballady* (Moscow-Leningrad).
Baxtin, V. and Moldavskij, D. (Comp.)
  1962 *Russkij lubok XVII-XIX vekov* (Moscow-Leningrad).
Berkov, P.N. (Ed.)
  1953 *Russkaja narodnaja drama XVII-XX vekov* (Moscow).

* Apart from full descriptions of all works referred to in footnotes the bibliography contains a selection of other works on the folk theatre and related topics.

240

1958   "Odna iz starejšix zapisej *Carja Maksimiliana* i *Šajki razbojnikov*", *Russkij fol'-klor: Materialy i issledovanija*. (A publication of the Institute of Russian literature, Academy of Sciences USSR), No. 4 (Moscow-Leningrad), 331-374.

Birjukov, V.P. (Comp.)
1936   *Dorevol'jucionnyj fol'klor na Urale* (Sverdlovsk).
        The two most important plays in this anthology are: –
        "*Šajka razbojnikov*", Variant 1, pp. 36-47.
        "*Šajka razbojnikov*", Variant 2, pp. 47-55.
1953   *Ural v ego živom slove: dorevoljucionnyj fol'klor* (Sverdlovsk). A revised edition of the above.

Brajlovskij, S.
1891   "Prazdnik Ripej", *Živaja starina*, Issue 3 (St. Petersburg), 223-224.

Česalin, S.
1910   "Novaja zapis' *Lodki*", *Etnografičeskoe obozrenie*, Book 86-87, Nos. 3-4 (Moscow), 100-116.

Čubinskij, P.P.
1872   "Materialy i izsledovanija: Narodnyj dnevnik", ed. by N.I. Kostomarov, *Trudy etnografičesko-statističeskoj ekspedicii v zapadno-russkij kraj*, Vol. 3 (St. Petersburg).

Dobrovol'skij, V.N.
1900   "*Mašen'ka*: materialy dlja istorii narodnogo teatra", *Etnografičeskoe obozrenie*, Book 46, No. 3 (Moscow), 117-124.

Dmitrieva, R.P. (Ed.)
1964   *Povesti o spore žizni i smerti* (Moscow-Leningrad).

Dostoevskij, F.M.
1956   "Zapiski iz mertvogo doma", *Sobranie sočinenij v desjati tomax*, Vol. 3 (Moscow), 389-702.

Drizen, Baron N.V.
1905   "*Ataman*", *Materialy k istorii russkogo teatra*, Supplement 2 (Moscow), 267-281.

Efimenko, P.E.
1878   "Svadebnyj obrjad arxangel'skoj gubernii", *Izvestija obščestva ljubitelej estestvoznanija, antropologii i etnografii*, Vol. 30, Book 5, Issue 1 (Moscow).

Eremin, I.N.
1940   "Drama - igra *Car' Irod*", *Trudy otdela drevne russkoj literatury* (Institut Prusskoj literatury Akademii nauk SSSR), Vol. 4 (Moscow-Leningrad), 223-240.

Franko, I.
1906   *Do istoriji ukrajins'kogo vertepa XVIII v.*, *Zapiski naukovogo tovaristva im. Ševčenka*, Vols. 71-73 (L'vov).

Galagan, G.P.
1882   "Malorusskij vertep", *Kievskaja starina*, Book 10 (October) (Kiev), 1-38.

Golovačev, V. and Lasčilin, B. (Ed.)
1947   *Narodnyj teatr na Donu* (Rostov-on-Don).

Gruzinskij, A.E.
1898   "K istorii narodnogo teatra: *Car' Maksimilian*", *Etnografičeskoe obozrenie*, Book 38, No. 3 (Moscow), 161-168.

Jacimirskij, B.M.
1914   "*Malanka* kak vid svjatočnogo obrjadovogo rjaženija", *Etnografičeskoe obozrenie*, Nos. 1-2 (St. Petersburg), 46-77.

Jastrebov, V.
1895   "*Tron*: svjatočnaja igra", *Kievskaja starina*, Vol. 48, Book 1-3 (Kiev).

Jaščurinskij, Xr.
1898   "Roždestvenskaja intermedija: *Koza*", *Kievskaja starina*, Vol. 63, No. 10 (October) (Kiev), 73-82.

Kallaš, V.V.
1899   "K istorii narodnogo teatra: *Car' Maksimilian*", Variants 1 and 2 (Moscow). Offprint from *Etnografičeskoe obozrenie*, Book 39 (Moscow, 1898).

Kolpakova, N.P.
1928 "Svadebnyj obrjad na reke Pinege", *Krest'janskoe iskusstvo SSSR: Iskusstvo severa*. Vol. 2 (Academia, Leningrad), 117-176. Published under the auspices of the State Institute for the History of the Arts.
Korinfskij, A.A.
1901 *Narodnaja Rus'* (Moscow).
Kostin, V.
1898 "K istorii narodnogo teatra: *Car' Maksimilian*", *Etnografičeskoe obozrenie*, Book 37, No. 2 (Moscow), 103-116.
Kudrjavcev, I.M. (Ed.)
1957 *Artakserksovo dejstvo: Pervaja p'esa russkogo teatra XVII veka* (Moscow-Leningrad).
Kudrjavcev, V.D.
1965 "*Derevenskij starosta*"(narodnaja drama)", *Fol'klor narodov Sibiri* ed. by L.E. Eliasov et. al. (Ulan-Ude).
Kulakovskij, L.V.
1946 "*Kostroma*: Brjanskij xorovodnyj spektakl' ", *Sovetskaja etnografija*, No. 1 (Moscow), 163-186.
1959 *Iskusstvo sela Doroževa: U istokov narodnogo teatra i muzyki* (1st edition, Moscow).
1965 (2nd edition, Moscow).
Kuz'mina, V.D. (Ed.)
1962 *Devgenievo dejstvo* (Moscow).
Levina, I.M.
1928 "Kukol'nye igry v svad'bu i 'metišče' ", *Krest'janskoe iskusstvo SSSR: Iskusstvo severa*, Vol. 2 (Leningrad), 201-234.
Listopadov, A.M.
1947 *Starinnaja kazač'ja svad'ba* (Rostov-on-Don).
Lopatin, N.M. (Comp.)
1885 *Polnyj narodnyj pesennik* (Moscow).
L'vov, N.A. and Prač, I. (Comp.)
1896 *Russkie narodnye pesni* (St. Petersburg).
Maksimov, S.V.
1903 *Nečistaja, nevedomaja i krestnaja sila* (St. Petersburg).
Malinka, A.N.
1897 "K istorii narodnogo teatra: *Živoj vertep*", *Etnografičeskoe obozrenie*, Vol. 35, No. 4 (Moscow), 37-56.
Markelov, M.
1922 "Narodnaja drama – *Šutki*", *Saratovskij etnografičeskij sbornik*, Issue 1 (Saratov), 163-165.
Markovskij, E.
1929 "Ukrains'kij vertep", *Materijali z ukrains'koj narodnoj drami*, Vol. 1 (Kiev).
Minx, A.N.
1890 "Narodnye obyčai, obrjady, sueverija i predrazsudki krest'jan Saratovskoj gubernii", *Zapiski imperatorskogo russkogo geografičeskogo obščestva po otdeleniju etnografii*, Vol. 19, Issue 2 (St. Petersburg).
Mjakutin, A.I. (Ed.)
1910 "*Car' Maksimilian*", *Pesni Orenburgskix kazakov*, Vol. 4 (St. Petersburg), 257-302.
Moldavskij, D.M. (Ed.)
1960 "Satiričeskie dejstva", *Narodno-poetičeskaja satira* (2nd edition, Sovetskij pisatel', Leningrad), 205-262.
Moxirev, I.A.
1965 "Vjatsko-poljanskij variant narodnoj dramy *Ermak*", *Učenye zapiski kafedry literatury Kirovskogo gosudarstvennogo pedagogičeskogo instituta*, Issue 20 (Kirov), 248-264.
Ončukov, N.E. (Ed.)
1911 *Severnye narodnye dramy* (St. Petersburg).

242

Peretc, V.N. (Ed.)
  1903 *Pamjatniki russkoj dramy epoxi Petra Velikogo* (St. Petersburg).
Pisarev, S.S. and Suslovič, S.
  1927 "Dosjul'naja igra-komedija *Paxomuška*", *Krest'janskoe iskusstvo SSSR: Iskusstvo severa*, Vol. 1 (Leningrad), 176-185.
Pomeranceva, E.V. (Ed.)
  1958 "*Car' Maksimilian*", *Pesni i skazki Jaroslavskoj oblasti* (Jaroslavl'), 111-151.
Propp, V.Ja. and Putilov, B.N. (Ed.)
  1958 *Byliny*, 2 Vols. (Moscow).
Putilov, B.N. (Ed.)
  1957 *Byliny* (Sovetskij pisatel', Leningrad).
Putilov, B.N. and Dobrovol'skij, B.M. (Comp.)
  1960 *Istoričeskie pesni XIII-XVI vekov* (Moscow-Leningrad).
Remizov, A.M.
  1920 "*Car' Maksimilian*"; *Teatr Alekseja Remizova* (Text compiled by V.V. Bakrylov) (Peterburg).
Romanov, E.R. (Ed.)
  1891 "*Car' Maksimilian*", *Belorusskij sbornik*, Vol. 1, Issue 5 (Kiev), 273-283.
Saxarov, I.P.
  1841 *Skazanija russkogo naroda*. 3 vols. (St. Petersburg).
  1885 2 vols. (St. Petersburg).
Ščedrin, N. (M.E. Saltykov)
  1951 "Igrušečnogo dela ljudiški", *Sobranie sočinenij*, Vol. 10 (Moscow), 357-383.
Šejn, P.V.
  1898 *Velikoruss v svoix pesnjax, obrjadax, obyčajax, verovanijax, skazkax, legendax i t.p.*, Vol. 1, Issue 1 (St. Petersburg).
  1900 Vol. 1, Issue 2 (St. Petersburg).
Šljapkin, I.A. (Ed.)
  1921 *Starinnye dejstva i komedii Petrovskogo vremeni*. A separate edition of *Sbornik otdelenija russkogo jazyka i slovesnosti rossijskoj akademii nauk*, Vol. 97, No. 1 (Petrograd).
Sipovskij, V.V.
  1911 "*Lodka*", *Istoričeskaja xrestomatija po istorii russkoj slovesnosti*, Vol. 1, Issue 1 (5th ed., Petersburg), 239-242.
  1953 Reprinted in *Russkaja narodnaja drama XVII-XX vekov*, ed. by P.N. Berkov (Moscow-Leningrad), 143-149.
Snegirev, I.M.
  1837-1839 *Ruskie prostonarodnye prazdniki i suevernye obrjady*. Issue 1-4 (Moscow).
Tereščenko, A.
  1848 *Byt russkogo naroda*. Parts 1-7 (St. Petersburg).
Tixanov, P.N.
  1915 *Odinnadcat' intermedij XVIII veka*. In the series, *Pamjatniki drevnej pis'mennosti i iskusstva* (published by the *Obščestvo ljubitelej drevnej pis'mennosti*), No. 187 (St. Petersburg).
Tixonravov, N.S.
  1863 "Nikitino mučen'e", *Pamjatkini otrečennoj russkoj literatury*, Vol. 2 (Moscow).
Turgenev, I.S.
  1955 "Burmistr", *Zapiski oxotnika* (Kiev), 118-131.
Vasil'ev, M.
  1898 "K istorii narodnogo teatra: *Tron*", *Etnografičeskoe obozrenie*, Book 36, No. 1 (Moscow), 76-100.
Vinogradov, N.N.
  1905 "Narodnaja drama *Car' Maksem'jan i nepokornyj syn ego Adol'f*" (St. Petersburg). Offprint from *Izvestija otdelenija russkogo jazyka i slovesnosti imperatorskoj akademii nauk*, Vol. 10, Book 2 (St. Petersburg, 1905), 301-338. Reprinted in *Russkaja narodnaja drama XVII-XX vekov*, ed. by P.N. Berkov

(Moscow, 1953), 180-199.

1914   "Narodnaja drama *Car' Maksimil'jan*" 4 variants, *Sbornik otdelenija russkogo jazyka i slovesnosti imperatorskoj akademii nauk*, Vol. 90, No. 7 (St. Petersburg), 17-188. Variant 3 reprinted in *Russkaja narodnaja drama XVII-XX vekov*, ed. by P.N. Berkov (Moscow, 1953), 199-251.

1905   "Velikorusskij vertep", *Izvestija otdelenija russkogo jazyka i slovesnosti*, Vol. 10, Book 3 (St. Petersburg), 360-382.

Volkov, R.M.

1912   "Narodnaja drama *Car' Maksimil'jan*", *Russkij filologičeskij vestnik*, Vol. 68 (Warsaw), 324-336.

Vsevolodskij-Gerngross, V.N.

1933   *Igry narodov SSSR* (Moscow-Leningrad).

PRIMARY SOURCES

Non-Slavonic materials

Baskerville, Charles Read

1923-24   "Mummers' wooing plays in England", *Modern philology*, Vol. 21 (Chicago), 225-272.

Boyd, A.W.

1931   "The Tichborne mummers' play", *Notes and queries*, No. 160 (London), 93-97.

Cruikshank, G.

1838   "*Polichinelle*: farce en trois actes" (Paris).

Ferguson, Lucille

1927   "Some early masks and dances", *Modern philology*, No. 24 (Chicago), 409-417.

Hardy, Thomas

1912   *The return of the native* (New York-London).

Harris, Mary Dormer

1925   "Christmas mummers of Stoneleigh", *Notes and queries*, No. 148 (London), 42-43.

Jenkinson, A.J.

1930   "Ploughboy play", *Cornhill magazine*, No. 68 (London), 96-105.

Manly, J.M.

1897   *Specimens of the pre-Shakespearian drama* (Boston).

1924   "Mummers' play", *Notes and queries*, No. 146 (London).

Newman, L.F.

1930   "Mummers' play from Middlesex", *Folklore*, No. 41 (London), 95-98.

Pigott, Stuart

1928   "Berkshire mummers' plays", *Folklore*, No. 39 (London), 271-279.

1929   "Mummers' plays", *Folklore*, No. 40 (London), 262-277.

Swift, Jonathan

1938   "Mad Mullinex and Timothy", *The poems of Jonathan Swift*, ed. by Harold Williams, Vol. 3 (Oxford), 772-782.

Tiddy, R.J.E.

1923   *The mummers' play* (Oxford).

244

SECONDARY SOURCES

Monographs

Adrianova-Peretc, V.P. et. al.
  1928 *Starinnyj spektakl' v Rossii: sbornik statej* (Academia, Leningrad). The 2nd issue in the series *Russkij teatr* edited by V.N. Vsevolodskij-Gerngross.
Afanas'ev, Λ.N.
  1865 *Poetičeskie vozzrenija slavjan na prirodu*, Vol. 1 (Moscow).
  1868 Vol. 2 (Moscow).
  1869 Vol. 3 (Moscow).
Alekseev-Jakovlev, A.Ja.
  1948 *Russkie narodnye guljan'ja* (Leningrad-Moscow).
Arxangel'skij, A.S.
  1884 *Teatr do-Petrovskoj Rusi* (Kazan').
Aseev, B.N.
  1958 *Russkij dramatičeskij teatr XVII-XVIII v.* (Moscow).
Atkinson, John Augustus
  1812 *A picturesque representation of the manners, customs and amusements of the Russians*, 3 vols. (London).
Avdeeva, E.A.
  1837 *Zapiski i zamečanija o Sibiri* (Moscow).
Baty, G. and Chevance, R.
  1959 *Histoire des marionettes* (Paris).
Beleckij, A.
  1923 *Starinnyj teatr v Rossii*, Part 1 (Moscow).
Bogatyrev, P.G.
  1923 *Češskij kukol'nyj i russkij narodnyj teatr* (Berlin-Peterburg).
  1940 *Lidové divadlo české a slovenské* (Prague).
Bogatyrev, Pierre
  1929 *Actes magiques, rites et croyances en Russie subcarpathique*, No. 11 in the series of works published by the Institute of Slavonic Studies (Paris).
Bogojavlenskij, S.K.
  1914 *Moskovskij teatr pri carjax Aleksee i Petre* (Moscow).
Bragaglia, A.G.
  1953 *Pulcinella* (Rome).
Brand, John
  1810 *Observations on popular antiquities* (including Henry Bourne's *Antiquitates Vulgares*) (London).
Bussell, J.
  1946 *The puppet theatre* (London).
Chambers, Sir Edmund K.
  1903 *The mediaeval stage*, 2 vols. (Oxford).
  1933 *The English folk-play* (Oxford).
Čičerov, V.I.
  1957 *Zimnij period russkogo zemledel'českogo kalendarja XVI-XIX vv.* (AN SSSR, Moscow).
Cohen, Gustave
  1951 *Histoire de la mise en scène dans le théâtre religieux français du moyen âge* (Revised edition, Paris).
Collins, Samuel
  1671 *The present state of Russia* (London).
Cruikshank, George
  1873 *Punch and Judy* (London).
Dawson, William F.
  1902 *Christmas* (London).

Efimova, N.Ja.
 1935 *Adventures of a Russian puppet-theatre* (Birmingham, Michigan). See also Simovič-Efimova, N.Ja.
Eremin, Igor' and Cexnovicer, Orest
 1927 *Teatr Petruški* (Moscow-Leningrad).
Evarnickij, D.I.
 1888 *Zaporoz'e v ostatkax stariny i predanijax naroda*, 2 parts (St. Petersburg).
Famincyn, A.S.
 1889 *Skomoroxi na Rusi* (St. Petersburg).
Filippov, V.A.
 1918 *Zadači narodnogo teatra i ego prošloe v Rossii* (Moscow).
Firth, Raymond
 1961 *Elements of social organisation* (3rd edition, London).
Fletcher, Giles
 1964 *The Russe commonwealth.* Republished in *The English works of Giles Fletcher the elder*, ed. by Lloyd E. Berry (University of Wisconsin press, Madison).
Franko, I.
 1906 "Do istorii ukrains'kogo vertepa XVIII v.", *Zapiski naukovogo tovaristva im. Ševčenka*, Vols. 71-73 (L'vov).
Frazer, Sir James G.
 1923 *The golden bough* (Abridged edition, London).
Gennep, Arnold Van
 1909 *Les rites de passage: étude systématique des rites* (Paris).
 1960 *The rites of passage.* Translated by M.B. Vizedom and G.L. Caffée (London).
Gołabek, Jozef
 1938 "*Car' Maksymilian*: Widowisko ludowe na Rusi", Polska akademia umiejętnoŝci, *Prace komisji etnograficznej*, No. 17 (Krakow).
Grekov, B.D.
 1959 "Kievskaja Rus' ", *Izbrannye trudy*, Vol. 2 (Moscow).
Haddon, Alfred C.
 1898 *The study of man* (London).
Hawkins, Sir John
 1776 *A history of music*, Vol. 3 (London).
Herberstein, Siegmund Von
 1852 *Notes upon Russia.* Translated from the *Rerum Moscoviticarum commentarii* by R.H. Mayor (London).
Kallaš, V.V. and Efros, N.E. (Ed.)
 1914 *Istorija russkogo teatra*, Vol. 1 (Moscow).
Kotljarevskij, A.A.
 1868 *O pogrebal'nyx obyčajax jazyčeskix slavjan* (Moscow).
Kulakovskij, L.V.
 1959 *Iskusstvo sela Doroževa: U istokov narodnogo teatra i muzyki* (1st edition, Moscow).
 1965 (2nd edition, Moscow).
Kuz'mina, V.D.
 1958 *Russkij demokratičeskij teatr XVIII veka* (Moscow).
Lejfert, A.V.
 1922 *Balagany* (Petrograd).
McNeill, F. Marian
 1957 *The silver bough*, Vol. 1 (Glasgow).
 1959 Vol. 2 (Glasgow).
 1961 Vol. 3 (Glasgow).
Magnin, Charles
 1852 *Histoire des marionettes en Europe* (Paris).
Mannhardt, Wilhelm
 1875-77 *Wald- und Feldkulte*, 2 Vols. (Berlin).
Maindron, E.
 1900 *Marionettes et guignols* (Paris).

Maksimov, S.V.
1903 *Nečistaja, nevedomaja i krestnaja sila* (St. Petersburg).
Minx, A.N.
1890 "Narodnye obyčai, obrjady, sueverija i predrazsudki krest'jan Saratovskoj gubernii". *Zapiski imperatorskogo russkogo geografičeskogo obščestva po otdeleniju etnografii*, Vol. 19, Issue 2 (St. Petersburg).
Morozov, P.O.
1888 *Očerki iz istorii russkoj dramy XVII-XVIII st.* (St. Petersburg).
1889 *Istorija russkogo teatra*, Vol. 1: "do poloviny XVIII st." (St. Petersburg).
Nicoll, Allardyce
1927 *The development of the theatre* (London).
1931 *Masks, mimes and miracles* (London).
Nikol'skij, N.M.
1956 *Proisxoždenie i istorija belorusskoj svadebnoj obrjadnosti* (Minsk).
Obrazcov, S.
1957 *Teatr kitajskogo naroda* (Moscow).
Olearius, Adam
1662 *The voyages and travels of the ambassadors sent by Frederick Duke of Holstein, to the Great Duke of Muscovy, and the King of Persia.* Translated by J. Davies. 2 parts (London).
Opočinin, E.N.
1902 *Teatral'naja starina* (Moscow).
Pekarskij, P.P.
1857 *Misterii i starinnyj teatr v Rossii* (St. Petersburg).
Peretc, V.N.
1895 "Kukol'nyj teatr na Rusi", *Ežegodnik imperatorskix teatrov* (Season 1894-5), Supplement, Part 1 (St. Petersburg).
Potebnja, A.A.
1865 *O mifičeskom značenii nekotoryx obrjadov i poverij* (Moscow).
Ralston, W.R.S.
1872 *Songs of the Russian people* (London).
Ridgeway, Sir William
1915 *The dramas and dramatic dances of non-European races* (Cambridge).
Rovinskij, D.A.
1881 *Russkie narodnye kartinki*, Books 1-5 (St. Petersburg).
Ščeglov, Ivan
1898 *Narodnyj teatr* (St. Petersburg).
1911 *Narod i teatr* (St. Petersburg).
Šljapkin, I.A.
1898 *Carevna Natal'ja Alekseevna i teatr ee vremeni* (St. Petersburg).
Simovič-Efimova, N.Ja.
1925 *Zapiski petrušečnika* (Moscow-Leningrad).
Snegirev, I.M.
1837-1839 *Ruskie prostonarodnye prazdniki i suevernye obrjady*, Issue 1-4 (Moscow).
Speaight, George
1955 *The history of the English puppet theatre* (London).
Stead, Philip John
1950 *Mr. Punch* (London).
Strutt, Joseph
1903 *The sports and pastimes of the people of England.* Revised by J.C. Cox (London).
Tereščenko, A.
1848 *Byt russkogo naroda*, Parts 1-7 (St. Petersburg).
Varneke, B.V.
1908 *Istorija russkogo teatra.* Part 1 (Kazan').
1939 *Istorija russkogo teatra XVII-XIX v.* (Moscow-Leningrad).

Veselovskij, A.N.
  1870 *Starinnyj teatr v Evrope: Istoričeskie očerki* (Moscow).
Vsevolodskij-Gerngross, V.N.
  1929 *Istorija russkogo teatra*, Vol. 1 (Leningrad-Moscow).
  1957 *Russkij teatr ot istokov do serediny XVIII v.* (Moscow).
  1959 *Russkaja ustnaja narodnaja drama* (Moscow).
Wilde, Lady Jane Francesca Speranza
  1890 *Ancient cures, charms and usages of Ireland* (London).
Zabelin, I.E.
  1915 *Domašnij byt russkogo naroda v XVI i XVII st.*, Vol. 1: "Domašnij byt russkix carej", Part 2 (Moscow).
  1912 *Istorija russkoj žizni s drevnejšix vremen.* Part 2 (Moscow).

SECONDARY SOURCES

Articles

Adrianova-Peretc, V.P.
  1928 "Scena i priemy postanovki v russkom škol'nom teatre XVII-XVIII v.", *Starinnyj spektakl' v Rossii: sbornik statej*, ed. by V.P. Adrianova-Peretc et al. (Leningrad), 7-63.
Alferov, A.D.
  1903 "Petruška i ego predki", *Desjat' čtenij po literature*, contributions by A. Alferov, A. Gruzinskij et. al. (2nd edition, Moscow), 175-205.
Alford, Violet
  1928 "The Basque mascarade", *Folklore* No. 39 (London), 68-90.
Avdeev, A.D.
  1960 "Maska", *Sbornik muzeja antropologii i etnografii*, Vol. 19 (Moscow-Leningrad), 39—.
B., I.
  1887 "*Car' Maksimilian* v Kovle", *Kievskaja starina*, Vol. 19 (December) (Kiev), 798-799.
Berkov, P.N.
  1957 "Verojatnyj istočnik narodnoj p'esy *O care Maksimiliane i ego nepokornom syne Adol'fe*", *Trudy otdela drevne-russkoj literatury instituta russkoj literatury akademii nauk SSSR*, Vol. 13 (Moscow-Leningrad), 298-312.
Bogatyrev, P.G.
  1947 "Otčet o poezdke v balkanskie strany: No. 1 - Po Bolgarii", *Kratkie soobščenija instituta etnografii akademii nauk SSSR*, No. 3 (Moscow), 82-94.
  1966 "Narodnyj teatr", *Russkoe narodnoe tvorčestvo*, ed. by P.G. Bogatyrev (Moscow), 97-118.
Boyd, A.W.
  1939 "The mummers' play", *Notes and queries*, No. 176 (London), 44.
Čičerov, V.I.
  1954 "Kalendarnaja poezija i obrjad", *Russkoe narodnoe poetičeskoe tvorčestvo*, ed. by P.G. Bogatyrev (Moscow), 149-171.
Dilaktorskij, P.A.
  1903 "Prazdnik Pokrova u krest'jan Dvinickoj volosti", *Etnografičeskoe obozrenie*, No. 4 (Moscow), 125—.
Dodds, M.H.
  1950 "A few notes on Yorkshire folk-drama", *Notes and queries*, No. 195 (London), 472-473.
J., W.H.
  1938 "Mummers' play at Christmas", *Notes and queries*, No. 175 (London), 453.

248

Kagarov, E.G.
1960 "Sostav i proisxoždenie svadebnoj obrjadnosti", *Sbornik muzeja antropologii i etnografii*, No. 19 (Moscow-Leningrad).
Kn. Dolgorukij
1870 "Materialy otečestvennye – žurnal putešestvija iz Moskvy v Nižnij Knjazja Dolgorukogo", *Čtenija v imperatorskom obščestve istorii i drevnostej rossijskix*, Book 1, Part 1 (Moscow).
Krupjanskaja, V.Ju.
1947 "Narodnaja drama *Lodka*, ee genezis i literaturnaja istorija", *Kratkie soobščenija instituta etnografii akademii nauk SSSR*, No. 3 (Moscow), 70-73.
1954 "Narodnyj teatr", *Russkoe narodnoe poetičeskoe tvorčestvo*, ed. by P.G. Bogatyrev (Moscow), 382-414.
Kulakovskij, L.
1953 "U istokov russkogo narodnogo teatra: zametki fol'klorista", *Teatr*, No. 8 (Moscow), 164-167.
Kuz'mina, V.D.
1955 "Ustnaja narodnaja drama v 18-om veke", *Russkoe narodnoe poetičeskoe tvorčestvo*, a publication of the Institute of Russian literature, Academy of Sciences USSR, Vol. 2, Book 1, ed. by D.S. Lixačev (Moscow-Leningrad), 386-395.
L., P.
1934 "The mummers' play", *Times literary supplement*, Jan. 4th, 12.
Laščilin, B.S.
1950 "Vozroždenie narodnogo teatra na Donu", *Kratkie soobščenija instituta etnografii akademii nauk SSSR*, No. 11 (Moscow), 31-33.
Lindsay, Jack
1940 "The English folk-play", *Times literary supplement*, April 20th, 195.
Martem'janov, T.A.
1914 "*Komedija o care Maksimiliane*", *Istoričeskij vestnik*, Vol. 136, No. 5 (Peterburg), 538-553.
Martinovič, N.
1921 "Zametki o narodnom kukol'nom teatre sartov", *Kazanskij muzejnyj vestnik*, No. 1-2 (a special issue on the peoples of the East) (Kazan'), 13-24.
Mepham, William A.
1934 "Village plays at Dunmow, Essex, in the 16th century", *Notes and queries*, No. 166 (London), 345-348, 362-366.
Morozov, P.O.
1914 "Narodnaja drama", *Istorija russkogo teatra*, ed. by V.V. Kallaš and N.E. Efros, Vol. 1 (Moscow), 1-24.
Ončukov, N.E.
1910 "Narodnaja drama na severe", *Izvestija otdelenija russkogo jazyka i slovesnosti imperatorskoj akademii nauk*, Vol. 14 (St. Petersburg), 215-239.
P.
1863 "*Car' Maksimilian*", *Iskra*, No. 6 (St. Petersburg), 82-85.
Pomeranceva, E.V.
1954 "Semejnaja obrjadovaja poezija", *Russkoe narodnoe poetičeskoe tvorčestvo*, ed. by P.G. Bogatyrev (Moscow), 171-188.
Puškin, A.S.
1950 "O narodnoj drame i drame *Marfa posadnica*", *Polnoe sobranie sočinenij v šesti tomax*, Vol. 5 (Moscow), 158-165.
Selivanov, A.
1884 "*Vertep* v Kupjanskom uezde Xar'kovskoj gubernii", *Kievskaja starina*, Vol. 8, No. 3 (March) (Kiev), 512-515.
Šeptaev, L.S.
1955 "Narodnaja drama v XIX veke", *Russkoe narodnoe poetičeskoe tvorčestvo*, a publication of the Institute of Russian literature, Academy of sciences USSR, Vol. 2, Book 1, ed. by D.S. Lixačev (Moscow-Leningrad), 395-407.

Sipovskij, V.V.
1912 "Začatki russkoj narodnoj dramy", Ch. 24 in *Istorija russkoj slovesnosti*, Part 1, Issue 1 (6th ed., St. Petersburg), 138-143.
Smirnickij, A.
1913 "K voprosu o vyroždenii vertepnoj dramy", *Izvestija Odesskogo bibliografičeskogo obščestva pri imperatorskom novorossijskom universitete*, Vol. 2, Issue 5 (Odessa), 194-211.
Sulockij, Protopop A.
1870 "Seminarskij teatr v starinu v Tobol'ske", *Čtenija v imperatorskom obščestve istorii i drevnostej rossijskix pri Moskovskom universitete*, Book 2, Part 5 (April-June) (Moscow), 153-157.
Tixonravov, N.S.
1898 "Načalo russkogo teatra", *Sobranie sočinenij v četyrex tomax*, Vol. 2 (Moscow), 51.
Varneke, B.V.
1913 "Čto igraet narod", *Ežegodnik imperatorskix teatrov*, Issue 4 (St. Petersburg), 1-40.
Wace, A.J.B.
1913 "Mumming plays in the south Balkans", *Annual of the British school at Athens*, No. 19 (session 1912-1913) (London), 248-265.
Žerebcov, B.
1940 "Teatr v staroj Sibiri", *Zapiski gosudarstvennogo instituta teatral'nogo iskusstva* (Moscow-Leningrad).

LIST OF TEXTS OF 'CAR' MAKSIMILIAN'

(with abbreviated titles as used in Chapters VII-XIII)

Abramov, I.S.
1904 *"Car' Maksimilian*: Svjatočnaja kumedija" (St. Petersburg). Offprint from *Izvestija otdelenija russkogo jazyka i slovesnosti*, Vol. 9, Book 3 (St. Petersburg, 1904), 266-298. (Abbrev. Abramov.)

Akimova, T.M.
1948 "Narodnaja drama v novyx zapisjax: *Car' Maksimilian*", *Učenye zapiski Saratovskogo gosudarstvennogo universiteta*, Vol. 20, philological issue (Saratov), 29-38. (Abbrev. Akimova.)

Berkov, P.N.
1958 "Odna iz starejšix zapisej *Carja Maksimiliana* i *Šajki razbojnikov*", *Russkij fol'klor: Materialy i issledovanija*. (A publication of the Institute of Russian literature, Academy of Sciences USSR), No. 4 (Moscow-Leningrad), 331-374. (Abbrev. Berkov, *Russkij fol'klor*.)

Golovačev, V. and Laščilin, B. (Ed.)
1947 *"Car' Maksimian i ego nepokornyj syn Adol'f"*, *Narodnyj teatr·na Donu* (Rostov-on-Don), 90-95.

Gruzinskij, A.E.
1898 "K istorii narodnogo teatra: *Car' Maksimilian*", *Etnografičeskoe obozrenie*, Book 38, No. 3 (Moscow), 161-168. (Abbrev. Gruzinskij.)

Kallaš, V.V.
1899 "K istorii narodnogo teatra: *Car' Maksimilian*", Variant 1 (Moscow), 6-13. Offprint from *Etnografičeskoe obozrenie*, Book 39 (Moscow, 1898). (Abbrev. Kallaš, Variant 1.)
1899 "K istorii narodnogo teatra: *Car' Maksimilian*", Variant 2 (Moscow), 13-18. Offprint from *Etnografičeskoe obozrenie*, Book 39 (Moscow, 1898). (Abbrev. Kallaš, Variant 2.)

Kostin, V.
1898 "K istorii narodnogo teatra: *Car' Maksimilian*", *Etnografičeskoe obozrenie*, Book 37, No. 2 (Moscow), 103-116. (Abbrev. Kostin.)

Mjakutin, A.I. (Ed.)
1910 *"Car' Maksimilian"*, *Pesni Orenburgskix kazakov*, Vol. 4 (St. Petersburg), 257-302. (Abbrev. Mjakutin.)

Ončukov, N.E. (Ed.)
1911 *"Car' Maksim'jan"*, *Severnye narodnye dramy* (St. Petersburg), 1-47. (Abbrev. Ončukov, Variant 1.)
1911 *"Car' Maksem'jan"*, *Severnye narodnye dramy* (St. Petersburg), 48-68. (Abbrev. Ončukov, Variant 2.)

Pomeranceva, E.V. (Ed.),
1958 *"Car' Maksimian"*, *Pesni i skazki Jaroslavskoj oblasti* (Jaroslavl'), 111-151. (Abbrev. Pomeranceva.)

Remizov, A.M.
1920 *"Car' Maksimilian"*; *Teatr Alekseja Remizova*. (Text compiled by V.V. Bakrylov) (Peterburg).

Romanov, E.R. (Ed.)
1891 *"Car' Maksimian"*, *Belorusskij sbornik*, Vol. 1, Issue 5 (Kiev), 273-283. (Abbrev. Romanov.)

Vinogradov, N.N.
1905 "Narodnaja drama *Car' Maksem'jan i nepokornyj syn ego Adol'f*" (St. Petersburg). Offprint from *Izvestija otdelenija russkogo jazyka i slovesnosti imperatorskoj akademii nauk*, Vol. 10, Book 2 (St. Petersburg, 1905), 301-338. Reprinted in *Russkaja narodnaja drama XVII-XX vekov*, ed. by P.N. Berkov (Moscow, 1953), 180-199. (Abbrev. Vinogradov, Variant 5.)
1914 "*Car' Maksimil'jan*", *Sbornik otdelenija russkogo jazyka i slovesnosti imperatorskoj akademii nauk*, Vol. 90, No. 7 (St. Petersburg), 17-52. (Abbrev. Vinogradov, Variant 1.)
1914 "*Car' Maksimijan*", *Sbornik otdelenija russkogo jazyka i slovesnosti imperatorskoj akademii nauk*, Vol. 90, No. 7 (St. Petersburg), 54-96. (Abbrev. Vinogradov, Variant 2.)
1914 "*Car' Maksim'jan*", *Sbornik otdelenija russkogo jazyka i slovesnosti imperatorskoj akademii nauk*, Vol. 90, No. 7 (St. Petersburg), 97-166. (Abbrev. Vinogradov, Variant 3.)
1914 "*Car' Maksim'jan*", *Sbornik otdelenija russkogo jazyka i slovesnosti imperatorskoj akademii nauk*, Vol. 90, No. 7 (St. Petersburg), 167-188. (Abbrev. Vinogradov, Variant 4.)
Volkov, R.M.
1912 "Narodnaja drama *Car' Maksimil'jan*", *Russkij filologičeskij vestnik*, Vol. 68 (Warsaw), 324-336.

INDEX

Abramov, I.S. 159, 193, 194
Academic Theatre 161, 167, 168, 169, 189, 190, 204, 215
Acting Methods 212-221; in *Car' Maksimilian* 211-220; conventional movements 214, 215, 216, 217, 218, 219; dramatic delivery 214; exits and entries 213; military influence 192; in *St. George* 182, 215, 217; in *The Ship* 215; special effects 220; speech 219-220; stage, use of 212, 213-214
Actors in Folk Theatre 187-195; 223-224; ages of 193; in *Car' Maksimilian* 179, 194; in marriage ritual 56-59; in *Paxomuška* 70, 71; and the public 225-226; remuneration of 195; in *St. George* 179; seminarists 190; in *The Ship* 128; soldiers 158, 190-191; women 192, 203; workers 128, 158, 190 (*See also skomoroxi*)
Afanas'ev, A.N. 145
Agreneva-Slavjanskaja, O.X. 45
Agricultural ritual 2, 3, 18-35; with anthropomorphic figures, birch tree 23; Ivan Kupala 30; Jarilo 28; Kostroma 24-25; last sheaf 31-32; Marena 30; *rusalka* 29; Semik 23-24; with human actors, Ivan Kupala 30; Jarilo 27-28; Kostroma 24, 26-27; *rusalka* 29; Semik 23
Akimova, T.M. 161
Aksakov, I.S. 211
Alekseev-Jakovlev, A.Ja. ix, 112
Anika the Warrior 164-167; as brigand 166; and Death 164-166; in folksong 166; influence of *vertep* 105 (*see also Car' Maksimilian*)
Animal masks 8-17, 32, 33, 35; and animal husbandry 2-3, 7-8; bear *see* Bear; bull 10; goat 9-10; horse 8-9, 16, 21

Anthropomorphism, Anthropomorphic 28 (*See also* Agricultural ritual; animal masks)
Antisemitism: (*See* Jew)
Audience 223-227; importance of 224-225, 227; participation in folk-theatre 208, 223, 224, 225-227; in *Paxomuška* 71, 223; in puppet theatre 113; in ritual 223
Avdeeva, E.A. 91
Avtomaty 84

Balagan vii, 120, 121
Banja (Ritual bath) 45, 48-49 (*See also* Bride and Rites of purification)
Barin (Folk-play) 143-148; and *Car' Maksimilian* 145; costume in 144, 205; humorous dialogue in 234-235; 'master and man' theme 145-146; shadow-theatre version 146; violence in 147-148; as *xorovod* 146 (*See also* Turgenev)
Bear(s) 10-16; Christmastide 'masked' 14, 15; fertility and good luck symbols 14, 15, 53-54; performing 12-14; as vegetation spirit 15; in wedding games 16
Bear-baiting, as public spectacle 12; at Royal Court 11-12
Benoit, Alexandre 237
Berkov, P.N. 13, 114, 117, 147, 161
Besedy (*See also Posidelki*) 47, 66
Betlejka 85 (*See also* Christmas crib and *Vertep*)
Blackening of the Face 6, 206; in *Barin* 144; The Black Arab 167-168; in *Paxomuška* 71
Bogatyrev, P.G. 7, 227
Bride, as actress 57, 59; bathing of 48-49, 60 62; bride's faction in marriage ritual 57, 66; bride's party (*devišnik*)